Enjoy the read

together we can to

peace to a troubled wo

Let me know if you

questions.

June 4 2017

Gladly,

Danielle

In the Crossfire of the Klans

BUDDY BLANCHE

ISBN: 978-1-4834-2389-0 (sc)
ISBN: 978-1-4834-2390-6 (e)

Because of the dynamic nature of the Internet, any web addresses or links contained in
this book may have changed since publication and may no longer be valid. The views
expressed in this work are solely those of the author and do not necessarily reflect the
views of the publisher, and the publisher hereby disclaims any responsibility for them.

Any people depicted in stock imagery provided by Thinkstock are models,
and such images are being used for illustrative purposes only.
Certain stock imagery © Thinkstock.

Lulu Publishing Services rev. date: 04/13/2015

FOREWORD

By Michelle Abramson, editor and friend

T his is a coming-of-age story with a twist. From earliest childhood to young adulthood, Buddy leads us through the society that was the Deep South in the tumultuous years preceding and immediately following the passage of the Civil Rights Act of 1964.

Buddy's parents were poor and moved frequently. He and his siblings introduce us to a world that seems much further in our collective past than it really is. This is a world of tight relationships between individuals of both races, but also a society where antipathy and bigotry pervade every aspect of life.

Buddy's father is a tire builder, a preacher in the Baptist Church—and a high-ranking member of the Ku Klux Klan.

Questioning, observant, and trustworthy, Buddy Blanche is a dependable guide. We follow him through some of our country's darkest times as he navigates childhood and adolescence. In the insightful and sometimes shocking dialogue, and the true events most of us witnessed from afar, his journey also brings us humor, warmth, and the positive hopes of all true Southerners.

In the Crossfire of the Klans is a compelling read. The characters - real individuals - are finely and compassionately drawn. They will remain with you.

INTRODUCTION

When writing this book, I had to visit some very dark places in the recesses of my memories. In the early morning hours of January 2009, I finished the first draft of this book then sat at my computer wondering, *How am I ever going to get this timeline vetted?* I was especially worried about the date on which my friend, Frank Morris, was murdered. I remembered that it was very near Christmas when he died, but I could no longer remember the exact date. I knew that there would probably be no old newspaper clippings to peruse, no obituaries, no magazine articles, and surely, nobody in my hometown was going to talk about it. I opened my browser and slowly typed "Frank Morris, Ferriday, LA" into the search bar, then pressed the Return key. I really wasn't expecting anything to come up, so I was shocked when a full page of Frank Morris articles populated my display.

Stunned, I scrolled through the list, reading the headline and first couple of lines that appeared before me, when my eyes settled on my father's name. I clicked on the link and the article opened with a partial image of Frank standing in front of his shoe shop. In the first line of the article, I saw my younger brother's name and my tears precluded me from continuing. I was overwhelmed with emotion, and sat nearly paralyzed for two hours, crying so hard at times that I couldn't finish the article. Someone had remembered; someone had it right. Someone was actually doing something about it. The timing was unbelievable!

Stanley Nelson, an investigative reporter for the Concordia Sentinel, and now my friend, had written a series of articles about the Frank Morris murder and about the events related to the case. He has doggedly pursued the truth regarding this and other civil rights related cases since his first

Frank Morris story headlined in early 2007. After you finish this book, enter "Frank Morris, Ferriday" into the search bar of your browser, and take a journey through Stanley's articles.

I am so very proud of my brother, Jimmy, for stepping up to the plate and taking a few swings when everyone else seemed to be ducking for cover. Hey, Brother, I am sorry that I left you holding the bag when I made my escape toward Vietnam. Don't worry, reader. This salutation will make much more sense after you read the book.

ACKNOWLEDGEMENTS

I thank Stanley Nelson, of the Concordia Sentinel, for helping me to vet the facts and timeline of the events in this book. I especially thank him for his courageous and determined efforts to unravel the long forgotten Ku Klux Klan murder of family friend, Frank Morris.

I thank my editor, Michelle Abramson, for her guidance and encouragement in preparing this book for press.

I especially want to thank my wife and children, for their love and support as I faced some very dark memories in the writing of this book.

To all of my advanced readers, thank you for your valuable feedback. You are awesome.

CHAPTER 1

Cora's Stories

Towering over me like a tree, Jackson snarled, "You nigger-lovin' little bastard."

After his threats from our last two meetings, I expected him to hit me, but I still wasn't prepared. At only 19 years of age, I had never been in a real fight, especially with a grown man. When I saw his arm flinch, I tried to step away but only backed into the side of the bin in which I had been inspecting table legs for my father. He must have enjoyed the panicked look on my face as I realized my dilemma – he was twice my size and I had nowhere to run. When he hit me, I reeled back into the large wooden bin and crumpled into a heap on a bed of unfinished table legs. The square, unlathed ends of the legs cut into me everywhere. I could feel blood running down the back of my neck from the gash that had just been opened in the back of my head. When I looked up, the bright July sun temporarily blinded me as I slipped into the edge of consciousness. Panic overwhelmed me.

I lay dazed, trying to make sense of what I already knew was senseless. Even though I had dealt with the unforgiving social attitude of racial prejudice all of my life, it still made no sense to me. I always tried to avoid the racial issues that divided my family and much of the south that I loved so dearly. Lying there, I reflected back to the simpler life of a four-year old in 1951, a time in which I was taught to respect people regardless of the color of their skin.

As I fought for consciousness, I could almost hear Aunty Luella chanting as she often did when we came calling so many years before. "Oh, here come my little white angels. Lordy, look here y'all, here come my little white angels."

My sister, Roxie, and I made the journey several times a week to retrieve the eggs and milk that Aunty Luella and Uncle Levi provided. Pulling an old Radio Flyer wagon behind an oversized tricycle, we must have been quite a spectacle in our bedclothes – converted hospital gowns that had been given to us by Mama's sister, Aunt Big Sis. Roxie was a precocious eight-year old with piercing brown eyes and a shock of curly brown hair. I was petite, tow-headed with blue eyes, and had a very shy smile, though it was never shy when we were going to see Aunty Luella. She declared us to be little white angels in our flowing gowns, and she treated us as such. Since Billy was not yet two, he didn't make the trips with us.

Aunty Luella always came out to watch over us as we walked the road between the two houses. As we pulled the rattling wagon down the gravel road, she stood on her front porch calling out to us, "Oh, Lordy, Lordy, here come my little white angels." She and Uncle Levi had been providing eggs and milk for my family since we moved to Fenwick, Mississippi, in the fall of 1949. Their home was about four hundred yards down the dirt and gravel road that passed in front of our house.

I never did find out if my parents actually paid Aunty Luella and Uncle Levi for the commodities; I do know how faithfully the old couple provided. When we made our visits, I had little concern for the commodities; my attention was focused on my gentle Aunty Luella as she picked me up and hugged me so tightly she seemed to warm my whole life. She was closer to me than either of my grandmothers, and definitely more affectionate. She made the quarter-mile walk seem like a stroll across the back yard.

Aunty Luella lived her entire life in the smoky, gray, one-room shanty with her husband, Uncle Levi, and her mother, Granny Cora. Her son, Perry, also lived with them but was very seldom at home when we made our morning visits. To my youthful eyes, Uncle Perry looked older than his parents, so I thought he was Granny Cora's husband when I first met him.

Their shanty, built on stilts that raised it several feet off the ground, smelled of smoke from the wood stove that stood in the back corner of the room. The lingering aroma of bacon grease and Granny Cora's pipe tobacco gave the room a delightful sense of home. There was a large bed in the middle of the room that always seemed overburdened with blankets and quilts, especially in the winter months. Granny Cora's bed was squeezed into the left side of the room with an old wooden chair at her bedside. The only other furniture in the room was a small table and a couple of rickety unmatched chairs under the front window. I never thought about it when I was younger, but I didn't know where Uncle Perry slept. I did wonder how four adults could live comfortably in such a small shack.

The house was bare of paint, inside and out. The boards on the inside walls were dark gray from decades of smoke, many of them with large splits caused by the hot summers. The gaps around the windows and doors were large enough to see daylight through them. The steps leading up to the porch were terribly warped and sloped downward, away from the house, making them dangerously slick on rainy days. The boards on the outside of the house were split and silver with age, giving the shack an aura of elderly dignity.

During the summer mornings, Aunty Luella often held us on her lap and sang as she rocked us in one of the two oversized rockers that sat on the front porch. Granny Cora sat in the other chair and told stories of her life as a slave, the Civil War, and her freedom. Those were special times for me. To a young child, love has no color. Luella treated us as her own grandchildren, probably because Perry never married and had no children.

When Granny Cora told her stories, we were especially attentive. As she talked, she puffed on an old pipe made of a hollowed stick and a corncob. Sometimes she curled her finger around the corncob bowl of the pipe and pointed with the mouthpiece as she accented some of her points.

"You know," she pointed at Roxie, "I wuz jus' about yore age when we wuz livin' on the plantation farm wit' Massa Doc Reed an' his family jus' before the Civil War. Massa Doc wuz real good to us, but he wuz gone mos' of the time. He had lots of business to take care of. My daddy taked care of the plantation, so we got to live in the 'back house' right tight with the big house."

"Yassah," Granny Cora continued, "Massa Doc owned my daddy an' mama, an' he taked care of us real good. He always maded sure we had plenty to eat an' good clothes to wear. Mostly we ate what they did, an' sometimes we gotted clothes from them when the young masters would git too big for them. My mama wuz real good at makin' everything fit jus' right. Massa Doc taked good care of me an' all my brothers and sisters. I got some schoolin' 'cause I goed to school wit' Massa Donny when I got ol' enough."

Granny Cora never told us how many brothers and sisters she had, but she talked about them often. She also talked about Doctor Reed and his family as if they were a part of her own. She considered having been a slave as a matter of fact; that was just the way things were in her youth. After the Civil War started, Doctor Reed freed her family, then hired them to continue their care of the plantation. Slavery was a concept that I couldn't grasp at my young age, but my memory was sharp and I remembered Granny Cora's stories in great detail.

Through the three years that we lived in Fenwick, Granny Cora continued her stories about her youth, the Civil War, and about her beloved Master Donny. She loved him as a child, she loved him while he was away during the war, and she loved him even more after his return home. During the war, he had been captured and held at the Union's Camp Douglas where he suffered horribly at the hands of his captors. When he returned home from the war, he was a changed man, frail and vulnerable. During the night, he suffered through terrifying nightmares, so Granny Cora moved into the main house to a room adjacent to Master Donny's. Though she had been a freedman for several years, she was devoted to the care of her master. After Master Donny recovered from his ordeal, he returned Granny Cora's love and attention in kind.

When Granny Cora related her favorite story, we paid particular attention. It was one that we heard many times through the years. "One night after he went to town, Massa Donny said he had a surprise for me. That night after I got his bath ready an' he wuz relaxin,' he gave me a box that he said he picked up jus' for me. He kept sayin,' 'Open it. Open it.' So I taked the paper off, an' I taked the lid off real careful. When I put my han' in the box an' touched the material, I started gittin' all 'cited an' started cryin' 'cause it wuz so pretty. I ain't never had a new dress before, 'specially not like that one. It wuz purple with fine cloth buttons all the way down the front. The top had a lacy, white bib that covered up the top buttons an' it had lace cuffs on the sleeves an' lace that hung on the front of it on both sides. It even had a bustle in it," she chuckled, "but I didn't need nothing to make my bottom stick out."

"'Put it on. Put it on,' he tol' me, so I went off to my room an' put it on; I wuz so 'cited I wuz shakin' all over. It taked me a long time to put the dress on, cause it had laces to tie an' lots of buttons that I had to do an' my han's wuz shakin' awful. I walked out in the hall an' looked at myself in the big mirra an' I ain't never seen myself so pretty – never. When I wore that dress, I always felt special. Massa Donny always maded me feel special, anyways."

Even as a four year-old, I understood that Granny Cora and Master Donny truly loved each other. I saw the sparkle of delight in her eyes when she mentioned his name; I heard it in her stories when her voice softened in sadness and delight. When Roxie retold the stories to me later, she would sometimes have the same look on her face as she went through the emotions. Granny Cora's stories and Auntie Luella's hugs made the three years in Fenwick pass quickly.

The years in Fenwick were years filled with firsts: first bee stings, first stitches, first dog, and Roxie's first perm. It was the first of my mother's pregnancies that I remember. Through the fall, her belly just grew bigger and bigger – I thought she would burst. On December 12, Daddy took her to the hospital. When they returned the next day, she looked so different – much thinner. Mama had a surprise wrapped in the blanket that she carried. She came in and sat in the large rocking chair that sat beside the old pot-bellied stove that stood in the middle of the room.

As she pulled back the corner of the blanket to reveal the baby's face, she said, "He's sleeping right now, so we have to be real quiet."

As she held the blanket back, Billy and I leaned in carefully to take a better look. Billy had several pennies in his hand so he put them in his mouth so he could use his hands to pull himself up a little for a better view. Just as his face came even with the baby's face, Mama said, "His name is James, but we will call him Jimmy."

As if on cue, Jimmy opened one eye, wriggled once, stretched real big, and gave a great yawn. Billy, delighted by the activity, jumped up and down, chanting, "He looked at me! He looked at me."

After jumping around for a while, Billy stopped and made several short gasping cries. He tried to scream, but nothing came out. Mama saw him and yelled, "Ed. Get in here fast; the baby is choking on something."

Before Daddy got into the room, Mama turned and laid Jimmy against the back of the rocker. She reached and picked Billy up by one arm, lifted him off the floor, turned him across her hip, and used the heel of her palm to give him a couple of sharp thumps to the back. Billy was still choking! She lifted him higher so that he was almost sideways across her hip, and gave him another couple of thumps, then squeezed him sharply right across his midsection. Billy gave a shallow huff. Mama lifted him up, stuck her fingers into his mouth, and dug out four of the pennies that he had shoved into his mouth earlier. Frantically, she demanded, "How many pennies did he have?"

"Eight," Roxie answered. "He had eight pennies, Mama."

Mama continued to dig around in his mouth for a minute or so, then declared, "I guess he swallowed the other four." She opened her hand to reveal four pennies.

Billy was still trying to recover after having lost his breath for the minute or so. After he caught his breath, he was also wailing at the top of his lungs. During the excitement, Jimmy had awakened and was in full wail. Daddy yelled at me, then at Roxie, demanding that each of us tell how Billy had gotten the coins.

After Mama composed herself, she yelled at Daddy, "Your brother came by the other day and gave them to him for singing 'Jesus, Jesus, Jesus'."

Mama was right. Uncle Raymond had come by for a visit and had paid Billy to sing because he sounded so cute.

After Daddy yelled at me about the pennies, the noise and the inequity of the situation overwhelmed me, so I went into the front room to escape into a quiet solitude. I felt guilty for what happened, but I also felt helpless to do anything about it. It was the first time I had been witness to what I perceived as brutality to one of my siblings, so this became another first: my first feeling of helplessness and cowardice. I felt that I could have done something if I had only tried. I hadn't understood that what Mama had done was necessary to save Billy from suffocation. Fortunately, time and distractions quickly heal the wounds of a four-year old. Baby Jimmy provided the distractions, and the approaching Christmas was the perfect time for forgetting the pains of the past.

Before Christmas, Mama gave Roxie and me a token amount of money with which we bought presents for Aunty Luella, Uncle Levi, and Granny Cora. She understood how important Auntie Luella and Granny Cora were to the two of us. She also appreciated the extra attention that they had been giving us since Jimmy was born. I don't remember what we got for Levi, but I do remember getting a blanket for Luella and a pair of black nylon stockings for Granny Cora. When we took the presents over for Christmas, Aunty Luella and Granny Cora made quite the fuss over them.

Granny Cora said "Lordy, Lordy. I got me some burying hose. You hear me, boy? I got me some burying hose. I ain't gonna use these 'til the day I die, then I'm gonna wear them when I go to meet my sweet Jesus. He gonna look at me an' he gonna say, 'Hoo wee, Cora. You look ready for heaven in them black hose.'"

Cora folded the stockings, carefully slid them back into the packaging, and put them in a large chest at the end of her bed. When she opened the chest, it smelled of cedar and mothballs. I could see the lace on a beautiful purple dress with cloth buttons and lace on both sides of the front folded neatly in one end of the chest. It looked so familiar to me that I knew it had to be the dress that Master Donny had given her. At my young age, I had no idea of the concept of how long ago it had been. How can a four-year old even imagine a time period of almost one hundred years?

For Christmas, our family loaded into the old black DeSoto coupe and we headed to Jena, Louisiana to spend the holidays with Grandma Blanche. Roxy, Billy, and I sat in the back seat, sharing space with a bundle of snowsuits hanging above the window on the driver's side of the car. Mama held Jimmy in the front seat to keep him quiet during the long ride. Immediately after we drove onto Highway 84, Daddy started laughing about how he was going to get that stupid mule that is always standing in the road in front of old man Taylor's house. As we drove for more than two hours, Daddy continued to plot and chuckle about what he was going to do to that mule.

When we reached the outskirts of Jena, as soon as Daddy turned the car onto the Old Harrisonburg Road, he pulled the car to the side of the road, reached into a paper bag that he had on the front seat, and pulled out a long string of firecrackers. He tore one end of the wrapper and pulled the fuse out so they would be ready for our approach to the mule. I don't know who was more excited as we drove the next three miles down the gravel road - Daddy or us kids.

As we approached the Taylor place, Daddy was giddy with the excitement. "There he is. There he is, standing right in the road just like he always is. I'm gonna get that jackass good."

Daddy drove slowly toward the mule, then as we approached, he rolled his window down a bit and pulled far to the right side of the road so that we would pass directly behind the mule. Just as we were going past the mule, Daddy took his cigarette and touched the exposed end to the firecracker fuse. As the fuse came alive with a hiss, he tossed the firecrackers at his open window, but the pack hit the doorframe and ricocheted into the snowsuits hanging in the back seat. When the first of the long string of firecrackers exploded, the three of us scrambled to the other side of the car to get away. Jimmy awoke and went into full wail. Daddy started yelling at us for waking the baby and making such a commotion. Soon the car was filled with fireworks discharging all around us. Daddy stopped the car and we all scrambled out as the last of the fireworks discharged.

By the time we loaded back into the car, all four of us kids were crying and Mama was still trying to explain to Daddy what had happened – he just couldn't believe that he had caused this fiasco. After we stopped sobbing, the rest of the ride to Grandma's house was rather quiet. When we arrived at Grandma's and unloaded the car, we could see the marks and small holes burned into the snowsuits by the fireworks. The interior of the car had not fared very well either; there were burn marks and shrapnel all over the upholstery.

When Daddy and his brothers got together on the front porch of the house, he told the story as if it had been one big joke. Mama was furious. During the stay, we recounted the story to all of our cousins, trying to impose upon them the horror of our experience. I still recall the story with great detail, but no longer with horror – it was a valuable lesson about my dad, and it was funny. That would not be the last time Daddy was to have a run-in with the mule.

After Christmas, Daddy came home one day excited about having been selected by a pulpit committee to become pastor of a country church near New Hope, Mississippi. He was looking for a place where we could live near the church, but from which it would still be practical to drive to work in Natchez. Roxie and I were both concerned with the news about moving away. What would happen to Aunty Luella, Uncle Levi, and Granny Cora after we moved?

CHAPTER 2

Life's Little Lessons

As children, we should be learning life's little lessons about singing, worship, fair play, innocent mischief, respecting elders, and unconditional love, but life isn't always fair. It occasionally hands us an experience that we shouldn't receive in a lifetime.

While Roxie finished the school year, we continued to live in Fenwick for those months. Cousins Michael and Missy had come to live with us for a while because Uncle Ace and Aunt Pearl had separated again. Michael was almost Roxie's age and played by himself most of the time; he didn't like to play with "girls" and he was too old to play with me. Missy was a lively, tow-headed three-year old who was the perfect playmate for Billy. The two of them played tirelessly and were full of that innocent mischief that would normally put a smile on the face of even the most somber of adults, but timing has its own mischief that can bring an end to innocence. We enjoyed having our cousins stay because we seldom got to spend much time with other children, especially cousins.

Each day before he went to work, Daddy gathered the family into the living room for prayer. It was a routine that brought a little order to the chaos of our household and a Christian comfort to us all since he had surrendered himself to the ministry.

As we gathered for prayer one spring afternoon, Missy and Billy came running into the room from the front porch. Daddy was standing behind the couch ready to pray while Roxie and I knelt at the ends, bowed against the large wooden arms. Missy and Billy took their places at the front of the couch but hadn't settled down for the prayer. Mama was in the bedroom with the new baby.

Daddy spoke to the two small children, "Bow your heads so we can pray."

Billy, still wound up from his frantic play, bowed his head with youthful enthusiasm. His head hit the board across the front of the couch with a loud "BONK!"

Missy giggled uncontrollably as Billy reached up to rub his head. Roxie and I snickered but knew that Daddy wouldn't be pleased by an outburst. Billy, however, did not have the experience that we had and he joined Missy in a duet of spirited giggles.

"Knock it off. Bow your head, now."

Neither of the three-year olds could control themselves and they continued to giggle with glee.

"Knock it off! Shut up and bow your head!" Daddy reached across the back of the couch to swat Billy across the back of the head, but his hand hit the board that ran down the back of the couch.

"Bonk!"

That was the undoing of the two children. Their giggling grew in volume and spirit. It infuriated Daddy.

"Knock it off." This time his hand didn't miss, striking Billy squarely on the back of his head, causing it to bump the board again.

"Bonk!"

I wanted to laugh, but I could see my father's rage growing. He reached across the couch and slapped Billy across the top of his head hard enough to knock him over on the floor, but not hard enough to stop the giggling.

"Shut up and bow your head, now!"

Both of the children tried to stop laughing, but each time they got near composure, one of them lost it and the other joined in another round of laughter. Daddy went into a rage. He reached across the couch, grabbed Billy by his tiny arm, yanking him off the floor like a rag doll.

"Boy, I said be quiet and I meant it! Stop laughing!" he spat venomously.

As Daddy held Billy in the air, he started swinging at Billy's backside with his other hand. Each time his hand came back, it struck the wooden frame with a loud thud, which seemed to incite the children even more. I recoiled in horror at what was happening before me.

After Daddy's hand hit the frame a few times, he became so enraged that he pulled his shoe off and started screaming at Billy at the top of his lungs.

"Stop laughing! You're going to stop laughing or I'll whip you 'til you cry."

Holding the shoe by the heel, he started beating Billy across his tiny backside. It only worked to make the situation worse because Billy had become hysterical and couldn't stop laughing, even when he started crying. Roxie, also in tears, yelled at Daddy, "He's just a baby, Daddy! Stop! You'll hurt him."

"I mean to hurt him. He is going to learn respect and reverence. He's going to learn to listen when I tell him to do something, or not to do something."

I couldn't say or do anything. I cowered from the room feeling helpless, ashamed, and guilty. I felt like there was something I should be doing, but I could think of nothing that could protect my little brother. I don't even remember which room I was in; I just sat in the corner and cried. After a short time, Daddy came to his senses and dropped Billy on the couch like a discarded toy. He walked out the front door, got into his car, and drove away without saying a word to anyone. I sat in the corner and cried myself to sleep. I was terrified of my own father. Though things could never be the same again, time and distractions helped to heal the wounds as they always had.

Since Auntie Luella knew that we were leaving soon, she seemed to try to make the best of our time together. The hugs were longer and warmer, the rocking was longer and more relaxed. Granny Cora took the opportunity to tell us her stories; repeating them and making them more intense as if she wanted to make sure we remembered the smallest of details. Even with the added attention, time passed too quickly.

After the school year, we moved from Fenwick to a rural home near New Hope, Mississippi. It was a new home that we rented from a man who had built it for his daughter. It had been vacant from the day it was finished. It stood at the end of a long red-clay road that was badly rutted by the heavy rains that had fallen through the year. It was a house that had few memories, so I gathered a few. Most of my memories of New Hope involved playing on a large toy tractor that we pedaled up and down the dirt road, sometimes pushing one another so we could get enough speed to kick up a dusty tail. Others involved being terrorized by the owner's old goat, which delighted in chasing us around the dusty driveway, butting us to the ground. We finally discovered that we could intimidate the goat using the big green tractor as a ram. We pedaled or pushed the tractor as fast as we could go, charging at the goat with mischievous intent. Somehow, the goat always turned to face the tractor, hitting it square in the grill with a loud bang followed by the laughter of delighted children. We were the only children for miles, so Roxie was the only one that had play time with other children while in school.

During the next year, we moved two more times. The first move took us to a small cinderblock house in Bude, Mississippi, where I started school in 1953. I had an advantage when I started because my older sister escorted me to school - and to my first classes. Bude School had all twelve grades in one building with about ten rooms and one large office. The lower grades were combined for the economy of the resources; first and second grades together, and the third and fourth together. The upper grades rotated teachers by disciplines: math, grammar, and social studies.

I liked my teacher, Mrs. Smith, so I delighted in helping her in the classroom. She was a young woman with blonde hair, blue eyes, and the patience of a saint. She spoke to us in a soft, even voice that made me feel reassured and confident. I had a crush on her from the first day of class, so I was elated each time she smiled at me for collecting papers or dusting erasers.

I enjoyed Bude because of the many friends in school and several playmates that lived on our street at the bottom of the hill that was the school's football field. Our house was a small light blue cinder-block house on a bare lot that wasn't much bigger than the house. Our closest neighbors lived in a trailer house that shared the lot. Their children were almost the same age as we were, so we became the best of friends. We spent much of our time exploring the small stream that ran through the ditch behind the house and the forest just beyond.

The school year was uneventful, until after the new year began. Daddy was driving home from a visit to one of the church members, when he was crossing a bridge on one of the country roads in Union Church. As he drove off the end of the bridge, another car rounded the curve from the opposite direction and they collided head-on at the end of the bridge. The car was destroyed, but Daddy survived with only a few cuts and bruises. After the insurance company settled, Daddy went into Natchez and bought a new 1954 Chevrolet Bel Air.

After he got his new car, Daddy wanted to drive to Jena to visit with Grandma Blanche and "break in" the engine. He got us out of school early on the following Friday and we made the three hour trip. As we drove down the Old Harrisonburg Road, there was a particular kind of excitement as we neared our destination, but fate had another lesson for us all. As we neared the Taylor house, Daddy muttered under his breath, "That stupid mule is out in the road again. I know how to take care of this."

As we approached the mule, he rolled his window down and slowed the car to a crawl until he was behind the mule. When his window was directly behind the mule, Daddy reached his arm out, banged loudly on the side of the car, and whistled sharply. The mule recoiled with a mighty kick that planted both hooves into Daddy's door; we were all shocked as the car rocked violently. This time, I was the one that started crying first. Something about that mule scared me witless. Fortunately, Daddy kept his wits and drove us away rather quickly. When we got to Grandma's house, Daddy got out in a hurry to assess the damage.

"Son of a bitch! He wrecked my new car!"

We all scrambled out of the car to take a look. I was still sobbing when I walked around the car and saw the damage. The door was dented badly, so I started bawling again. I was sure that it was so badly bent that it could not be fixed. Mama and Daddy both had to explain to me that they would have it fixed just like new again. I wasn't so sure. For the second time in two years, Daddy had been bested by the same mule. Mama and Daddy didn't lie to me; they had the car repaired as soon as we returned home to Bude.

At the end of the school year, we moved to the small rural community of Quentin. The move from Bude seemed more traumatic than the previous two. Not only were we moving away from friends, but each move seemed to take me farther from Aunty Luella, Uncle Levy, and Granny Cora. I missed the long walks down the road where I got the attention that I relished so deeply. I never heard any more of Granny Cora's great stories.

The house in Quentin was built on pillars that raised it about three feet off the ground. Even on the hottest of summer days, the ground under the house was cool and soft, making it the ideal place to play "cars and trucks." We used small boards to make towns, construct bridges, and grade roads that weaved between the pillars from one end of the house to the other, avoiding the areas with the heaviest spider populations. We carried an old shoe sole with us to smack the spiders that dared to intrude on our play area.

The house had no paint inside or out, so the boards on the outside were faded and cracked with age. On the south side of the house, they were cracked so badly that light shone through the walls and the wind whistled a miserable course of discomfort during the cold winter nights. In the winter, the house was heated by a double-sided fireplace with one side in the master bedroom and the other in the living room. The back bedrooms where the children slept were not heated. Since the boys' room was next to the master bedroom, we got some of the heat that escaped through the open doorway between the two rooms. Unfortunately, Roxie had the small bedroom at the very back of the house, behind the kitchen. She had her privacy, but she also had the leaky walls, squeaky door, and creaky floor.

The electrical wiring ran along the ceilings and down the walls of the house, routed from room to room through rough holes chiseled through the tops of the walls. In each room, a crude double-knife switch allowed us to turn the lights on and off. If we were careless when turning the lights on or off, we received a terrible shock. The house had no electrical outlets. To run the two small oscillating fans that cooled the house in the summer, Daddy had to screw special adapters with electrical outlets into the light sockets that hung from the ceilings.

Our room had a double bed in which Billy, Jimmy, and I slept together. Our toy trucks and cars were lined up against the wall across the room. Neither of the inside doorways actually had doors in them; they were just open portals between our room and the kitchen and the master bedroom. The outside door was in the middle of the back wall. Our only decoration was the razor strap that hung on the door frame between our bedroom and the kitchen, always ready for Daddy to administer a little discipline if we got out of hand – "spare the rod; spoil the child."

Like the house in Fenwick, this one had no indoor plumbing, so we had a two-holer outhouse located about 200 feet behind the house. During the warmer months of the year, spiders and wasps competed for space in the outhouse. They seemed to have worked out an arrangement, since the spiders populated the lower half of the space and the wasps built nests in the upper half. I don't know which was worse, being dive-bombed by the wasps while trying to take a pee or trying to keep the spiders at bay when we had to sit. For inclement weather, we used a slop-jar which was nothing more than a ceramic-clad metal pot that had to be emptied in the outhouse at the beginning of each day - a duty that we shared with disgust. Because I was so afraid of the wasps and spiders in the outhouse, I had a tendency to use the slop jar or go out into the edge of the forest.

Quentin wasn't really a town; it was just a dying community that was once a whistle stop on the main rail between Natchez and Brookhaven. It had one road that turned off between the "shotgun shacks" that lined Highway 84. The gravel road ran about a half mile from Highway 84 to a junction with the railroad tracks. At the junction, there was an old mill on the east side of the road and the trading post - which served as the train station and post office - on the other. All of the colored people lived in shotgun shacks along Highway 84 and along the road to the mill near the railroad tracks. All of the white people lived on the other side of the tracks, where the road split into a T, each side of which doglegged around a field that was farmed by sharecroppers living along the two roads.

Before moving to Quentin, Roxie and I had been enrolled in Bude School, so we continued to attend even after we moved. We rode the school bus with the other kids from the neighborhood, but we were dropped off at the school in Bude while the remainder continued to Meadville. I never knew where all of the colored kids went to school; I just knew that they did not ride the bus or go to school with us. I never really thought about it until the summer after I completed the second grade. That was the year that I met Clarence White, who was not. He became the first colored kid with whom I ever talked or played.

One afternoon I was walking up to the trading post to spend a dime I had earned. When I got to the railroad tracks I decided to walk a short distance along the tracks instead of along the road. As I walked, I occasionally picked up a rock and threw it into the thick brush along the other side of the tracks. At one time, I threw a large rock into the bushes with a particular enthusiasm, as if I were pitching for the New York Yankees. I was pleased with the accuracy and velocity of my pitch, so I stood there and reflected on the mechanics of my throw. Though lost in thought, I saw a missile launch from the bushes right toward me. Puzzled, I ducked to the side and peered into the bushes to see who, or what, had launched the rock at me. I hesitated a bit before I picked up another large rock and hurled it back into the bushes from whence the rock had been launched. After a short delay, another rock was hurled from the bushes and I ducked to give myself a safe distance from where I thought the rock would hit. That marked the beginning of an all out rock war. I dodged and took cover behind a telegraph pole as I threw rocks into the bushes for what seemed like hours. Though I ducked efficiently, I was hit several times on my back and leg during the war. I was sure that I heard several cries of pain as I struck my hidden target so obscured by the bushes. After one loud cry, the war was over; no rocks were returned after I threw in my volley.

I continued to the trading post where I saw a colored boy sitting at the edge of the porch crying. I could never stand to see anyone cry, so I walked over and asked him what was wrong. I was about to get my first lesson in discrimination.

"I can't go in the store 'cause I don't got no money. They don't want no colored people around 'cause they say we bother people."

I was shocked and a bit confused. I went into the store and got a bag of marbles, and, with the change, bought myself a Coke from the chest on the porch. I sat on the edge of the porch near the colored boy and we began to talk about playing marbles, baseball, and going to school. After I drank most of the drink, I noticed how he was looking at it each time I put the short bottle to my mouth. I handed the bottle over to him and said he could have it because I was full. When he smiled, I could tell he was about my age. Even though he was much bigger than I was, he had large front teeth that had not grown in fully, just like mine. When I handed the bottle to him, a white lady leaving the store said, "Boy, don't you go givin' that little nigger anything, or else him and his kind will be havin' everything you git in no time flat."

I watched his face to see how he would react to her accusation, as he lowered his head in submission and shaded his eyes from view with his large hands. It was then that I noticed two large marks on his arm and realized that he had been the one at whom I had been throwing rocks for the past hour or so.

Well, the lady was partially right. Over the next couple of years Clarence got all of my marbles – every time I bought any. Occasionally we met in the field next to the old mill across from the trading post, drew a circle in the dusty ground, and "knuckled down" for some keepers; he had the strongest thumb I have ever seen. When he knuckled down and shot, he blasted several marbles out of the circle on almost every shot. He even won the marbles that I won from the kids at school and from the kids on my end of the road. Somewhere in Mississippi is a colored kid named Clarence with the biggest marble collection in the state. I owned some of those marbles for less than twenty minutes.

We also played baseball together through that summer and the next. We learned the fundamentals of baseball together, practicing in the large dirt field at the old mill across from the trading post - a neutral territory that was claimed by neither the colored people or the white. Occasionally we played an impromptu game of ball when some of his friends - seeing us playing in the field - came to join in. None of the kids on my end of the road would join us. They said they didn't want to play ball with "the niggers" because they didn't know how to play – they played "nigger ball."

Since we were playing together much of the time, I thought it was only right that we should also go to school together when school started in 1956. Knowing that there was no way to go to his school, we concocted a scheme so he could go to school with me. We were going to make him look white so he could come down to the bus stop and ride to school with me.

The year before, I had seen Aunt Phyllis use bleach to turn her hair blonde, so I thought we could do the same for Clarence. He said that his uncle had some process that would make his hair as straight as mine. One day, when no one was paying attention to us, he took an old wash tub from his house and I took a large bottle of bleach from mine and we met at the base of the water tank of the mill. We drained some water from the big tank until the tub was about half full and then he climbed into the tub, still in his shorts. After he got in, I poured some bleach into a cup and poured it into the water with him, not knowing what to expect. I also poured a cup of it into his hair very slowly and rubbed it around like shampoo, being very careful to keep it away from his eyes. I was surprised at how soft his hair felt; I always thought his hair would be wiry and coarse. Clarence wanted to get out of the tub because he said it burned a little, but I explained to him that the bleach took a little while to work because I had seen my mama and my aunt use it before, on clothes, of course. He sat on the edge of the tub, occasionally dipping himself into the water to stay cool on the hot summer afternoon. After he had been in and out of the water for about an hour, we dumped the tub and ran it full of fresh water. When Clarence got in, I used the cup to pour water over his head as he dunked himself several times.

After his bath, the only change that we noticed in him was that his fingers and toes were extremely wrinkled. We left the remaining bleach under the tower while we returned the tub to his house. We walked the tub up the steps of the shack and dropped it onto the back porch with a thud.

Someone in the house yelled, "What y'all doin' out there?"

Suddenly a large colored woman came out the door and froze as she saw me standing on the top step. I think I managed to say "Hi," but I'm not sure. She stood long enough to compose herself then she spoke directly to me, "Boy, do your folks know you down here? I don't want no trouble here 'cause you down here with us colored folks."

After that she turned to Clarence and looked at him as if she had seen a ghost. "Lordy. God Almighty. Boy, what you done did to your hair?" I turned and looked at Clarence then froze in shock, not believing what my eyes were showing me - I knew this wasn't right. His hair had turned bright orange! It wasn't just orange, it was mottled and uneven with patches of black. She persisted, "What y'all done did here? What y'all tryin' to do? How'd y'all do that to him anyhow?" Clarence tried to explain it to her as best he could, but after he started talking, she started laughing like no one I had ever heard before - it was a laugh that filled the air with surprise and joy, the kind of laughter that everyone should share at least once in a lifetime - and this one was mine! I didn't understand what was so funny, nor did I understand why she wasn't yelling and scolding us both.

I followed her laughter as she walked into the house and yelled out, "Etta. Come out to the porch. You gotta see what these boys done did."

When the other woman reached the porch, she looked at Clarence, looked at his mother and said, "Claudine, what done happen to your boy?"

When Claudine tried to explain, she laughed so hard that she couldn't get the words to make sense, so Clarence started explaining. Now Etta was laughing too; the same laugh that just seemed to come from the bottom of her soul. After Etta called out to the house next door, it seemed like all of the colored people were out laughing and talking to each other, trying to understand how something like this could happen – it was a spectacle.

After the shock wore off, Claudine came and sat on the edge of the porch with her feet on the steps. She looked at me and said, "Boy, you a white folk and you don't un'erstan' what it's like to be a colored folk. We has to stay in our places or else we gits lots of problems with some of the white folks. You a good boy for playin' with Clarence an' all, but y'all has to be careful that it don't cause no problems for us with all the white folks that lives 'roun' here." Then she turned and put her arms around Clarence. "Boy, you colored an' you always be colored. You live with colored folks and you go to school with colored folks. Tha's the way it is and tha's the way it will always be. So be what you is an' be happy 'bout what you is." Then, after she thought about it for a minute, she said, "Well y'all done made his hair lighter, but what wuz y'all gonna did about his skin. It still been colored."

"Paint," I said under my breath.

She said, "What did y'all say."

I said it loud and clear this time, "Paint."

She said, "Boy, you can't be paintin' him with no paint, that stuff could hurt him bad."

"No ma'm. We use it at school. It's tempera paint, and it comes in bottles, and you can mix it, and it doesn't hurt if you get it on you, because I get it on me all of the time at school. So I wuz gonna get some of the paint bottles from school and we were gonna mix a little red in with some white paint to make it the same color as me. After we get it the right color, we gonna smear it all…"

My explanation got lost in the laughter. His mama could laugh! When she laughed, everybody laughed – and they did. I will never forget the ring of the laughter at that house on that special day. No matter where I am, I can recall the ring of that laugh and it brings great joy to my heart.

It was also at the beginning of the school year that Hurricane Flossy hit us. It was the first hurricane I remember, probably because it had such an impact on us. When the wind picked up and it started raining, it literally blew rain through the walls of our house. The wind also blew some of the tin roof from the top of the house, so we had several spots in the house where it was raining inside almost as hard as it was raining outside. We weren't very concerned until the power transformer on the pole out by the road exploded. When we lost the electricity, I got scared, even though it was in the middle of the day. We knew that the lights would probably be off for a couple of days.

Because of the inclement weather, we were using the chamber pot more often than we were going out to the outhouse. Since we were using it both day and night, it filled up rather quickly. During what seemed like the worst of the storm, someone yelled, "Buddy, the slop jar is full and it is your turn to take it out!"

Emptying the slop jar was not a job that I relished in any circumstance, but the storm took it to another level - I was terrified! I just knew that the wind would blow me right out across the field behind the house. After I donned my sister's rain boots and a slicker that was about three times too large, I stood at the back door of the house dreading my assignment. I was even more concerned because the storm had broken one fork of the large sweet gum tree that grew at the back of the house, felling it right across the back yard where I needed to go. I would have to go all the way around the fallen tree to get to the outhouse! I stood frozen at the back door and planned my route to the outhouse. "I will push the door open, go down the steps, run around the top of the tree to the right side, then cut across the yard to the outhouse, set the pot down, open the door, then pick up the pot and empty it into the open pit below." I stared at the steps that were now my first obstacle and noticed how they were so warped and seemed to slope downward worse than ever.

Finally, I composed enough courage to push the door open and start my journey, but things went wrong right away. The wind caught the wooden framed screen door and slammed it open against the back of the house with a resounding bang. I was scared to death. I carefully took my first step out onto the top step, but as I did, my foot slipped on a slimy cedar seed pod and shot out from under me so fast that I couldn't catch myself. Thinking quickly, I set the slop jar down on the top step. My butt hit the top step with a thud, and then I bounced down each of the eight steps until I was seated on the bottom. I sat there for only a second before I realized I was witness to the most awful sound in the world – a full slop jar falling down eight steps! It crashed against my back and discharged its contents over everything – including me. I always had a weak stomach, so this was just too much for me to handle. Gagging, I turned and started back up the stairs to get back into the house. However, the rest of the family was blocking the back door, shouting for me to stay outside until I was washed off. Someone even handed out a bar of soap and instructed me to strip and wash. After that, I really didn't care if I blew away; I just wanted this to end. I stripped down to my birthday suit and let the warm rain shower me clean. Suddenly I realized how comical the situation was and I started laughing. I couldn't laugh as well as Claudine, but I felt her kind of joy and started clowning around as I washed myself with the soap in the pouring rain. I danced naked while the heavy rain washed the excrement from the steps.

Life was already proving to be a tough teacher, but it was at school where I was to have one of my most traumatizing accidents. Most of my life I had worn elastic top pants, usually shorts that my mother made for me. After having graduated to the fourth grade, I started wearing real blue jeans that had a snap at the top and a zipper in the fly. I didn't, however, start wearing underwear on a regular basis. I paid for that combination dearly one day when we were let out for recess and I rushed into the bathroom. I was in a hurry because I wanted to get out and play for a while. I stepped up to the urinal, which was nothing more than a tiled trough on one end of the room, unzipped, and took a quick pee. In my haste to finish, I must have gotten steps out of order, because I grabbed the zipper pull and gave it a yank before I had things properly put away – "Oh my God, that hurts!"

I let out a loud whimper as I tried to pull the zipper back down, but it was to no avail. After a few more loud cries and whimpers, I had attracted the attention of all of the boys in the room. One of them ran out into the hallway toward the office and yelled at the top of his lungs, "Buddy caught his wiener in his zipper!"

The next thing I knew, I had an even larger audience. It wasn't long before the principal came into the room. When I turned and saw him I thought I would faint; he had pliers in one hand and a pair of scissors in the other. He made the other boys leave the room then he tried to assure me that everything was all right; I wasn't convinced. He turned me around, away from the urinal, then I was truly shocked and mortified; there was my sister with one of her friends and Miss Jones, my teacher. Miss Jones walked over, kneeled in front of me, and grabbed my waistband with a tight grip while the principal grabbed the tab on the zipper with the pliers. He pulled firmly on the zipper and I mustered as much courage as possible to keep from crying harder. Suddenly, the zipper released and I was free from my tormenter, but not from my embarrassment.

The principal left the room and returned shortly with a tube of salve and a Band-Aid brand adhesive strip; all I wanted to do was leave. They made me drop my pants, then washed away the blood using a dampened towel that seemed to appear from nowhere. Miss Jones, still kneeling beside me, took the tube of salve from the principal, removed the cap and squeezed out a dab of the salve on the end of the tube; I was so embarrassed. I think she sensed my embarrassment, because she took my hand and wiped the dab of salve onto my finger and told me to rub it onto my new wound. It soothed everything except my horror. I still carry the scars to remind me to take my time at the toilet and to wear CLEAN underwear wherever I go.

By Thanksgiving, Mama was showing – she was expecting again. I think Mama and Daddy were trying for a girl after having three boys in a row. The pregnancy was happening without announcement or fanfare. She continued to grow through the fall and into the winter. While at church service on a cold winter morning, someone drove up to the church in a rush of dust and sliding gravel. The man burst through the front doors of the church and ran up to the pulpit where Daddy was still preaching. After he whispered something to Daddy, they walked to the back of the church for a moment, then Daddy walked back up to the pulpit after the man left. He looked pale but tried to act as if nothing had happened as he continued the worship service. After the service, Daddy informed some of the congregation that our house had burned to the ground and we needed a place to stay. Before we left church, we had a place to stay that night and for several weeks in the future. The congregation was gracious with their offers and care for us over the next few weeks.

The fire investigator determined that the fire started when a brick fell out of the fireplace and into the adjacent closet in the master bedroom. Since the fireplace had no firebrick liner and no other layer of containment, the fire set something in the closet on fire. None of our neighbors had telephones at the time, so someone had to go to the trading post to report the fire and have them call the fire department. Since the nearest fire department was in Bude, it took them 20 minutes to respond, so the house was fully ablaze when they arrived. They parked a tanker and a pumper in front of the house. Just as they started spraying water on the house, a sharp explosion sent a piece of brass shrapnel through the front of the house where it wrapped itself around one of the large pipes on the pumper truck. That was followed by several smaller explosions that sent shrapnel in all directions, sending firemen scrambling to disconnect hoses and move the fire trucks to a safe distance from the house. They could do nothing but let the house burn to the ground because the old ammunition that Daddy kept stored in a large chest in his bedroom was exploding from the intense heat.

I had seen the old World War II ammunition while looking at some pictures taken while Daddy was in the Philippines during the war; gruesome pictures of Japanese soldiers impaled on bamboo poles, or heads on stakes put there by the Filipinos in reprisal for atrocities committed by the Japanese during their occupation. I remembered five large rounds of ammunition about three inches in diameter with about twenty 50 caliber rounds stored on one end of the chest. On the other end, he had several metal canisters of ammunition that had been loaded in belts for use in a 30-caliber machine guns used on the LCVP and LCM amphibious landing craft he piloted in the US Navy. It was easy to understand why the firemen pulled away when the ammunition started discharging.

After the house burned, we stayed the night with the Simons family; a large family with three sets of twins. It is always easy to remember the day the house burned because it happened on Mama's birthday, plus it was also the second time that Elvis Presley was to have appeared on the Ed Sullivan show - January 6, 1957. To distract us from the trauma of the day, the adults gathered us in the living room around a small television for the Sunday evening programs, *Disney's Wonderful World of Color* and *The Ed Sullivan Show*. When *The Ed Sullivan Show* started that evening, we waited with great anticipation while the adults gathered around the dining table for coffee. After Ed Sullivan introduced him, someone struck a guitar chord, and Elvis grabbed the microphone and started, "You ain't nothing but a hound dog..." Silvia Simons, one of the 15-year-old twins, dived at the TV stand screaming, "I love you, Elvis. I love you." The small stand collapsed, sending the TV to the floor with a crash. Needless to say, we did NOT get to see Elvis perform that night. I was sure that Silvia would get a beating for her assault on the small television, but Mister Simons took her aside and calmly scolded her for what he understood was an accident resulting from her unbridled enthusiasm.

How different things were in the Simons' household. As an eight-year-old, I knew that had I been responsible for something like that, I would have been sent into our room for the razor strap and Daddy would have employed it with his own special enthusiasm. Then it hit me; there was no razor strap now, only ashes. I remember having said a prayer of thanks for the small blessing hidden in the catastrophe of our fire. Daddy would never use the razor strap on us again.

I don't know if it was the naivety of my youth or if I had simply been numbed by the impact of the catastrophe that had befallen us, but I seemed unaffected by our dilemma. I was not concerned with where we would live or what we would wear; I knew that everything would be made right again. This was not the first time we had been left homeless. When I was but 18 months old, Daddy gambled away our house, our furniture, the car, all of his money, and a parcel of land that, years later, would be converted into a subdivision worth hundreds of thousands of dollars. With nowhere to go, we had moved into the end of a Quonset hut that had been converted to a chicken house on my uncle's egg farm and chicken ranch. Though I was only 18 months old at the time, I can still recall the cool dampness of the dirt floor and the single light that hung by a rope from the ridge pole in the top of the Quonset hut. I also remember how barren the end of the hut had been, with only a bed, one shelf, and the crib that held my four month old baby brother. We had lived in the hut for about 3 months when Mama found a snake skin that had been shed around the bottom of the rocker on one end of Billy's basinet. That was one of the few times when I had seen my mother put her foot down and make demands of my father, but it was most effective because we were moved into another house before nightfall.

CHAPTER 3

Change Is Coming

After the house burned, we moved into some apartments in Natchez where, for a time, every day was an adventure. The move was simple because we had nothing left after the fire. The only things that were saved were the clothes that had been drying on the clothesline and a lawn mower that had been stored under the front porch. At the apartment, we had electricity in every room, running water, and indoor facilities – no outhouse and no more slop jars! Living there was great for us because there were a large number of children with whom we could play and make friends. We had a parking lot and common areas where we could play ball, sidewalks for skating, and a convenience store where we could buy the latest comic books.

Right after we got moved into the apartments, Mama had to leave us for a short stay at the hospital. When she returned a few days later, she was carrying another small bundle. She pulled the corner of the blanket down to reveal a tiny face and said, "This is Johnathon. He was born yesterday. He weighs seven pounds and six ounces. Now there are four of you boys and only one girl."

That further complicated our initial arrangement at the apartment, which was rather unique. There were no three-bedroom apartments available when we moved in. To have enough space, we were moved into two 2 one-bedroom apartments that shared a common entryway. Since Roxie was going through puberty, she was afforded her own room for privacy. The boys slept in the living room of the same apartment. Mama and the baby slept in the bedroom of the other apartment, while Daddy slept in the living room to rest undisturbed by the baby. After a few months, we finally moved into a three-bedroom apartment where we could all be together again.

It was while we were living in Natchez during 1957 that I first became aware of integration and the desegregation efforts in other parts of the South. At the beginning of the school year, nine colored students were enrolled in Central High School in Little Rock, Arkansas, as a result of a Supreme Court ruling on desegregation three years earlier. Though only ten years old, I followed the story with great interest because it seemed to have everyone in my family and all of our friends upset with the government and with colored people in general. On the first day that the nine were supposed to attend the school, many of the segregationist groups in the area had vowed to block their entrance. To support the segregation, the governor of Arkansas ordered the Arkansas National Guard to block the entrance of the school so that the students could not enter as planned. The Supreme Court immediately declared the use of the National Guard unconstitutional, so the soldiers were removed almost immediately. Nobody I knew was in favor of the desegregation of the school because they assumed that the schools in Louisiana and Mississippi were destined for the same fate; they were ready to draw a line in the sand.

Though I didn't really understand what was happening, it seemed that everyone I knew was upset with someone in the government. They were upset with the Supreme Court for making a ruling that required the governor to remove the National Guard from the school. They were angry with the Arkansas governor for complying without putting up more resistance. They were upset with the police for sneaking the nine students into the school, only to remove them later in the day because it caused several riots with the white citizens of Little Rock. Most of all, they were angry with President Eisenhower for putting the entire Arkansas National Guard under federal jurisdiction, removing them from the command of the Arkansas governor. He deployed the National Guard and a division of the Air Force to provide an armed guard for the students as they entered Central High School again in late September, 1957. Though they were intentionally intimidated by the other students in the school; all but one of the nine made it through the first year. In the following year, the Little Rock School Board cancelled the entire high school year to prevent the desegregation of the schools, forcing most of the students to transfer to schools outside the Little Rock School District or to enroll in private white schools to continue their educations. I was very afraid that the South was entering its darkest period. It was a continuous topic of discussion any time we got together with friends or family. I could feel the rift growing between the white community and the colored community around me. With the cold war growing too, I didn't know which to be more concerned about: the looming threat of desegregation of our schools or the ever-present threat of a nuclear attack by those "godless communists" in Russia.

While we were living in Natchez, we occasionally visited my aunt and uncle who lived in a new subdivision in Fenwick, not far from where we lived many years before. I liked visiting with Uncle Sherm and Aunt Milly because they had five kids; all but one of them older than me. The older kids and their friends played games with us around the neighborhood. It was especially fun when we got to play Capture the Flag or "Jack, Jack, show your light" on the visits that lasted until after it got dark.

I enjoyed the time of the year when the Mississippi summer heat gave way to the brilliant colors of fall. The evenings became cooler and the night skies always seemed to grow darker as the leaves began to fall. The darker nights made the games more challenging and added eeriness to the play.

One night after we had been playing outside for a while, Mike, one of the older boys, said, "Let's go down the road and roll tires at the niggers." I had no idea what we were doing, but I followed along with the rest of the gang. We took a couple of flashlights and walked down Jack Kelly Road where we could look down a steep bank and see a wide, gravel road below us. Neither of the roads was lit, so it was pitch black except where the flashlights shined. There at the top of the hill was a stack of old tires that had been staged by some of the other kids earlier in the day. Mike took another flashlight down the bank and retrieved several more tires from the road below. Mike lined us up along the top of the bank, gave each of us a tire, and told us to stand them up and be ready to roll them down the hill. After we had the tires ready, he had us turn out all of the lights.

We stood waiting in silence for about 10 minutes when the command came, "Get ready, here they come."

I looked carefully until I was finally able to see the glow of a couple of cigarettes carried by persons approaching on the road below. I couldn't see the people, but as they got closer I could hear their voices - two colored men talking as they walked in the darkness. When they were on the road almost directly below us, Mike barked, "Now!"

Everyone pushed their tires off the top of the bank and I stood silent, listening to the crashing of the tires as they accelerated through the brush toward the people below. I suddenly panicked and started screaming as if my hair were on fire. Instead of investigating the reason for my screaming, everyone joined in. In a matter of seconds, all the children at the top of the bank were screaming with one breath after another. Mike and one of the other boys turned on the flashlights and started waving them around so that they flashed on the tires and the people running below. He was yelling at the top of his lungs, "Run, niggers, run!"

I could also hear the men on the road below as they screamed and yelled at one another, trying to dodge the tires as they cascaded all around them. All I could see was a lit cigarette that had been dropped on the road below and another disappearing down the road as they made their escape.

After everyone else stopped screaming and yelling, I continued to scream and cry. Finally, Roxie grabbed one of the lights and came down to see if I was hurt. She said, "Buddy, what's wrong?"

"I'm scared. I don't want to do this no more."

Mike piped in, "There ain't nothing to be scared of. They the ones that have to be scared," as he pointed down the road where the men had run.

"I don't want to be out here no more. I'm scared. I want to go back inside, NOW."

Roxie said, "What are you afraid of? You ain't never been afraid of the dark before. Why didn't you roll your tire when the rest of us did?"

"Roxie. What if they was Uncle Levi and Uncle Perry? They would be real scared and I was scared too. I think it could have been Uncle Levi and Uncle Perry. They could be hurt."

Roxie understood, but the rest of the kids were unimpressed and less than forgiving. They taunted me as Roxie walked me back up the road toward the house. After we got inside, she and I sat and worried over the possibility that the colored people we had been tormenting could have been the very people that we loved so much. I never played outside in the darkness with our cousins again.

After we lived in Natchez for a year, Daddy was called to pastor a church in Olla, Louisiana, so we moved to Jena to be midway between Olla and Natchez, where he still worked at the tire plant. We lived in town for a while before we moved into an old home just down the road from my grandmother in 1959. She seemed to hate me and took pleasure in bullying me because I was a "runt." She and my Aunt Jean delighted in teasing me about my size and my shrill voice, telling me that I was too much like a little girl. Grandma led me to believe that I was not worthy to be my father's namesake.

Our new house reminded me of the one in which we had lived in Quentin. It had no paint inside or out, barely had electricity, and – once again - no indoor plumbing. We had propane for the stove and heating, so we had no fireplace. We had to draw our water from a well that was 138 feet deep – 138 feet! A pulley was suspended from a pole just above the well casing to hold the long bucket we used for hauling water from the depths. To draw water, we had to place the bucket into the well casing and lower it carefully so the rope didn't catch in the pulley. When the bucket hit the water, the rope would go slack as a valve in the bottom of the bucket opened, allowing it to fill. As the bucket filled, it sank and pulled the rope tight again, letting us know that it was time to draw the bucket back to the top. Though I was small, I could pull the bucket to the top faster than anyone but my father. It took me 51 hand-over-hand pulls on my best day.

Washdays and bath days were always especially hectic because each washer load or bath required about 10 gallons of water – five bucket loads each. In addition to drawing the water, we had to heat it for most of the wash and for all of the baths, especially during the colder months of the year. We heated most of the water in a large pot on the kitchen stove. Sometimes we used a large black caldron that we kept over a fire pit near the well. Because it was such a chore to draw bath water, we bathed only on Saturdays when we had time to draw and heat the amount of water required to bathe two adults and four children. During the warmer months we bathed more often because we went down to the shallow creek at the bottom of the hill and bathed as we splashed about and caught crawfish.

Attending school in Jena became a special chore. We lived about five miles out of town, so we had to be bused to and from school. Though we were only five miles from school, the bus made a loop that took us another 12 miles after we got picked up at the end of our road. With all the stops that we made and all the little detours that we had to make for the more remote homes, it took more than an hour each way. During the winter months, we had to walk down to the main road and wait at the intersection to be picked up, rain or shine. A cold, rainy morning could be especially miserable. During the warmer days, the bus was like an oven. We would lower the windows as far as possible, but the windows were so high there was never enough airflow to cool us, especially when the bus was fully loaded after school.

Each year in Jena, the children around me grew, but I seemed to be destined to be the smallest in my grade. Two of my younger brothers were bigger than I was. Larry was born in June of 1959, so I still had two smaller brothers. It didn't seem very important through the sixth, seventh, and eighth grades that I was so petite.

However, by the time I started high school in 1961, things were very different – I was the smallest student in school at only four feet, eight inches, and 83 pounds. Most of the high school students treated me with parity, but I did have my antagonists, the worst of which were the Paroda brothers, Josh and Richard. Both of them were senior classmen, but they attended several classes with me; a fact which I think they both resented. One of our shared classes was physical education, which I hated because we had to dress out in a common shower and locker area. I was especially shy about dressing out with the other guys because they were all so much larger and all of them were already going through puberty. I seemed to be lagging behind at everything!

One day during physical education class, we were playing football, which I especially enjoyed; I was quick and had good hands. Josh was on my team and had been giving me a bad time from the moment we dressed out for class. During one of the plays, Josh turned to me and said, "Hey, Squirt. Go out wide and run a ten yard button-hook."

I put my thumb and forefinger together to make an "O" and replied, "Otay, Buckwheat," doing my best impersonation of Porky, Spanky's little brother, of *The Little Rascals*.

Josh flew into a rage and yelled at me, "What? You called me a butthole? I'll kick your butt up around your ears." As he yelled, he started running toward me with fire in his eyes.

I took off like a shot because I knew he was very capable of kicking my butt and very determined to do just that. I shouted back over my shoulder, "I didn't call you any names. I didn't call you anything. What are you talking about?"

"You called me a butthole! You held your fingers up and made a butthole sign and you pointed it at me."

"I did not. I said, 'Okay.' I didn't call you any names. I just tried to let you know I was going to go out wide like you said." It was then that we both realized that I could avoid him as long as I darted about because I could change directions so much quicker than he could. I knew that I could not outrun him if I tried to get away. I was arguing my case desperately as I dodged left and right trying to stay out of his grasp. "You know. I was holding up the 'Okay' sign like they do in the *Little Rascals* and *Our Gang* shows. I wasn't calling you any names."

"Where I come from, that means you are calling me a butthole. If you ever do anything like that again and I think you are calling me a name, I'll kick your butt so hard, I'll knock the leaves off your family tree!"

At about that time, the coach walked out onto the field and blew his whistle to let us know it was time to go shower. I was never so glad to see the coach in my life. I was sure he had just saved my bacon. As we went to the showers, all of the guys were hooting and getting a laugh out of my predicament. "You better watch it, Buddy. He is twice your size and you shouldn't mess with him. He'll make mincemeat out of you if you get him mad."

After I showered, I walked out into the locker area and put my underwear on. As I was standing in front of my locker, Josh walked up behind me and gave me a little shove and said, "Hey, Squirt. You better watch it. The way you were screaming out there, everyone will think you're a girl. You were squealing like a little girl being chased by a spider."

My heart sank – they sounded just like my grandmother's words. I turned to face him just as he started to give me another shove, so I quickly put my hand up to catch his. I caught his hand so square that our fingers interlocked. Shocked, he said, "So you want to hand wrestle, huh? Or are you just queer and want to hold my hand?"

"I am not queer. I don't even know what that means!"

With that, Josh held his left hand up as an invitation to engage my other hand in a hand-wrestling contest. I was hesitant, but I raised my right hand up into position to interlock his fingers again. Suddenly the locker room was filled with tension. All the guys were shouting at me. "Buddy. You are about to get your arms ripped off. He'll tear off your hands and feed them to the pigs."

"Say you are a queer, Squirt." Josh squeezed my interlocked fingers as he applied pressure to twist my hands into a submissive position.

I held my hands in position at almost shoulder height and prevented him from twisting my hands around or from bending my wrist. As he applied more and more pressure, his face began to show the strain and surprise of his inability to break my hold or bend my wrist. As he strained, he repeated, "Say you are a queer, you little pipsqueak or I'll break your wrists."

I was just as surprised as he was about his inability to break my wrists, because I wasn't really straining yet. After I could see him straining, I began to apply pressure to his fingers and wrists, though I was afraid that he would get angry and really hurt me. As I applied the pressure to lower his arms, I also twisted his hands downward where I had an advantage since I was so much shorter. After I pulled his hands all the way to the bottom, I pressed my hands in toward his and started bending his wrists so that his hands went backward under his arms. With that I thought, "If he was going to kick my butt, I may as well make it worth my effort." As I applied more pressure to his wrists, I watched the surprise on his face when I said, "Say I am not a queer. Say it. Say, 'Buddy is not a queer.'"

The entire room fell into a shocked hush as Josh shouted out, "Okay. Okay. Buddy is not a queer." With that, I raised my arms and released his hands fully expecting him to hit me. Instead, he looked down at me, gave a little chuckle, then reached out and tousled my hair with his big hand.

High school changed on that day. Josh still teased me, but the teasing was no longer antagonistic; it lacked the previous maliciousness. In fact, Josh became protective of me. He could pick on me, but nobody else dared.

He treated me like a little brother for the rest of the year. I finally felt safe in high school.

The security I gained in high school didn't last long. In the spring of 1962, we moved to Vidalia, Louisiana, a small town directly across the river from Natchez, Mississippi. We moved into a new home in the Taconey subdivision built on a concrete pad – no more playing under the houses. We had it all: a garage, a sidewalk, central heating, and two bathrooms! The front of the ranch-style home was bricked up to the bottom of the windows, which were framed by shutters against a plain white wall.

The inside of the house smelled like fresh paint and linoleum glue. The only floor in the house without linoleum was in the garage. The living room, dining room, and kitchen wrapped around a common wall on the west end of the house where all of the outside doors were located, the front door into the living room, the garage and back doors into the dining room. A narrow hallway led to the master bath and the bedrooms. Mama and Daddy had the master bedroom at the back of the house, just past the bath. Roxie had the middle room at the front of the house, across from the bath, and we – all five boys – had the last bedroom at the end of the hall, just past Roxie's.

In our room, we had two sets of bunk beds and a large chest of drawers. Billy and Jimmy shared one set of bunks; I had the top bunk of the second set, while Johnny and Larry, the two youngest, shared the bottom. We had a common closet where we stored our shoes and hung our Sunday bests. It was a very tight fit for five active boys.

When we moved into the house in Vidalia, Mama and Daddy got a new bedroom set, so Daddy was trying to sell the cedar set that they had before. Not long after we moved in, one of Daddy's Armstrong coworkers, Jerry Minor, came by the house to check it out. At six foot, four inches and 220 pounds, Jerry was a large man with a broad smile and neatly trimmed sandy, brown hair. When he and Roxie met, it was love at first sight. I don't know which of them was more immediately and completely smitten, but their attentions toward one another was immediately apparent.

As weeks went by, Jerry came calling more often - not that it upset anyone. He seemed to get along well with Daddy and had a great sense of humor. I could tell he had a genuine affection for Roxie, but he seemed to have another mission, too – recruiting Daddy for some kind of KKK activities with several of their other coworkers from Armstrong. Though I knew my father's philosophy on integration, I was still taken aback by his participation in the Ku Klux Klan. I never understood how he could reconcile a philosophy of hatred and oppression with his role as a minister, where he taught weekly about the infinite love of God. It made no sense to me.

One night in June Daddy came home particularly upset about something. He asked where Roxie was, then went ballistic when he found out that she was out for the evening with Jerry. He said something rude about them messing around with fire, got into his car, and left in a huff. I could only guess that Jerry said something to upset him while they were at work, for I hadn't seen him this disturbed about anything for a long time. When Jerry returned home with Roxie, they sat in the driveway and talked secretively for about twenty minutes. They were still sitting there when Roxie saw Daddy coming home. She got out of the car in a panic and hurried into the house, locking herself in her room. I panicked also - Roxie normally had a steely resolve and was not easily shaken. As Daddy pulled up next to him in the driveway, Jerry backed out and left in a haze of smoking tires.

Daddy got out of his car, slammed the car door, and hurried through the front door toward Roxie's room. Though I was still standing outside, I could hear him shouting at the top of his lungs, but I couldn't discern what he was yelling about. I walked into the house just in time to see him with his shoulder against her door, pressing against it with all his might. He continued to yell at her, "Open this door right now, or I'll tear it off its hinges! I'm gonna whip your ass, you little slut! I saw you parked down behind the levee with Jerry. I knew he was going to be trouble – he's eight years older than you and experienced. He has a reputation all over Natchez for messing around over there. I ain't letting no daughter of mine run around acting like that; ruining my good name while you're acting like some kind of dog in heat. Open this door now!" As he yelled, I could see how much harder he was pressing against the door. When Roxie answered, I could tell that she was leaning against the door from the other side and she was resolved to keeping him out.

Mama and I were both trying to calm Daddy, but it was to no avail; with each passing moment he became more hysterical and more insistent in getting into the room. Suddenly he went into a rage so violent that I feared for all of us. Mama approached him from her bedroom and put a hand out on his shoulder, but he half backhanded her hard enough to send her reeling into their bedroom. I started in his direction, but froze when he turned and looked at me. His eyes were full of rage and I felt as though he looked right through me. I felt hollow and stood frozen at the end of the hall, chained by my own cowardice. I wanted to go to my room but Daddy was blocking the entire hall as he leaned against the door. He was screaming obscenities through the door at Roxie, but I couldn't understand most of what he said. As he continued to push on the door, his language became fouler, and his voice became hoarse and hateful. Soon, I felt as if I had gone into shock because I could hear him, but could no longer understand anything he was saying. As he ranted, he backed away from the door and hit it with his shoulder so hard that I could hear the wood frame splintering. He bashed at the door for several minutes while I stood there wondering what to do, wishing that Jerry would come back to rescue us.

When the door frame finally gave way, Daddy fell though the door and I took advantage of the moment to run past him toward my room. As I passed the door, I glanced into the room to see Daddy pick himself up and launch at Roxie. I hardly recognized him; his eyes were glassy with tears and he was actually frothing at the mouth. I rushed into my room and slammed the door just in time to hear my youngest brother, only a toddler, crying – it was coming from Roxie's room! His cries had become hysterical; one frantic scream after another. I could also hear Roxie pleading, "No, Daddy. Please. Don't do this." Suddenly, my heart almost stopped when I heard Roxie's door slam. Mama started rapping on the door, pleading with Daddy to stop hitting Roxie and bring the baby out of the room. Daddy yelled something unintelligible at her then I heard him slap Roxie so hard that it resonated through my brain like a gunshot.

After that, the noise from the room was a barrage of slaps and screams as Daddy mounted his assault on her. I could hear him hitting her as she continued to plead with him to stop. His yelling had grown hoarse and profane, but I could understand it better by now. He kept repeating, "Is this what you wanted? Is this what you really wanted? Well I'm gonna give it to you."

"No, Daddy, please don't. Daddy, please stop. You're hurting me. Daddy, please."

I tried to ignore the pleading and the assault, but it just seemed to grow more frantic; the baby continued to cry hysterically, Roxie screamed and pled for an end to the madness, and my father continued his onslaught. I was at the point of losing my mind. I had to find some way to end the madness. I walked to my closet and reached inside to retrieve my 22-caliber rifle with which I was an expert shot, having proved it several times in Boy Scout competitions. I grabbed a few bullets from my ammunition box, slid the bolt back on the gun, and planted a bullet into the chamber. After closing the chamber with determination, I started out of my room when I saw my mother propped against the door in a heap of total resignation. Hysterical at that point, I alternately yelled at my father and cried inconsolably while I tried to apologize to my sister for what I had allowed to happen. I walked back into my room like a rooster that had been defeated in a cock fight; there was nothing I could do, and nowhere to escape. I walked back to the closet, closed the door, squatted in the corner, put the barrel of the gun under my chin, and started praying for God to stop this insanity. Several times I tried to pull the trigger, figuring that if I killed myself it would end the assault. Surely my death could serve some purpose, even if it could just stop my own pain and be forever on my father's conscience for what he was doing. Finally, the noise in the next room quieted to the sound of Roxie's sobbing and an occasional moan from Daddy. I had to do something - I didn't know whether I was going to shoot him or myself.

When Daddy opened the door to Roxie's room, I got up and went to my door with the rifle still in my grasp. Mama was still in the hall, but was propped against her own bedroom door. Roxie was pleading with my father, "Daddy please don't take those. They belong to Jerry. That is his high school ring and he can't get another one." It was then that I noticed that he had something clutched in his right hand, which was swollen from the beating he had just administered.

I stepped out into the hallway just as Roxie stepped toward the door, I was horrified; her clothes were torn, her lip was bleeding, one of her eyes was swollen almost closed, and her face was horribly bruised. She sat baby Larry out on the hallway floor then closed the door with a bang before I could even get an apology out of my mouth. I followed Daddy to the back door where he opened the sliding glass door, stepped out, and threw the rings out into the field behind the house. I was sure that I heard one of the rings hit a board on the fence at the back of the yard. I started toward the door when he turned to me and snarled, "If I ever catch you looking for those, I'll tear your butt up." I knew what that meant because the double-tongued belt that he used for beatings terrified me – it was his tool of choice after the razor strap was destroyed in the fire. I did go out and look for the rings several times but never made a big deal of it; I was afraid of attracting the attention of our neighbors who were sure to report it to my father.

The next week, Roxie and Jerry eloped. Nobody would tell any of us boys what was happening or where Roxie had gone because they were afraid that Daddy would find out. I walked around the house as if I had lost my soul. I missed Roxie so badly that I cried myself to sleep every night in waves of guilt and shame at what I should have prevented. I found no peace in sleep.

My family never recovered from that event; we were a household of victims. I could no longer look my father, my mother, or my brothers in the eye. My shame for my cowardice was unbearable. My mother tried to be strong for all of us, but it was more than she could handle. She tried to maintain our normal schedule and activities around the house, which had fallen silent of laughter and fun. In addition to trying to keep the household together, Mama also had to try to keep Daddy healthy and distracted in the aftermath of the attack. My brothers were so traumatized that there was hardly any play or laughter around our household. Most of our play through the following weeks involved sports and friends that took us away from the house.

For as long as I could remember, Daddy had come and gone to work on a predictable, regular schedule. For several days after the beating, he went to work on schedule, but returned to the house right after noon as if trying to catch us doing something wrong. Our paranoia was made complete; Daddy's was only beginning. His behavior became more erratic and extreme with each passing day.

Things got so crazy around the house that I lost track of time as the summer came and went. Daddy became obsessive about Roxie, but nobody would tell him where she was living because of the threats that he continued to make. To keep him functional, the doctors had prescribed medications that kept him under control. As his obsession and anger escalated, the doctors increased his dosages and the strength of his medication. I tried to busy myself with mowing lawns and doing odd jobs to earn money to get the things that I needed for the upcoming school year. With the continuing drama of Daddy's obsession, I was numb and depressed. I felt so isolated because Daddy demanded more and more of Mama's attention, reducing the amount of attention that she could give to us. As my father's behavior became more predictable, my mother's time was monopolized by her caring for him.

In the fall of 1962, when we started school again I became the smallest kid in yet another high school. I was still only four feet, eight inches tall, but this, my sophomore year, was to become my year of change, which started almost immediately. The racial issues of the area had already been charged by a lawsuit, then the appeals to the Supreme Court, for the enrollment of a black man, James Meredith, at Ole Miss, our beloved University of Mississippi - a school that still identified its alumni as "Rebels."

When the Klans in our area heard that Meredith would be attending the university at the end of September, Daddy started meeting with some of his friends to plan a strategy to prevent his enrollment. One day in mid-September, one of those friends, R. J. Glover, came to the house to show off something that he had in his car. I followed Daddy and Mister Glover out to his car where he unlocked the trunk and revealed a large load covered by several military style wool blankets. When he tossed the blankets aside, I was stunned by what I saw – a box of guns and ammunition - machine guns. Mister Glover reached into the box and retrieved a Tommy gun and a German MP40 machine gun. He handed one of the machines to Daddy, who ratcheted back on the receiver ejecting a cartridge onto the ground at my feet. Alarmed, Mister Glover said, "Careful with that Ed, that thing is loaded and ready to go."

Daddy quickly put the machine gun back into the box when Mister Glover grabbed it and said, "Don't put that thing back in there like that; one bump and it could shoot up your whole neighborhood."

One of our neighbors, with whom Daddy also worked, strolled over to the back of the car and picked up one of the machine guns. The three men stood at the back of the car until each of them had picked up and examined each of the guns from the box, dry firing some of them toward the field at the end of the street.

Though they sent me away before they started talking, I could still hear them well enough to understand the gist of their conversation. They were part of a group of men that was going to the University of Mississippi at the end of September to block Meredith's enrollment and attendance. Mister Glover stated that they wouldn't be using any of the guns at the university; they would be carrying new weapons that they could throw at the "agitators," and liquids that they cold spray on the them, to really "fire them up." With that, he produced a small bottle from the back of the car and said, "This High Life will put the fear of God in some of them. If you get their hair wet with this stuff, it smells to high heaven and it burns like hell." I knew High Life to be an unpleasant concoction of many uses and applications. I had heard my uncles talking about how they used it to get rid of undesired animals around their homes and neighborhoods. High Life was one of the few things that would even exterminate fire ants.

After Mister Glover left, Daddy went into the house and made a number of telephone calls to some of his other friends, telling each of the details for the upcoming demonstration to be held in Oxford, Mississippi in late September. While he had their attention, he also made a point of bragging about the arsenal that he had just seen, hinting about how they may be employed if things were to get worse.

As planned, they were ready at the end of September. They received word that the US Attorney General was sending troops and federal marshals to make sure that Meredith made it into college as scheduled. On September 30, a large group of the men from our area joined forces with several other groups from all over Mississippi at the university campus. At first, the demonstration consisted of shouting at the marshals, troops, and supporters that had gathered on the campus for the enrollment. However, things got out of hand rather quickly with a melee of rock throwing, fist fights, and even gunshots. During the ensuing riots, two federal agents were killed and more than a hundred people were injured.

When the men returned from Oxford with Daddy, I saw that a couple of them were injured. Mister Glover had a gash across his right cheek, both eyes blackened, and bruises on both sides of his face. Mister Brady also had a black eye and a large bump on the side of his head. As they treated their wounds, they talked excitedly, so I was surprised when none of them talked about the incidents of the day with any detail; it was as if they just wanted to forget about it. They considered the day's events a victory because Meredith was unable to complete his enrollment at the university. After everyone else left, Daddy went straight to bed so I didn't get any of the details about what happened.

The next day, we heard that James Meredith was successfully enrolled in the university. Daddy skulked about the house like a large cat itching for a fight. After dinner, he said something about going to a meeting, then disappeared until almost midnight. Daddy came into the house with a bundle of clothes and a handful of papers, which he set on the dining table. As he rifled through the sheets, I noticed that one of the papers had a header, "The Fiery Cross." I tried to get a better look at the paperwork, but Daddy picked them up quickly when he noticed that I had taken an interest.

Mama was trying to hold us all together but she knew that things were beyond her control, so she called on one of my uncles for help. Uncle Raymond, Daddy's brother, was one of only two uncles that I trusted or respected at that time. He was a barrel-chested, round-faced man with a ready smile and arms as thick as the legs on most men. When he showed up at the house one day, I think we all breathed a sigh of relief because Daddy's behavior had become so erratic. However, my father went berserk. He leaped out of his bed and charged at Mama, accusing her of plotting against him. When Uncle Raymond saw Daddy move toward Mama, he stepped between them, a move that only incensed Daddy. He reached out and swatted Uncle Raymond across the face and called him a name. Uncle Raymond was unfazed by the blow. "Ed, don't you hit me again, or I will hit you back." Daddy hit him a couple of times more while Uncle Raymond kept warning him, "Ed, stop hitting me. Don't hit me again." Finally, the big man had enough. He rolled his big hand into a maul, and threw a short, powerful punch that hit Daddy right between the eyes. Daddy fell backward and slumped across the bed, no fight left in him.

Mama and Uncle Raymond walked into the kitchen and sat at the table to talk. Recovering, Daddy started rifling through the drawers in his bedroom. I knew what he was looking for, but I had already removed all of the guns and ammunition from the house, not because I was afraid of what Daddy would do, but because I was afraid of what I might do. One day I might get the courage to carry out the threat I made when I took the rifle from my closet a few nights earlier. I heard Uncle Raymond explaining to Mama how Daddy's health insurance from the tire plant would cover his hospitalization and what she would have to do to have him admitted.

During the following week, Daddy went to work one day and didn't return home in the afternoon. Mama matter-of-factly explained that he had been admitted into a special hospital in Jackson, Mississippi, and he wouldn't be home for a while. I could see that the stresses of our family situation were wearing heavily on Mama. She tried to keep a brave face on for us, but I could see her sadness and feel her grief. Jerry and Roxie came by the house to pick up the rest of her clothes and what was left of her hope chest, loading them into the back of Jerry's car. I tried to apologize for not having helped her but could never make the words come out. Jerry didn't say much but did make a comment about how Daddy would settle down after he got those shock treatments for a few weeks.

My Daddy is in a mental institution! I was genuinely surprised. After the reality settled in, I thought, *Well, here is one more thing for the Blanche family to talk about. Every time they all get together, I hear my aunts and uncles talk about how none of us boys are going to be worth anything – there are just too many of us. Now this is just one more thing for them to throw up into our faces. I can just hear it now, 'These boys are going to be less than worthless, their daddy was institutionalized.'*

Nature can be so cruel sometimes. Mama was gone much of the time to be with Daddy during his recovery. Since she didn't drive, she had to be shuttled to and from Jackson for several days at a time during which we were left to fend for ourselves. Fortunately, I knew my way around the kitchen so I did most of the cooking and cleaning while she was away. It was during this time that I started to grow, REALLY grow. There was a monster inside me that was trying to outgrow my skin. During the next six months I grew from four feet, eight inches to five feet, six inches – ten inches in six months! Every joint in my body ached and there was not enough food in the house to keep my appetite sated. Since Daddy was not working, we had no money to speak of and we were falling behind in the house payments. The cupboards were often bare. I was so thankful that Vidalia had a school lunch program because I got at least one good meal on schooldays. I grew so fast that I got stretch marks on the backs of my legs and my pants were looking more like knickerbockers.

I never paid much attention to the inadequacy of my clothing until Mister Lindley, my geometry teacher, came up to me one day and said, "Buddy, I'd like to do something for you. Do you mind if Ophelia and I help you? We've seen what is happening to you and would like to help you some way."

I was taken aback by the offer because I had no idea who Ophelia was. He explained to me that Ophelia was his wife and that she wanted to make sure that we had enough to eat and clean clothes to wear.

I liked Mister Lindley better than any of my other teachers because he always had a word of praise for me, having tried to move me into a more advanced mathematics class earlier in the year. After school that day, he drove me to the Vidalia General Store and had me fitted for three pairs of new blue jeans that were so long, I had to roll the bottoms up two cuffs to make them the right length. After he paid for the pants, he smiled and said, "Those ought to keep up with you for a while."

On the way back to the school, I told him that I wanted to repay him some way for what he had done, offering to cut his grass or wax his car. He gave me a big, knowing smile and said softly, "No, Buddy. I have a son that already takes care of those things. One day you will be in a situation where you will be able to do the same thing for someone else. All you have to do is pass it on; help someone else when you get that opportunity."

That was one of two impossible challenges Mister Lindley gave me that year. The other was to trisect an arbitrary angle using nothing more than a compass and a straight edge – an impossible operation for which I would get an "A" if I could make it work for any angle. Of course I did not complete either challenge during that year, but I did trisect the angle while in a mechanical drawing class in college – I just had to do a little cheat and fold the paper. For the challenge of passing on the good deed, I've yet to find a way to redeem a debt of infinite value.

While Mama and Daddy were away, each of the boys found ways to cope with the situation. Johnny and Larry weren't in school yet, so they were watched by one of our neighbors during the day. They had many young friends to play with while the older children were in school. Billy, always the entertainer, bought a dummy and took up ventriloquism. He attracted a crowd and charmed the girls wherever he went. Jimmy, who we had taught to play baseball when he was only three, immersed himself in the sport. He could already throw a curve ball that would impress the pros and had a pitching coach who was working with him several days each week to get him ready for baseball season. I was the only one that still seemed disconnected to the people and things around me. I owed a debt to Mister Lindley that I could never repay, I no longer had Roxie to help me make sense of my life, I was outgrowing my skin, and I was alone. My life had changed in ways I could not understand, having consequences with which I could not cope. I had an ominous feeling that the changes were not going to end soon.

CHAPTER 4

Divergence

While Daddy was away for treatment, we fell far behind in the mortgage payments, eventually falling into default. After they released him from the hospital, he and Mama sold the house as quickly as possible to prevent foreclosure on the property. With the proceeds from the sale, they bought a small house in Ridgecrest, a subdivision on the outskirts of Ferriday, Louisiana.

At first, Ferriday seemed to be a town divided against itself; even in the outskirts. We lived in a subdivision on the south side of Highway 84 where no colored people lived in the eight mile distance between Vidalia and Ferriday. Like a bad cliché, all of the colored people in our area lived on the other side of the tracks on the North side of Highway 84. However, things got reversed as you went into town. The first thing you saw after you crossed the tracks that guarded the entrance to Ferriday was the bayou with a prominent sign stating, "Ferriday is a Bird Sanctuary." The area always seemed to look as if it were being used as a dumping ground; strewn with trash and old appliances. Behind the bayou was an old sawmill that was open on three sides, exposing the mill machinery like a museum proudly displaying antique hardware. Past the sawmill, the first true glimpse of Ferriday revealed "Bucktown" - the colored quarter - which populated the south end of town with houses that varied from nice brick homes to those that were dilapidated and on the edge of condemnation. Local businesses lined both sides of the highway, though many had been closed and boarded up for as long as I could remember. The other three quarters of Ferriday were all white with most of the businesses located in the north and east sides of town.

I don't know how I made the transition to Ferriday. I still bore the humiliation and shame of my failure to act when Daddy attacked Roxie. I had become withdrawn and shy, fearing that everyone could see my cowardice. I had to find something else that I could focus on. In addition to everything else, at 15, I was finally beginning to go through puberty.

As soon as we got settled in Ridgecrest I got my driver's license – driving was my escape and freedom. I had been driving with a permit for more than a year, and found that I loved driving, anywhere, for any reason. When Daddy needed to go across state for anything, I went along to do the driving. Even before I got my license, he trusted me enough to sleep while I navigated and drove to church functions and to some of his Klan meetings, even though I would not participate in any of the events. At the Klan rally, I stayed with the car, pretending I was a chauffeur. Every Sunday, it was my job to drive my father to and from the new church near Olla, Louisiana. I enjoyed the drives because it was the only thing for which my father gave me continued approval. It also gave me special time with Daddy during which I could try to reconnect with him after his assault on Roxie. When he told me I could get my own car, I was ecstatic. That meant that I would need to get a job to pay for gas and insurance, and it meant that I would be driving myself to school!

I found a job very quickly at the Shell service station near our subdivision and started working immediately. I enjoyed working at the service station because it gave me a sense of freedom and a distraction from the scenarios I continuously built in my head - scenarios about what I would do next time. At the station, I was allowed to do any kind of automotive work for which I felt qualified, so I studied auto and service manuals diligently to become qualified on all of the services that were offered at the station. I worked shoulder to shoulder with the two colored men who worked in the two stalls outside: washing cars, changing oil, lubricating, and occasionally changing batteries or alternators when customers would bring them to us in desperation. The owner, J.D. Mills, and his mother managed the station and did most of the sales from inside the front office.

The two men I worked with were as different as night and day. Wilbur Jones was a big, soft-spoken man with a gentle manner and a belly laugh that would entertain even the most serious of people. His skin was chocolate brown, his eyes a light brown. His hair was full, thick and wiry, and his teeth were perfect with a bright white luster. He was a full-time employee at the station and quickly became my mentor and trainer. James Gorham was gaunt looking with deep set eyes that were as dark as coal and skin that was darker than any colored person I had ever known. His mouth seemed too big for his face and when he smiled; his teeth were stained brown from coffee and heavy smoking. He only worked at the station on the weekends or when they needed help for special projects. He was loud and boisterous, laughing aloud at everything and anything.

Summer at the station was very busy, so I took advantage of it by working every available hour I could get. Since I spent so much of my time with Wilbur during the summer, we were getting to know each other very well. Every day that I worked with him became more comfortable and productive because we worked cooperatively, sharing the responsibilities of the rack areas equally. Wilbur enjoyed it because I was so willing to take on the responsibilities and share the credit for our accomplishments. I enjoyed it because Wilbur treated me with parity; he never talked down to me because of my youth. As we worked out in the racks, we talked freely and cracked jokes to one another to break the monotony of the mundane work. After a while, he began to feel like a trusted friend instead of just someone with whom I worked.

When I wasn't working, I spent much of my time fishing on Lake Saint John or at home reading the classics or the blue books from a biographical series about the boy heroes: *George Washington, Boy President*; *Abraham Lincoln, Boy President*; *Thomas Edison, Boy Inventor*. I found it relaxing to lie on the cool concrete floor under the carport and enjoy my books in the breeze that usually came with the heat of the day. I also spent more of my time studying racially motivated violence in the south and the charged racial dichotomy of my own household. Daddy became more involved with the Klan activities, spending more time at the rallies and meetings in Mississippi than at those in Louisiana. Since he worked at the tire plant in Natchez, he joined the Klan klavern there. Several of the men who worked with him at the tire plant had also been recruited into the same klavern, so he already knew most of the men in the local klaverns. At first, the Klan meetings seemed more social than functional, but that changed during the year. In 1963, the Klans stepped up the violence against the colored activists and outside agitators in Mississippi; but we didn't seem to be as affected in Louisiana. On June 12th, someone shot and killed Medgar Evers by a sniper outside his home in Jackson, Mississippi. I knew who Evers was because I had been reading about his Civil Rights activities around Jackson and his involvement in the National Association for the Advancement of Colored People – an organization which Daddy and many of his Klan cohorts detested.

The day after Evers was killed, R. J. Glover came to the house to visit with Daddy. I was stretched out in my favorite cool spot in the corner of the carport when Mister Glover and Daddy leaned against the car parked in the driveway and started talking secretively. At first, I wasn't paying attention to what the two were talking about, but when Mister Glover mentioned Medgar Evers, I was all ears. "You know who did it don't you? You met him before at the rally that we held a couple of months ago in Jackson. Do you remember that old Marine that talked to us for such a long time after the rally was done? I think his name was Beckham or Beck-something-or-'nother. Anyway, some of the guys over in the Jackson klavern are saying that he done the shootin'. They're sayin' that he SAID he done it. I always thought that guy was a little messed up in the head, but never figured him for that kind of guts."

Daddy replied, "I heard a few of the boys at the tire plant talking today and they said the same thing. A couple of them know the marine well enough to know that he is capable of doing that kind of thing, and some even heard him admit to actually shooting that nigger. By the way, his name is Beckwith – de la Beckwith. He'll be all right if he just keeps his mouth shut. There ain't a jury in the whole south that would convict him for killin' that nigger agitator."

As they continued their discussion of the assassination of Evers, I tried to move closer to them while they talked. Mister Glover saw me trying to eavesdrop so they moved out to the end of the driveway to continue their conversation.

After the Klan violence started, Daddy became more distant as if to isolate us from his involvement in the Klan activities and the violence that was sure to come. I had already become vocal about my concerns for his participation in the Klans and his growing involvement in the union activities at the tire plant. Because of all the Klan activities and freedom marches, the summer of 1963 was full of distractions and concern.

During the last part of the summer, the two girls that lived next door provided the greatest distraction, having taken it upon themselves to tease me to the edges of sanity. It seemed that every time the younger girl saw me outside after it started getting dark, she would go into her room and start undressing, pulling her blouse off in full view of her window to expose her ample breasts. She would then come to her window, give a "shy" wave, then pull her shades down. I would get so boiled up I didn't know what to do; I knew what I wanted to do. Though she was my age, she was much more developed and precocious than I. The older girl was more overt in her attentions and intentions. When she caught me reading in the shade of the carport, she would come sit or lie next to me with her bare leg across me, usually against my bare back or chest. She would rub the soft part of her forearm or the inside of her thigh on my bare skin watching for any sign of my excitement. She seemed delighted if she got me stimulated or when she got me to fidget enough to try to hide it. I always felt that she was teasing me for my humiliation and embarrassment more than she was for my pleasure. I figured they were so relentless because they knew how easily excited I had become as puberty had its way with me. Before they moved at the end of the summer, both of them had confessed to my mother that they were crazy about me because I was so nice and was the smartest boy they knew. Unfortunately, my mother didn't tell me about how the girls felt until after they had moved away. After Mama told me what the girls said, I didn't feel very smart at all – I felt I had missed out on something good.

While we lived in Ridgecrest I met a few kids my own age so I was looking forward to attending school. The only high school kids I already knew were those that lived in my immediate neighborhood and a few whose cars I serviced at the Shell station. I began to make preparations for school by buying school supplies and a few new clothes. I had several pairs of work shoes, but only one pair of dress shoes that were not in the best of shape. The stitching on the sole on the right shoe had worn out, so the bottom layer of leather flapped loose, slapping against the insole with each step. When Daddy saw the condition of the shoes, he suggested that

I take them to Frank's Shoe Shop in Ferriday. He said, "That darkie can make them look and feel like new. Just take them down to Frank and let him know who you are. He will fix them for next to nothing."

I knew Daddy was right about Frank fixing my shoes because he had been fixing our shoes for many years. He and Frank Morris had been friends for as long as I could remember. When we lived in Natchez years earlier, Daddy dropped in to see Frank when we passed through Ferriday on our way to Jena to visit Grandma. When we lived in Jena, he stopped by Frank's Shoe Shop when we traveled to Natchez. It seems that they always had something to talk about, just another part of the enigma that was my father. I knew that Daddy admired and respected him because Frank was the only colored person that had ever been invited to sit at our dinner table. Sometimes I think Daddy respected him more than he respected some of his own brothers.

One afternoon I took the shoes to Frank's shop which was located just inside town on the right side of Fourth Street, the main street through Ferriday. I felt uneasy as I pulled up into the alleyway next to his shop and parked. Though I had been to Frank's shop before, I had never been there by myself nor had I ever been in any other part of the colored quarters by myself. When I got out of the car, I walked back toward the street to the front of the shop where I hardly had the front door open when Frank popped through the door at the back of the shop. He came to the gate that separated the workshop from the display area and greeted me with his patented smile. As usual, he was impeccably dressed, with spit-shined shoes, creased pants, and a bright red vest over a white dress shirt and tie. He wore an apron to protect his clothes from the shoe polish and grease on the machines in his shop. His hair was glistening and slick with Royal Crown Pomade. The only discrepancies to his usual formal dress were his cuffed sleeves which he had rolled up past his elbows.

"How y'all doin', Master Blanche? I see you done wore through another pair of shoes. Yo daddy always said you wuz hard on shoes, so I always done made them extry tough 'fore he took them home to you." He reached across the gate, took the shoes, and gave them a cursory exam before remarking, "These is some nice shoes y'all got here. Next time y'all gets new shoes like this, bring them to me first and I'll make them strong as you. Y'all can jus' wait if y'all ain't in no hurry. I can fix this in no time."

As Frank worked, I looked around the shop at his machines and cobbler stand where he was applying glue to the loose sole. He had several pairs of used shoes for sale at the front of the store where they were displayed to all who stopped in front of the large plate glass window. I looked at the shelves of shoes on the back wall and started to read the names on the tags that identified each pair with a customer. I counted at least three pairs that belonged to known Klansmen and two that belonged to Concordia Parish Sheriff's Deputies. As I studied the back of the shop, I felt someone studying me from the bedroom at the back of the shop. As I peered into the darkness, a very pretty colored woman came to the door and peeked out at me before fading back into the darkness of the room. Frank noticed as I stood mesmerized and said, "Don't pay her no never mind. She jus' waitin' on a friend to git here. Y'all don't pay her no never mind 'cause yo daddy would come down here plenty mad if he saw y'all looking at her that way."

I had heard that Frank was a lady's man, but never thought about it when he was around me before; he had a way about him. I had also heard that he acted as a go-between, providing women to the local law enforcement officers in the small room at the back of his shop or in his house which was located about a few hundred feet from his shop. In one moment he could be as humble as a country preacher and in the next as self-confident as a city politician. He was strikingly handsome with a ready smile that revealed a mouth full of perfect teeth. I knew that there was something going on when he went to the door of the bedroom and said something reassuring to the lady. I couldn't hear what he said, but I heard the reply as she giggled back, "Honey, I got as much time as you got shoes to shine." He went back to the sewing machine and ran stitches around the soul of each of the shoes, then turned to me and said, "Y'all want me to put some taps on here so you don't wear out the heels so fast? They gonna make people stan' up and take notice in that new school." Before I could answer, he turned and put one of the shoes on the shoe form and nailed a horseshoe shaped metal tap to the back of the heel. When he finished with the second shoe, he handed them over the counter to me with a big smile.

"How much do I owe you, Mister Frank?"

"Boy, you don't have to call me 'mister.' You jus' call me Frank."

"If my daddy heard me calling you Frank, he'd kick my butt then make me apologize. I think I better call you Mister Frank or Uncle Frank."

"Uncle Frank? Uncle Frank?! Make me sound like some kinda darkie in a movie or somethin'. Soun' like Uncle Tom! Y'all call me what you has to, but don't call me Uncle Frank." He laughed and said, "If you calls me Mister Frank, then you owes me two dollars. If you jus' calls me Frank, then you owes me only a dollar.

I reached for my wallet and handed him two dollars and replied, "I owe you two dollars then, because I ain't riskin' another fight with Daddy for just a dollar, Mister Frank." He laughed as he took my money and said, "I always knowed you wuz a good boy. One day you an' me gonna be friends like yo daddy an' me. He a good man, too." When I looked at the shoes carefully, I was surprised at how fresh they looked; they really did look new. As I left the shop, I examined the stitching in the souls and knew that I would wear them out before they came loose again.

When school started at the beginning of September, 1963, I was ready. I drove my two-tone blue '54 Ford through Ferriday with pride as I made my way to my new high school for the first time. It was on the north end of town with the length of the school's gravel parking lot having access to the main road. Most of the classrooms were lined along either side of the hallway in the long building that ran parallel with the road. It reminded me very much of Bude School where I had attended my first grades. It felt like home to me.

Shortly after school started, all hell broke out in Alabama when four young colored girls were killed in an explosion at the Sixteenth Street Baptist Church in Birmingham. When I got home from school that afternoon Daddy told me he needed me to drive him over to Vidalia for a meeting. I drove him to the Shamrock Inn where he met with six other men in the back room of the restaurant. I sat at the front by myself as he and the other men had an animated discussion about the events happening in Alabama. I could occasionally hear some of the conversation when one of them would carelessly raise his voice high enough to overcome the noise of the traffic at the front of the restaurant.

"It's their own damn faults, them and the courts for starting all this shit."

"It's them same agitators that keep comin' over here in Mississippi and stirrin' things up. Them agitators probably blew up the church themselves just to stir up more trouble."

I tried to move closer to the door to understand more, but one of the men snarled at me, "Move your ass back across the room."

I moved, but I wasn't pleased. As I took my seat, I began to fume as they justified the actions of the Klansmen that had perpetuated this travesty. I don't think any of them knew about the bomb beforehand, but they seemed to know exactly who was involved after the explosion. After I moved away, I ordered another cup of coffee and sat quietly. I could still hear as the men as they traded agitated comments.

"You know that it won't be long before we have to deal with more of those agitators right here on our own front porch."

"We have to tighten our own ranks and make sure that this integration doesn't even get a start around here. They're over there rioting right now, tryin' to tear up the whole city. If they try to bring that shit over here, the streets are gonna run with blood."

"I hear that the FBI is working to get stool pigeons to report on us all over Mississippi and Louisiana. How we gonna stop these stool pigeons from gittin' in on us?"

"We already got a way. We got our own club to keep out all those we don't trust until they prove themselves worthy. Each person in the club carries one of these." The man produced a silver coin from his pocket and showed it to the table with pride. Two more of the men produced the same silver coins and placed them on the table next to the first. "And they ain't no good if they don't have your birth year on them. That's part of the secret identifying mark. We all know each other already, but this just makes sure that it stays that way."

"Nobody gits in and nobody gits out without one of these. The only way to git in is to earn the trust of someone that already has one; you got to prove yourself."

I tried to see if Daddy also had one of the silver coins, but he was completely hidden from my view. On the way home, I tried to question him about the coins but he stifled me quickly. "Boy, don't you ever mention any of that to anyone. Not to me, not to anyone. Those men are dead serious and just knowing about those silver dollars can get you stuffed down an abandoned oil well. They even have police that work with them. Don't ever mention it again."

As we continued home, I tried to make sense of what was happening with the Klans, so I pressed on, "But Daddy, that was a church that they blew up in Birmingham. It was a Baptist church like your own. How would you feel if they decided to blow up one of our churches?"

That did it! He was immediately in a full rage at my audacity, but I wasn't through yet. No! I had to go one more step. "Those were children; little girls. They were all about Jimmy's age. How can any of those men – anyone at all - justify killing little girls?"

At that point, I don't know if he was enraged at me because I was asking all the wrong questions or if he was afraid that I might say something to someone else to get my answers. I really wasn't looking for answers from him, I just wanted him to examine his position in what was happening and think about where it might take us all. I am sure it was more wishful thinking than reality, but I was hoping that part of his rage was motivated by guilt over the Klan's participation in the death of four young girls.

After his meeting with the men in Vidalia, my relationship with my daddy became even more strained. Though I worked very hard to gain his approval in whatever I did, nothing seemed to matter. He became even more critical of almost everything I did. Mama and my brothers must have thought we had become sworn enemies. I spent a lot of time in tears. I was not physically or emotionally strong enough to fight back effectively. And since my voice was changing, any argument I made sounded like it was played through a saxophone with a broken reed. My voice didn't seem to know what range it should be playing, especially when my emotions came into play.

I tried to lose myself in my work and school where I tried my best to fit in socially, but how does one with few social skills fit in? Things got even worse for me as I became paranoid from the social stress. I made friends, but I was afraid to get too close to anyone because I was sure they would see my cowardice; my fear seemed to live on me like an old jacket. I tried to make up for my lack of skills by telling tall tales of my accomplishments, which usually painted me as the hero. While I was trying to escape my own problems, I learned a couple of lessons about people with bigger problems than my own.

The first lesson came during the first day of November when I went to work. Wilbur was agitated and sober; something was really eating at him. It seemed that he was only using the work that we had as a distraction. Later when things around the station settled down, I approached him. "Hey Wilbur, is everything alright?"

"They done beat up that boy over in Natchez. They beat up him and that other boy out at Port Gibson, then they shot his car. They shot that car full of holes."

"What are you talking about? I ain't heard nothing about a beating or shooting in Natchez or Port Gibson."

"All they wuz doin' wuz tryin to get them people over there so they can vote. They jus' boys."

"Who shot at them?"

"They wuz four or five men done tracked them boys down and beat them real bad. They beat them up in a service station jus' like this one, then they shot they car all over."

I apologized to him about what was happening and told him I would find something out for him. It didn't take long before I found out that I didn't really want to get more information. During the week, I went with Daddy to some kind of meeting at a rod and gun club in Natchez. I recognized many of the men that were there, but that means that many of them also recognized me. They were all men who worked with Daddy or with whom he frequently met at the Shamrock Inn. The beating of the two men in Port Gibson was the topic of the day.

"Did y'all see what them boys from over at the paper plant did? They done put the fear of God in a couple of them agitators."

"It wuzn't just the boys from the paper plant that done that. One or two of them wuz from the tire plant," someone said in rebuttal, as if this were some kind of competition for who should get credit.

"We want to thank our brothers from Concordia for givin' us their support in all of this, too. We couldn't have done any of this without them," the man nodded in the direction of my father. It was the first time I had seen any indication that Daddy was involved directly with anything like this in either Mississippi or Louisiana.

"Well, I don't think we gonna have no more problems out of those boys. I think they got the fear – they got some respect for our local rights."

"This is just the beginning, boys. This group is gonna grow – the south is gonna rise again! It is gonna start right here in Mississippi."

A loud whoop of approval went up. The noise in the room climbed to a roar; the din made it almost impossible to separate one conversation from another. I watched as a few of the men circulated around the room as if they were receiving accolades for a job well done. As I watched the room, I could see that Daddy was not being given the same accolades and took some comfort that he had not been present at the beating of the two men.

On Friday, I told Wilbur what I knew about the incident, but not how I got the information. I tried to reassure him that there was only a small group of men in Mississippi that were involved with the beatings and burnings that were being reported. "I don't think we have anything to worry about on this side of the river. The people over here have a little more sense than that."

Wilbur was not convinced. "We got as much Klans over here as they do anywhere else." He looked at me as if he suspected me of having been in the Klans. Somehow, I was sure he knew about my father's involvement. His pain and concern was obvious – Wilbur wore his heart on his sleeve. This was all hitting too close to home for me. It was but a premonition of the violence that would soon follow.

My second lesson on the afternoon of November 22, 1963. I was entering my fifth period Spanish class when one of the girls in the class said, "Buddy, did you hear that President Kennedy was shot?"

Thinking that she was joking, I shot back, "It was probably Joe DiMaggio after he found out the president was messing around with Marilyn." Of course I chuckled at my own joke. "Maybe he wasn't shot. Maybe he just fell out of his rocking chair."

"No. He was shot in Dallas and I heard that he is already dead, but they had to take him to the big hospital in Washington, D.C. so he could get special treatment to save his life."

I turned to her and said, "You are kidding, aren't you?"

"No. He was shot while he was visiting in Dallas. I heard that Governor Connolly was shot too because they were both in the same car."

I sat through class in disbelief of what I was hearing, feeling guilty for having made the cruel statements about him earlier. I admired President Kennedy though he was an unpopular president with the white people of the South. He had become one of my World War II heroes after I read of his heroic actions in the book *PT109, John F. Kennedy in World War II*. I also admired him for the way he handled the backlash after the fiasco at the Bay of Pigs and for having backed the Russians down during the Cuban missile crisis. At that time, I probably respected him more than I respected anyone in the world.

On the afternoon of the assassination, I could hardly wait to get home and watch the news. I didn't have to wait. All of the television channels were continuously broadcasting the breaking news and the actions that were being taken to find the assassin. Almost immediately they announced that they had captured Lee Harvey Oswald in a movie theatre, revealing pictures of his capture and incarceration on the television. When Daddy got home, he watched for a little while then made me turn the TV off because there was nothing else on. I went out to the back yard and sat at the edge of the slough and wept. I had never felt such a loss before. Now I had only one great World War II hero left – Audie Murphy, the youngest, most decorated soldier of the war.

During the next week the news carried a flurry of activity associated with the assassination. On the night of November 24, I was watching a news special as the police were leading Lee Harvey Oswald down the corridor of the parking structure at the police station when someone stepped out of the crowd and shot him. They captured the shooter on the spot and identified him as Jack Ruby, a night club owner who was disturbed by Oswald's assassination of the president. I had trouble understanding how he made his way through the throng of officers to take the shots and wondered at the miracle that none of the officers were struck by stray bullets. Beginning with Kennedy's assassination, each new circumstance increased my sadness and my feelings of insecurity. Each new incident strengthened my belief that it was all a conspiracy. How could anyone be safe if the president of the United States was not safe, if the governor of Texas was not safe, if a person was not safe when surrounded by scores of armed policemen? It had to be a conspiracy set up by several agencies.

None of the other events surrounding the assassination affected me as much as did the grace and dignity of the Kennedy family members during the week that followed. Jackie Kennedy held her composure as if she were trying to comfort the entire country on the loss of our beloved president. Even young Caroline held her composure like a young princess bred to slough off pain and loss with the dignity of an adult. I think the entire country was brought to tears as the gun carriage carrying President Kennedy's coffin, followed by a riderless black horse, drew near the Saint Matthews Cathedral for his memorial service. I held my own composure well until after the ceremony when young John Kennedy Jr. stepped forward and saluted as his father's coffin was being removed from the cathedral after the service. It is an image that is indelibly stamped into my memory and emotions for a lifetime. I tried to hide my tears from the family, but it was impossible to do since we had only one television and everyone was gathered in the living room to watch the small black and white TV for the coverage of the events.

At school, I was spending more time to myself or with a very few select friends. I don't know how I would have made it through those tough days were it not for the friendship of my two closest Spanish class cohorts, Katherine and Candice. I admired them for their intelligence, sensitivity, and popularity.

Katherine Leigh was a beautiful blonde daughter of the high school math teacher. She was dating the acknowledged smartest boy in school. Not only were they the brightest couple in school, but also one of the most popular.

Candice was the socialite of the group. She played coronet for the high school band, was a star member of the Bulldogs Booster Club, and seemed to be involved in the organization of every high school event. She was dating the football captain, but I could never see what she saw in him. I think my feelings about him involved some jealousy because I had fallen for her.

If it had not been for the two girls, I don't know how I would have gained any social skills at all. During the Christmas break, I missed them because my family went off in all directions as each of us followed our own interests.

In January, 1964 events heated up the racial issues of our area again. Congress passed the Twenty-fourth[h] Amendment abolishing the poll tax, thus making it possible for colored people to vote. Louisiana had not used the poll tax since the Huey P. Long administration, when he implemented a receipt system so voters no longer had to pay the poll tax. Instead, local law enforcement was responsible for distributing the two-year receipts to all eligible voters. No receipt, no vote. The receipt system was also abolished by the Twenty-fourth[th] Amendment, qualifying any person over 21 without a criminal conviction to vote in Louisiana. I was very worried about how this was going to affect my family and friends during future elections, and about reprisals that were surely forthcoming from the Klans.

My father was especially bitter about the passing of the amendment. He made threat after threat about how he and his friends were going to make sure that none of those "lazy bastards" were going to vote in this state. He started meeting regularly with Jerry, R. J. Glover, Sam Tanner, and several other men who I had not met. I heard them talking several times about how the state organization had grown to several thousand Klansmen with more klaverns than ever. The Klans were growing stronger by the day. They had become more secretive in their meetings, regularly changing their times and locations. However, he continued to meet weekly at the Shamrock Inn with the men of the Silver Dollar Club, as they now called themselves. They seemed to flaunt their exclusivity and disregard for any form of authority. I saw one of them literally thumb his nose at two FBI agents that had followed one of them to a meeting.

I tried to overlook my father's activities, but each day it became more difficult as his activities became more invisible and more secretive. My resentment for him was already deep after what he had done to Roxie, but now it became more open. I began to express my disdain for his activity and for the Klan organization to which he was so devoted. We regularly argued about his involvement in Klan activities and his reconciliation of those activities with his role as a minister. I think it became apparent to the rest of the family that we were on opposite sides of the political and racial issues of those times.

On the days that I worked, I could see the tension growing in Wilbur and James. Wilbur told me how things were getting worse for them since the amendment had been passed. They complained that none of the white people they knew treated them the same anymore, even those who had trusted them explicitly in the past. I could see JD, the owner, treating them differently at the station also, giving them less responsibility and more work, assigning more authority to his mother. She became less tolerant of the decisions that Wilbur made while working out in the racks, reprimanding him harshly and often. When James was there, he simply stayed out of the way and avoided any contact with JD or his mother.

On a Friday night after we had a particularly busy day, I thought it would be good for us to wind down a little after I closed the station. We closed the office and the bay doors then raised the grease rack just high enough to sit on it. I gave Wilbur some money and asked him to go over to the Stop and Go Mart for some vodka. While there, he also picked up a couple of packs of cigarettes and two six-packs of Fresca. We sat on the grease rack, where each of us grabbed a soda, drank a little to make room, then topped off each of the drinks with vodka. I poured a small pack of peanuts in mine. We sat and talked about the issues for a while, then we started telling jokes – any kind of joke was fair play. I thought it great sport when Wilbur started telling me about how the colored people would do the same thing, but when someone made an insult, they would turn it into another game of insults they called "the dozens." The object of the game was to escalate the level of the insults with which you barbed your opponent until one of the players could not think of an insult without saying something about his opponent's mother, thus conceding defeat. If you were simply conceding your loss, you could avoid insulting your opponent's mother by simply stating "yo mama." I could not even imagine getting into a game of insults with my family or with any of my friends – things would get ugly too quickly.

After we drank for a while, James's composure began to slip. He began to challenge some of the jokes as not being funny or as being stupid. Each time he would have an outburst, Wilbur would calm him down and get back into the revelry of the moment. After we drank for a while longer, James began to cry for no apparent reason. I moved over near him and asked him what was wrong. He told me that his baby son had recently died and that he was sure that something could have been done to save him. I felt so bad for him, but didn't know how it felt because I had never lost someone so close to me. Wilbur and I tried to console him, but I was also curious about the circumstances of his son's death. Innocently, I asked him how his son had died. He said, "Gonorrhea." In my ignorance and under the influence of the alcohol, I blurted out, "Gonorrhea? You can't die of gonorrhea, it is a venereal disease. It just makes you drip. If you catch it all you have to do is get a couple of penicillin shots to cure it."

James came unhinged. He jumped up, stood over me and put his face right in front of mine shouting, "You just a boy. What do you know about life and death? What do you know about my son? What do you know about gonorrhea? What do you even know about sex? You prob'ly ain't even got none yet." I quickly apologized for making the remark and admitted that he was right. I really didn't know much about anything. I suddenly felt ignorant and overwhelmed at the same time. My apologies seemed to exacerbate James's anger. He pressed his face so close to mine that I had to lean backward over the grease rack to avoid bumping his head. When I fell backward off the rack, James jumped on top of my chest, pinning my arms with his knees, and put his hands tight around my neck.

Wilbur came over and stood over the two of us and started yelling at James, "Let him go. Leave him alone James. He said he wuz sorry for what he said and he done admitted that he didn't know what he wuz talkin' about."

Wilbur's instructions agitated him even more; James yelled back, "I'm gonna show him somethin' alright. He needs to learn what he done talking about. I'm gonna show him that you can die from sex. I got enough here to choke him to death." At that, he reached for his zipper as if he was going to expose himself and continued, "I got enough here to choke him good. He gonna learn somethin' about mouthin' off about things he don't know about."

Wilbur looked horrified. He grabbed James by his shirt and picked him straight off of me as he continued to dig at his zipper. "You can't treat that white boy like that. Don't you know who you messin' with? He got people that can make you disappear. Oh, God! What you done did?"

He dragged James across the concrete floor toward the front door of the bay, unlatched the door, raised it about four feet and threw James out in a heap. As James collapsed and rolled across the driveway, Wilbur began a panicked rant. "Man, what you done did! Git your black ass across the tracks and stay hid, 'cause they could come after you tonight! You can't treat colored people that way, and you sure as hell can't treat white people that way. That can git you killed. That can git your whole family killed. You gotta know better than that."

As James staggered off into the darkness, Wilbur turned his attention to me. "Buddy, you alright? He didn't mean it. He's drunk and he didn't know what he was doing. I'm sure he didn't mean nothin'. Here, let me help you up. You alright? Don't go gittin' all mad at him 'cause he havin' a bad time right now. We don't want nothing to happen to James. You hear me, Buddy?"

He reached down and offered me a hand up. "You gonna be alright with this?"

I was still a bit dazed by the incident, so I couldn't compose myself quickly enough to make Wilbur feel comfortable. I tried to reassure him, parroting back to him some of the things he had said to me, "He's so drunk he don't know which end is up. I know him well enough to know he didn't really mean anything by it, but man! He went off his rocker there for a while. Is he gonna be alright? We better go check on him. If he gets out on the highway, someone could run him down before he gets halfway across." Wilbur and I ran out of the bay toward the highway which had recently been improved into four lanes with a median strip dividing the opposing traffic. Wilbur ran out to catch James and escorted him across the highway, holding him in the median until traffic cleared enough to allow him to cross safely. "Go on across the tracks an' git yourself in bed. You don't be goin' out nowhere tonight. You go straight home and stay there."

When Wilbur returned, I walked back into the bay, feeling a bit shaken. Together we closed and locked all of the doors, turned the compressor and lights off, then pulled the bay door closed behind us. After I locked the last door, Wilbur said, "James just ain't right after his son died. He just ain't right. Buddy. He didn't mean nothing an' I'm sure he didn't mean to hurt you. He got too much liquor in him. He done lost control. Don't git too mad at him."

Again, I tried to reassure him. "Wilbur, it's alright. I ain't mad at him. I feel real bad about what I said. I never even knew that his son had died; and I certainly didn't know he died from gonorrhea. I didn't even know that was possible! We'll talk about it tomorrow. My head is too messed up right now. I need to get home and get my head straight before I can even begin to think about it."

I don't think the last statement was very comforting to Wilbur; he hung his head and trudged away as if he were carrying the weight of the world on his back. I could tell that he was very troubled but I didn't know what to say to assure him that things were alright between us. I watched as he walked toward his home across the highway and railroad tracks. As he disappeared into the darkness, I got into my car and drove home slowly and carefully as I tried to sort things out. When I got home, I went straight to my room, avoiding everyone else in the house. I didn't want anyone to notice that I had been drinking – all I needed was another confrontation with Daddy. I was not sure that, if asked, I would be able to resist telling what had happened at the station. I don't think anyone would have understood my situation. I was sure that they would have thought even less of me for not having defended myself better in the situation. I was also sure that if Daddy found out about it, someone would die that night. I just wanted to go lie down and clear my head. More than anything else, I needed to find a way to get through my continued embarrassment for my inability or unwillingness to fight back. My inadequacy was being made more public and more complete.

After I went to bed, I fell into a troubled sleep. My younger brothers, with whom I shared the room, later told me that I was talking in my sleep. My concern became even deeper because I was afraid that I might say something in my sleep that would indict James.

When I went to work on Saturday, neither James nor Wilbur was there as expected. At midday, Wilbur drove up the driveway and parked his old Plymouth coupe in front of the wash bay door. Though Wilbur kept the car impeccably clean and shiny, it was smoking badly and had a rough idle that was accented by a hollow knock each time the engine turned over. The car was packed to the roofline with only enough room for Wilbur, his wife, and two small passengers. He said he was there to pick up his check because he had to go to Chicago for a family emergency, but I knew better. That look in his eyes was not concern for an ailing relative – it was fear. His eyes looked as if he had not slept for days, hollow and full of sadness that I had never seen in him before. JD was quite upset with Wilbur for leaving and even more upset that he had to pay for an incomplete week of work. After Wilbur received his pay, he headed back to his car to check the oil and radiator level. While he was checking everything, I tried to talk with him, but he couldn't even bring his eyes to meet mine. He simply said, "I know it ain't your fault what happened. It was James, but I can't stay 'round here right now. He went out and started talkin' to everyone 'bout what happened over here last night. He done said some things that's gonna git someone killed if he keeps on talkin'. That fool done been talkin' like he's proud – like he wuz braggin'. I can't stop him, so I have to git somewhere safe for a while. You a good boy an' you gonna be a good man some day. Don't let this taint your thinkin' 'bout me or any other colored folks. He just ain't right in the head no more."

I tried to talk him out of leaving, but I understood why he felt he had to leave. He had himself, his wife, and two children to protect from the possible repercussions of the actions of someone incapable of controlling his false bravado and loose tongue. If the Klans heard that James had attacked a white boy, they'd kill him and anybody that they felt was party to it.

When Wilbur cranked his car, the knocking was particularly loud, so I was even more concerned about his leaving with his family. I suggested that it sounded like a rod knocking and his car was probably not road-worthy enough for such a long trip. He just hung his head and repeated that he had to go. The only way he could feel that he and his family were safe was to leave and get as far away as possible. I started to walk away, when I realized that I still had most of the money from my last paycheck. I reached into my back pocket, pulled my wallet out, and handed him a wad of twenty dollar bills as I shook his hand. He reluctantly accepted the bills, "I'll pay you back for this one day."

When he finally looked up at me, I could see the tears welling in his big brown eyes; tears that made his eyes look even darker, deeper, and hauntingly sad. I stood there in front of the bay as he backed out the driveway, pulled out onto the highway and started his long drive. As Wilbur drove off into the distance, I could hear JD swearing under his breath as he watched from the door of the office.

Things weren't the same around the service station without Wilbur. He had always been a hard worker and now it fell to me to take up the slack caused by his loss. I didn't mind the extra work but I was frustrated that JD was not in a hurry to hire a replacement. James stopped coming by the station for work or for his usual social visits. Work became a drudge. I really missed Wilbur's company as I worked in the bays doing wash jobs, lubes, and tire repairs. I especially missed the daily banter that kept us entertained through our mundane tasks and daily chores. JD would venture out of the office to pump gas occasionally, but never helped out in the bays. His mother was essentially useless for anything except tendering money.

After two months at the station without any help, I was fed up. I had begun to resent the station, the job, and the owner. I had been offered a job at a competing station in the middle of Ferriday where the manager said I could earn a commission for all of the parts and consumables that I sold, including headlights and fan belts. That seemed like a lucrative deal to me. I was ready to leave anyway after a small altercation with JD's mother escalated into a major fiasco.

One day while I was working under a car in the grease rack, she called out for me to stack some cases of oil that had just been delivered into the office. I tried to tell her politely that I was busy and had oil all the way up to my elbows, but she insisted that I come and stack the oil cans immediately. When I didn't respond right away she came to the door of the lube bay and started screaming at me. After I finished putting the oil plug and filter back into the car, I walked past her and stacked the oil cans into a pyramid stack on the lower shelf at the back of the office. As I worked, she stood behind me and ranted about everything I was doing. Finally, after I had reached a boiling point, I stalked out of the office and continued my work in the lube bay.

She continued to rant until I flipped the control lever for the grease rack to the down position, releasing a loud rush of air that drowned her rants out for a minute or so. I completed my chores and was well into completing all the tasks that had to be done before closing the station for the night when JD drove up. I paid no attention as JD's mother unloaded on him about my evil plot to overthrow her and cause chaos at the station. JD had me come into the office and demanded an apology to his mother then explained to me that while she was there, she was the boss. "If she says jump, you jump. Don't give her any lip and do not disobey any command she gives you."

I explained that I had been working on a rush job for one of our most valued customers and that, under the same circumstances, I would do it again. As his mother flew into another tirade, JD suggested that it might be time for me to think about the security of my job there and hinted that I could be replaced. I was not one to keep my composure very well, so I think he was quite surprised when I smiled and said I wasn't worried about it. I think he was even more shocked when I bid them goodnight and walked out the door for the night.

After I opened the station the next day, JD came in early to continue his supervision and instruction for me. It was as if he no longer trusted me to do the work I had been doing for almost a year. I became so frustrated that I avoided any contact with him for most of the day. It was mid-afternoon when things fell into place like only God could do it. While I was working under the grease rack again, JD came out and started asking me questions about what I was doing and why I was doing it that way. At almost the same time, Wilbur drove up and parked his car in its usual spot just outside the wash bay. When I saw him, I dropped what I was doing and ran out to say hello. When I approached him, I reached out to shake his hand but just as I reached, Wilbur reached out and grabbed me in a big bear hug. I was so shocked and embarrassed that I stood there with no response at all. I felt terrible about it later. JD walked out and said, "What are you doing here? I thought you were long gone?"

"I need a job Mister Mills. I got to git my family back down here as soon as I git settled in. We just can't live up there in Chicago."

"Well, I hope you ain't thinkin' about workin' here again, 'cause you already burned that bridge when you left before. I don't need no more help around here right now so you can just go on down the road and find something else."

"I really need this job Mister Mills. Me and my family, we ain't got nothin' right now 'cause I couldn't get no steady work in Chicago."

"Well, you ain't gonna find no steady work around here either. We ain't had no colored people workin' here for a couple of months now, and I'm gonna keep it that way."

That is when it hit me. I already had another job offer and I certainly didn't need this one anymore, so I chimed in, "You know Mister JD, you told me last night that I need to think about my security here and that I could be replaced. Well I thought about it and I've taken a job at Spruill's Texaco in Ferriday. I just don't think I can put up with you and your mother anymore, so I think this is a good time for you to replace me. Wilbur can have my job. I'll bet he can even tell you what he is doing and why he does it that way when he finishes that lube and oil change on the rack in there." I lied about taking the job at Texaco, but I was sure Mister Spruill still wanted me to work for them. With that, I wadded up the grease rag that I had in my hand and put it into JD's hand.

JD shot back at me, "When did you get a chance to talk to Bill Spruill? He closes that place up an hour earlier than we close here. I'll call him and let him know what you did here and he won't let you near the place."

"I'll come by later and pick up any money you owe me. Better yet, give it to Wilbur and I will pick it up from him." I got into my car and drove directly into Ferriday to talk to Mister Spruill. He said, "What happened over at the other place? Did you just walk off?" I explained Wilbur's situation and told him what I had done as best I could. My explanation must have been adequate because he started asking me about my shirt and pant sizes so he could order uniforms for me. Wow. I was going to get uniforms. I was going to wear the Texaco star!

I started working at the Texaco station right away, and immediately doubled my pay because I could spot the discoloration of a burned out headlight as customers drove into the driveway and I checked the belts on every car as I checked the oil. I also took the opportunity to check tire tread and condition when I did a quick air pressure check on each of the tires. I exceeded Mister Spruill's expectations for sales, so he increased my pay and my commission rate.

I also enjoyed working at the Texaco Station; it made me "the man who wore the star" in all of the Texaco television ads. We kept the station clean and painted with the Texaco trademarked white, green, and red. When someone drove up to the pumps, I jogged out to let them know that we were on the ball – we were a full-service station. I especially enjoyed the trust that Mister Spruill had in my ability to do the work.

I hadn't worked at Spruill's Texaco long before I took notice of a couple of 1964 Chevrolet Impalas that came to the station for fuel and service. Each of the cars was outfitted with an array of antenna and heavy-duty alternators to provide extra current that would be required by radios which were housed in the trunk. I also noticed that the well-dressed men sometimes paid for their services with a government sponsored Texaco credit card. As they came into the station week after week, I made a correlation between the drivers and the cars, noting that there were two different cars, but three different drivers. I felt smug feeling that I was the only person in Ferriday that knew we had FBI agents living and working around us all of the time now. What I didn't know was who they were investigating and for what reasons.

CHAPTER 5

Hitting Closer to Home

My first year at Ferriday High School was going well, which pleased me immensely. I had several friends in school now, but none as close as Katherine and Candice. Two months earlier, when we returned to class after Christmas break, the two of them started grilling me about who I intended to take to the Junior-Senior prom. Both of them were going steady at the time, so they already knew who was taking them. I really had no plans for going to the prom at all, so they chided me about my situation.

"You are going to deprive some poor underclass girl from going to the prom?"

"You know that any freshman or sophomore would say yes in a minute – they wouldn't even think about it."

"April sixteenth is going to be here before you know it. You need to start asking now."

I thought about the prom for a while and decided they could be right. There were two sophomore girls I liked, but I was too shy to ask either of them out. One of the girls had transferred to the school at the same time I had; the other had lived in the subdivision in which I worked when we first moved to Ferriday. I couldn't work up the courage to talk to either of the girls, one because she was new and I didn't know her at all, and the other because I did know her, but considered her too popular to ask. Katherine and Candice finally filled me with enough courage to ask – going to fifth period Spanish was like walking into an interrogation chamber. After a month of their encouragement, I asked Gloria Poole to escort me to the prom. I felt more comfortable asking her, because I had known her longer. Much to my surprise, she accepted.

The next three months felt more like three weeks. Even though I had my own car, my brother-in-law, Jerry, offered me the use of his car for prom-night. It was a beautiful 1963 Chevrolet Impala Super Sport convertible, with dual deck mirrors on the front, dual raked antenna at the back, and fender skirts that made the car look slick and formal. The car was a metallic aqua blue with a white vinyl interior and wide chrome bars that ran across the backrest of each of the front seats. I promised to take good care of his car.

On prom day, I drove to Natchez to pick up the convertible from Jerry who had cleaned and polished the car to look like new – I felt like Cinderfella. I carefully drove the car back to Ferriday where I picked up her corsage and my boutonniere and then dressed up in my finest suit. When I went to Gloria's house, I was not prepared for how stunning she looked – I felt completely unworthy! I remembered few details of the night except how beautiful Gloria looked and how out of place I felt. I really didn't know how to dance and I was not a very eloquent conversationalist. I don't remember if I even asked her to dance or if we had our picture taken for the occasion.

When we left the prom that night, I drove Gloria directly to her home where I bade her goodnight without touching her – no hand holding, no hug. Afterwards I drove home to change clothes and pick up my younger brother. We got into the car and, for the first time, let the top down on the convertible and headed toward Natchez. When we reached Highway 84, I turned on the radio and we talked about how much we felt we were missing because Ferriday and Natchez had few radio stations, all of which played only country-western music. Billy leaned forward to tune the radio between presets and found one that we had never heard before – WLS in Chicago was playing rock and roll.

As we settled into the music, I moved into the left lane to pass a semi. After passing the truck, I moved back into the right lane when the front of the car dipped and we suddenly lurched to the right. I tapped the brakes, which only exacerbated the pull to the right as we drifted onto the shoulder of the road, too close to the drainage ditch. I shifted the car into second and stomped on the accelerator pedal, which lifted the front of the car. I managed to straighten the car up on the shoulder, but I couldn't get it back onto the highway in time to avoid the brand new 1964 Pontiac Bonneville that was parked on the shoulder. The right fender of the car dived hard as we struck the left rear of the Pontiac, crushing it right to the rear window. The convertible flipped into the air and vaulted over the Pontiac, landing in an open space in the parking lot of the Stardust Nightclub. The car landed hard on the right side then rolled over on the top as it slid through the parking lot. All I remembered after the impact was the shower of sparks that came off the hood and windshield frame. Then things got weird.

The next thing I remember was looking down on the mayhem below as they dragged my body from the car – I was sitting atop the billboard that held the sign for the nightclub! One of the wheels on the car was still spinning and there was smoke coming from the undercarriage, which was now exposed to the dark sky. As I sat there observing from the top of the billboard, I felt the presence of someone else; a bright, ghostly image of a man sitting to my right who repeated, "You'll be all right, son. Just stay right there, you'll be just fine." I sat silently and watched as they pulled my body away from the car and sat me out at the front of the parking lot and propped me against some stranger that kneeled beside me. I heard him repeating, "You'll be alright son. Just hold your hand right there and you'll be alright. They got someone coming for you."

Suddenly, I awakened to find myself seated on the pavement near the highway, propped against a stranger who continued to repeat, "Just hold your hand right there and you'll be just fine." It was then that I became aware that he was holding my hand against my right ear. I turned my head, leaned to my left, and looked at my right hand in which I was holding a handkerchief saturated with blood. The crimson stream ran down my arm and dripped off the end of my elbow. I leaned back against my hand and drifted into unconsciousness.

When I gained consciousness again, I was still propped against the stranger's knee when I heard someone say, "Was there anyone else in the car?"

I tried to tell them that my brother was in the car, but nothing intelligible came out of my mouth.

Someone answered, "If there was anyone in that car, they are dead now. That car is so flat on the ground it woulda taken their head off."

Oh, God. I killed my brother. My brother was in the car with me. He was in the car with me. "Billy. Billy! Billy!" I shouted his name several times before I drifted into unconsciousness again. My mind would not grasp what had happened to me nor the possibility that I had killed my brother.

I gained consciousness again just in time to hear the car horn blowing continuously. Someone blurted, "The battery is shorting out, get back 'cause it might catch on fire." I became even more confused and disoriented when I heard a string of profanities coming from under the car. The familiar voice woke me fully and I realized it was Billy.

"Let me go, you bastard. Let go of me. I'll kick your butt, you son of a bitch. Let go of me." With that, several of the men that were standing nearby raced over to the car and pulled the door open wide enough to reach in and help him.

"He's caught up on something in here. Somebody hand me a knife." When someone handed a knife to the man, he reached as far into the car as he could and sawed at something for a few seconds, which seemed like an eternity. Suddenly there was a loud cheer as they pulled Billy from under the car. They helped him out to the edge of the highway and sat him beside me. I became overwhelmed and started crying. I sobbed, "You're alright. You're alive." That turned into, "Oh no. I wrecked Jerry's car. I wrecked Jerry's car. I don't know what happened, but I wrecked Jerry's car."

A patron from the bar recognized me and made a call to my home. Before I knew it, my parents were at my side. My mother grabbed my hand and held it tight as she talked to my brother and me. It seemed that everyone was trying to talk at the same time; trying to explain the details of the circumstances to my parents as they tended to us. I kept slipping in and out of consciousness as the air filled with the wailing of a siren that grew louder and nearer. Flashing lights were all around us now, adding to the confusion of my mind. Police were asking questions and trying to control the traffic, and ambulance crews were tending to Billy and me. Onlookers surrounded us; some were drunk and a little too helpful, some were trying to help tend to us, and others were trying to tell everyone else what they should be doing.

The drive to the hospital took an eternity. The driver didn't use the siren but a couple of times until we got to the railroad tracks just before entering Ferriday. After we reached the city limits, the siren wailed all the way through town. When they had bandaged my head at the scene, they wrapped the bandage over my eyes, so I couldn't see Mama during the trip, but I could feel her presence. I could hear Billy complaining in the background because someone was still trying to tend to his head.

At the hospital, they took me into the emergency room where they cut the hair from the right side of my head, cleaned the gravel and sand out of my wounds, and sewed the top of my ear back into place. I held on to the bed frame and my mother's hand as they cleaned and sewed the multiple cuts on my shoulders and behind my right ear. I was sure that I had crushed Mama's hand into the bed frame as they started cleaning before the local anesthesia took effect. After they closed about four open gashes on the side of my head, they wrapped it, strapped me to a hospital bed, and took me into a room where my brother was already resting. I think all of us said it at the same time, "Thank God."

I discovered the next day that, in addition to having gained a head full of scars, I had broken my two front teeth when my mouth hit the chrome horn ring in the center of the steering wheel. My beautiful bunny teeth were now blunted in an arc causing me to look like some kind of vampire with my oversized canines - one more thing to add to my self-consciousness.

Billy was released from the hospital but I was kept for observation since the damage to my head was so extensive. I was lying in bed with my upper body inclined when a colored lady in a hospital uniform stepped to the foot of my bed.

"Boy. You know who I am?"

I looked at her and had not the slightest recognition. I lay their wondering for a moment when she said, "I am your Aunt Sandy. I am your daddy's sister. Your daddy and I have the same daddy." I don't think I had a reaction; I just lay there dumbfounded. I think she expected me to get upset and throw something, because she stood there looking as puzzled as I felt. I think I was in too much pain to even care at that point. I don't think I was surprised because I had heard rumors about my grandfather's indiscretions for most of my life.

As Aunt Sandy left the room, a familiar red-head entered the room and lit it up like sunlight. I had always considered Patricia unapproachable because she was so pretty and one of the most popular girls in school. When she called me by name, I tried to smile and reached down to make sure that I was properly covered. I wasn't aware that she even knew who I was. She asked how I was doing then told me as much about my accident as she had heard; it sounded awful. She said she was very glad to see me alive, then she handed me a copy of a Natchez Democrat newspaper that had the news of my death. I guess someone at the club the night before had too much to drink and reported that I died at the scene of the accident. We both laughed about it before I realized how awful it must have been for any of my friends to have read the erroneous report before knowing the truth. She said that there were a lot of rumors around school that I had been racing, drunk, and that my prom date had still been in the car. I think Gloria did a good job of letting them know the truth – none of the rumors were true.

While we were talking, I mentioned that my brother may have been saved because he was bent over, still messing with the radio when we crashed. She blurted out, "Did you hear the Beatles?"

"Beatles? What are the Beatles?"

"They are a new band that just came over from England. They are very popular and they have two songs that are at the top of the charts. I just love their music."

"I don't recognize them at all. What kind of music do they play?"

"They did 'She Loves You' and 'I Want to Hold Your Hand,'" she said excitedly. "There are four of them: John, Paul, Ringo, and George. They are all dressed up in suits and they have special haircuts that really make them look neat - different."

After hearing her excitement about the Beatles, I could hardly wait to hear them. When I got out of the hospital and returned home, I tuned the radio in our bedroom to WLS every night to hear the latest rock. I heard two Beatles tunes the first night I tuned in and immediately understood the excitement. Their music was so different from everything we had been listening to for the past few years. Even more than the Beatles, I like the rhythm and blues sound of the colored groups – a new sound they called soul or Motown. I had to play the radio very softly so Daddy wouldn't hear. If he had heard us listening to either rock and roll or soul, he would have taken the radio from us.

I didn't have long to feel sorry for myself over the tragedy that was my prom and the car accident. Jerry and I both lost our licenses because neither of us had liability coverage for his car when I had the accident. I had to apply for a hardship permit to drive so I could get to and from work and school. I was despondent over the loss of my driving privileges.

It wasn't long before I had more than enough diversions to distract me from my woes. If I wanted to go to Natchez or Vidalia, I had to hitch a ride from friends or family members. That meant I would be spending more time riding around with my father. I often had to tag along with him as he visited his friends or attended his meetings in Natchez.

While I was still wearing the bandages around my head, I went with him to Vidalia so I could see my insurance agent. After getting my insurance needs adjusted, I joined Daddy at the Shamrock Inn where he was meeting with some of his friends. When I got there, I sat at a table close to a counter toward the back of the restaurant. After studying the menu for a while, I ordered a hamburger and a cherry Coke. While I was waiting for my food, I noticed a young colored fellow watching me from behind the counter. His lips looked too big for his face; his dark skin glistened with sweat and struck a stark contrast against the white jacket that he wore. I could tell that he was studying me, and I was sure that he was curious. It didn't take long for the questions to start.

"Are you the one that wrecked up on Highway 84, by the night club?"

"Yeah."

"I drove by there right after you wrecked. I jus' finished up my stuff here an' I wuz driving home when they had you out by the road and the police wuz talkin' to you."

He came over and propped himself with his forearms crossed on the counter. As he leaned over the counter, I could see a light colored, map-like scar on the right side of his neck, disappearing under the collar of his jacket. When he got settled, he pointed to my head and said, "I done got scars on me like that, too. Seem like somethin' always happenin'."

"Yeah." I acknowledged. "I got scars on my chin, under my nose, and on the side of my head already; and now this. It durn near turned my ear to hamburger meat."

"Then you Mister Blanche's boy."

"Yeah. I'm Buddy. I am his oldest boy."

"I'm Joe. I been knowin' your daddy for a long time. He come by here a lot. He always meetin' with peoples in here. How fast wuz you doin' when you wrecked?"

"I was doing about sixty-five."

"I heard you wuz doin' over a hundred."

"No. The only time I ever went that fast was out on the road through the pecan orchard goin' out to Lake Saint John. I like that stretch of road because it is smooth, straight, and you can see for a couple of miles. There ain't no roads cross it through that whole stretch. There is only that levy that runs along the north side."

"I know that place. I lives out there with my gramma and grampa sometimes. They lives out on that road that comes in at the other end of the pecan groves."

"I can't drive out there anymore because they took my license away from me."

"I shore hope that never happens to me, 'cause I couldn't work here no more if it did. I am the driver. I drives the girls ..." He stopped mid-sentence when he realized what he was going to reveal. I had heard about the colored man that drove white women to and from Natchez and the Shamrock Inn, with occasional runs to a sports club in Deer Park, south of Vidalia. I also heard rumors that he had been involved with one or more of the white women that he escorted from place to place.

Just as my food arrived, Daddy appeared with several of his friends close behind. "Show Warren and Charles the stitches in your head."

I reached up and unwrapped part of the bandages on my head. Joe stepped back into the doorway and disappeared into the kitchen.

"Boy, you lucky to be alive."

"That damned near took off your ear didn't it?"

"Took off his ear? It damn near took off his whole head."

I felt like some kind of spectacle. As soon as they made their comments, I rewrapped the bandages and gulped my food down as quickly as I could. As I washed it down with the Coke, Daddy related the gory details of the wreck, embellishing as he usually did. After telling his story, Daddy and the men disappeared to the back of the restaurant again and continued their talk.

When we left that day, I didn't think we would be back so soon. Since I could not return to work yet, I accompanied Daddy to the Shamrock the following week after he received a coded message from someone in Natchez. One of the men from the group was already there when we arrived. I don't think Daddy recognized him because he greeted him with, "Hello. Mister AYAK?"

The man responded with, "AKAI."

It was a code that the Klans in the area had begun to use. AYAK was code for "Are you a Klansman?" AKAI is the proper reply meaning, "A Klansman am I."

I sat at my usual table and they made their way to the back of the restaurant.

I watched as more men arrived and joined the men at the back of the restaurant. I recognized some of them as they arrived from Ferriday, Vidalia, and Natchez. I also recognized one from Franklin County. As the men arrived, they all seemed to want to talk at once, so the discordant discussion was very loud.

"Do you realize what this means? We have to tighten our ranks and we have to be vigilant in our efforts to keep the authorities confounded."

"What is this all about anyway?"

"Haines will tell us when he gets here."

I watched the cars as they arrived, reading the license plates carefully. I couldn't identify the home parishes for the cars with Louisiana tags because they had no identification marks on the plates. However, the Mississippi license plates had the county of registration stamped into the bottom of the plate. I noticed that they called the meeting to order when a man from Franklin County arrived and was identified by several of the other men from Mississippi.

Since most of the men recognized me by now, I think they just ignored my presence at the table. They could have ignored me because I still looked wounded with half my head shaved, bare scars over the right side of my head, and a goofy smile that revealed my chipped teeth. I didn't have to sneak closer to their conversation because it was loud and filled with excitement.

One of the local men blurted out, "What is this all about? Why are we here?"

A tall, thin man from Mississippi responded, "Have any of you heard what happened over in Franklin County? Meadville?"

"I heard someone over there took care of a couple of them nigger agitators they picked up on the highway."

"Well, it is more than that. You are going to hear a lot about this because someone is already talkin' and they pointin' fingers at people here in Adams county and over at the mill. They are gonna be digging through all of your shit to try to get to the bottom of this. They are gonna talk to anyone who will talk to them. Don't talk to no one."

"We don't know anything. What are we gonna talk about?"

The man from Mississippi spoke up again, "I don't know what you know. I don't know who knows what. I do know that some of you will find out what happened soon and we don't want nobody talking to no one. Them local yokels already know enough."

"If you don't know 'em, don't talk to 'em."

"We got to stay close on all this, because we fixin' to have a shit-storm in Franklin County, and we don't want it to spill over into Adams County and Louisiana."

"Sounds like it's already spilling," someone rang out in a sarcastic tone.

"Just keep your mouths shut and you got nothin' to worry about."

"What the hell are we talkin' about anyway? I still don't know what you are talkin' about."

I was also curious about the subject of their discussion. I thought I would soon find out. After Daddy and I left the meeting that night, we drove home in silence. I related a little bit about what I heard and understood about the discussion when he cut me off, "Don't talk about this to anyone. Listen to what that man said. These people can make you disappear! Some of those men over there would beat you to death just for asking questions about some of the things that are going on now and things that are gonna be happening soon."

That was a rather ominous warning. I decided to let it lie. Daddy actually looked concerned about this. I think he knew just enough to know how dangerous the situation was.

It wasn't long before I found out that they had been talking about the disappearance of two young colored men from Meadville on the second of May. It was said that they had been taken to a farm between Natchez and Meadville where they were beat into submission with beanpoles and tree branches. After they were beaten, they were wrapped into tarps and put into the trunk of a red car and driven away. They hadn't been seen since. The Franklin County Sheriff's Department and the Mississippi Highway Safety and Patrol were beating the bushes for any evidence that would reveal the fate of the two men. Even more importantly, the FBI was now investigating for the same evidence. Because of the added attention of the FBI, the man who had picked the two men up from Meadville was very concerned that his role in the disappearance would be revealed. One of the Franklin County sheriffs told one of the youth's mothers that he had run away and was probably in Birmingham or Chicago. The sheriff also made a statement that he was not concerned with the investigators from the FBI or the Highway Patrol because "the Klans will be here a long time after they are gone." Nobody was talking about the event, so the investigation was going nowhere.

Because of his stance on the integration issue, the Klans already hated President Johnson, who took office after Kennedy was assassinated. They also felt that he had betrayed the South, since he was from Texas. At the end of May, President Johnson made a speech at the University of Michigan in Ann Arbor that particularly inflamed their hatred. He had a plan that he thought would put an end to the violence and bring about equality in the South and throughout the nation. This was to include a series of meetings and studies regarding our cities, their natural beauty, the quality of education, and other emerging challenges. He said that from these we would bring about the emergence of a "Great Society." I remember some of the comments I heard from Klansmen at a Natchez meeting in the week that followed.

"He ain't talkin' 'bout no Great Society, he is talking about a Gray Society. He figures to mix the races so that there ain't no black and no white, just gray."

"We got to draw together and fight back against this mixing of the races. We don't want our children and our grandchildren mixin' with these niggers."

"We have to make a show of force in our cities, in our states, and all over the country to let these people know that we are here and we have teeth."

Then they repeated in unison, "A Klansman I am, and a Klansman I will always be." I had heard that slogan in greetings before, but this was the first time I had heard it used as a chant of any kind.

Daddy's status and involvement in the Klans grew. His activities weren't just visible to our white neighbors, but also to the colored people around us. Wilbur often asked me questions about Daddy's activities or raised concerns about any of the Klan involvement in the area as if they thought I could do something about it. He told me that James was hearing a lot of talk about the Klans over in Ridgecrest where he worked for the water department.

I never knew the extent to which Daddy was involved with some of the Klan activities and the violence associated with the demonstrations and marches across Louisiana, Mississippi, Alabama, and Arkansas. I also never realized the position of authority and power he had attained in the Klans due to his organization and activity. At some point during his tenure with the Klans, he had attained the position of Grand Titan, a position that I understood made him the second highest-ranking Klansman in the state.

In June, Daddy joined the United Klans of America, a new faction of the Klans which was headquartered in Alabama. It was a conglomeration of klan groups, such as the Original Klans of America, the White Knights of the KKK, and the Alabama Klans. They had become "The Invisible Empire," the United Klans of America, and they were a particularly brutal group indeed. They had been responsible for the bombing of the 16th Street Baptist Church in Birmingham, Alabama that killed four young girls the year before. Many of the older Klansmen in the area were disappointed that the local klaverns were not being aggressive enough; they wanted to do something to stop the tide of integration where it stood, so they started joining the new klaverns of the UKA.

Because of the UKA's reputation for action, they were very successful in recruiting local Klansmen and entire klaverns from the area klan factions. Daddy was already a Grand Titan with the Original Klans in Concordia Parish. During the time that he was recruiting for the UKA in Louisiana, E. L. McDaniel was recruiting in Mississippi. I think they were so successful because they worked together closely to coordinate their recruiting and organization efforts.

When I realized how far he had risen in the ranks of the Klans, it explained the increased presence of the FBI in our small town and their increased interest in my family's activities, especially Daddy's. I also think that their occasional visits to my house were intended to make their presence known to neighbors and friends, intimidating those who might be inclined to get involved with the Klans.

Since my father was now prominent in the local Klans, he also had the collateral duty of an investigator. When charges were filed to the Klans about the activities or behavior of local citizens, he and several other Klansmen investigated the circumstance to determine if the local Klans should take some action, or if they should have a wrecking crew hit the offenders to make an example of them.

A wrecking crew was a despicable gang of thugs selected from the Klans to do "enforcement," usually in another region so they wouldn't be recognized. For instance, if the Klans in one town needed an enforcement gang, they arranged to have a wrecking crew from distant klaverns do the hit, usually from a distance of more than 60 miles. The men selected for the wrecking crews were large and brutal, often men with records and a long history of violence. Usually they weren't very careful in their selection of targets nor in the way a hit was executed.

As luck would have it, someone filed charges against Frank Morris in July and wanted to have a wrecking crew hit his business. Daddy called Mister Nugent, of the King Hotel, to set up a meeting for the following day. After he set up the meeting at the hotel, he called E. L. McDaniel and a local Klansman whom he called E. G.

Since the King Hotel was less than half of a block away from Spruill's Texaco, I met Daddy for a hamburger before his meeting with the Klansmen. While we were eating, Doug Nugent, the manager of the hotel, came over and plopped down at the table with us. At over 350 pounds, Mister Nugent was a very large man, so his presence at the table made it feel crowded with only the three of us. He started talking to Daddy about the ensuing investigation of Frank Morris as if I were not even at the table.

Mister Nugent started, "I don't know what started this investigation, but I think I know who is behind it. I don't know what started the row between Big Frank and Morris, but I think that deputy is out to get him for something."

I knew who he was talking about immediately. Big Frank was what the locals called Deputy Sheriff Frank Delaughter. At six foot, four inches and more than 250 pounds, he struck an imposing figure. He had a reputation for being brutal and corrupt. He was known to have beat prisoners in the Ferriday jail and he seemed to have no respect for anyone. I knew him by his reputation and because he occasionally came to the Shell station in Ridgecrest when I worked there the previous year. If he viewed you as important, he'd smile and joke with you; if not, you were just something to scrape off the bottom of his boots. If he had somehow crossed Big Frank, Morris was in trouble. After Mister E. G. got to the meeting, they were joined by another Klansman that I had seen before, but did not know. I left the meeting and went back to the Texaco station after they started talking about the charges against Frank.

Several weeks later, Daddy and the group of investigators met at the King Hotel. Nobody could substantiate the charges against Frank Morris, so they determined that no wrecking crew would be called to hit him or his business.

Mister E.G. said, "But someone called a hit on that nigger, so they ain't gonna be happy about it."

E. L. McDaniel replied, "I already told you and the Klansmen that brought these charges to us. We will not bring a wrecking crew in here for this. I told them once that we would not send one from Natchez."

After they made their verdict, I felt like celebrating. I could tell that Daddy was pleased with the verdict, too. As the men talked freely about the investigation, I finally got the gist of the charges that had been brought against Frank Morris. Someone had charged him with making inappropriate remarks to a white woman who had been parked at the front of his shop while she waited for him to finish some work that she brought to him.

Before I even thought about it, I blurted, "That is a damned lie. Frank is a businessman who would never say anything to anybody, colored or white. He would never do anything to hurt his business, and he definitely would not take the chance of offending any white person."

Finally I had some good news that I could share with my friend Wilbur. Since I was working in Ferriday, I didn't see Wilbur or James very often. When I did see James, he was especially humble and made it a point to be very polite and respectful to me. Though it made me very uneasy, I understood his position and reason for fear. He never did offer a real apology to me, but I could see it in his eyes every time we talked. Sometimes I thought he would burst from the pressure of his unspoken apology. Wilbur said that James had long since stopped bragging or talking to his family or friends about the incident at the station. Both of them drank more heavily than they had before, but neither of them seemed interested in drinking with me when I stopped at the station. Though Wilbur and I talked at length sometimes about the racial strife that surrounded us, we never talked about the private things that really bothered us anymore. His jovial demeanor had been replaced by the sober sadness of our changing situation. I missed my friend.

The addition of the UKA into the area set a flurry of activity into motion. Many of the Klansmen from the previously established White Knights and the Original Klans were defecting to the new UKA because they were increasingly dissatisfied with the lack of action by the older groups. Because of the feedback from those that were defecting, leadership in the OKA and White Knights was being challenged. Groups were scrambling to establish themselves as the true leaders and recruiting very heavily at the Armstrong Tire Plant, the International Paper Plant, and Johns Manville in Mississippi, because these were the largest pools of skilled men. In addition to the increased focus on building their strength, the Klans stepped up their violence in Louisiana and Mississippi. They had made the threat that "blood was gonna flow" and they set about to prove it. They were set to show Lyndon B. Johnson that there would be no Gray Society in the south.

In June, another Meadville man was abducted and taken to a farm between Natchez and Meadville where he was also beaten, but this time there was a big difference. The man that they abducted and beat was Ally Allison, a white man that someone had accused of fraternizing with the colored people in the area. We knew some of the Allisons when we lived in Quentin; they were good people, but were as poor as church mice. They lived in the Ediceton area, and for at least one year, the Allison children had gone to Bude School with us, usually in tattered clothes and bare feet. They didn't do very well in school, so when they stopped attending, I didn't know if they had simply quit or if they were attending a different school. Mister Allison drove an old pulpwood truck, a job usually done by the poorest of white men or one reserved for colored men. The truck that he drove was dilapidated and missing half of the exhaust system, so it must have been deafening to ride in the truck for much of the day.

I asked myself, "What could they gain by beating someone who was already beat? He called everyone Mister and Missus; he always said, 'Yes, sir and yes, m'am,' and he never did anything disrespectful to anyone, including the men who had attacked him." In the atmosphere of the growing violence, I guessed things didn't have to make sense. In this cowardly act, nine or ten men stood by and watched while a sadistic Klansman, Paul Banner, tried to impress them with his power, prowess, and control because Mister Allison had been fraternizing with colored people. He and his family were forced into the situation because he worked shoulder to shoulder with the colored men every day. Because of his social status, very few of the white people in the area treated his family with any regard or respect. He was one of the most humbled and submissive men I had ever met.

After they beat and tortured him, they dropped him off along the roadside in Meadville near to where they had abducted him. He must have suffered intensely because his family could not afford to get medical treatment for him. Neither the Meadville Police, the Franklin County Sheriff's Department, nor the Mississippi Highway Safety and Patrol investigated the beating with any real intention of bringing charges against the perpetrators.

During his recuperation, Mister Allison decided that this kind of beating would never happen to him again. He decided to exact his revenge on Paul Banner and remove the threat of future beatings forever. Shortly after he could get up and about, he took his shotgun into Meadville and waited for Mister Banner to return from Natchez. When he saw the man, Mister Allison pointed his shotgun, and with an oath of revenge, pulled the trigger. Nothing happened. To his horror, his trusty shotgun had failed him. While he was still trying to figure out what had caused the shotgun to misfire, Mister Banner walked up to his still weakened victim, wrenched the shotgun from his grip, and proceeded to beat him with it. Again Ally Allison was beaten within a breath of his life and no one came to his aid. Again, no one sought justice for him.

During the week that followed, a Mississippi Highway Patrolman pulled a young colored man over on the main road through Meadville for running a red light. He arrested the young man and took him to the Franklin County Jail in Roxie. They held him at the jail for several days even after his father paid the $10 fine. When they finally woke him up early one morning and told him he was free to leave, he ran into more trouble than he ever expected as a result of his simple traffic infraction. Several hooded Klansmen armed with baseball bats blocked the only exit from the hall of the jail cells. As he stood frozen in fear, the hooded men rushed him, beating him with the bats. After they knocked him to his knees, nearly unconscious, they put a hood over his head, pulled it tight, carried him out of the jail, and threw him into the back of a car.

They drove him to a forested area, took him out of the car, and dragged him away from the road. Even though he was still hooded, he could tell that there were many more men standing around him now. He could hear their comments and threats as they led him the last few steps where they leaned him against a tree. "Hug it, nigger. Hug it like you love it." He wrapped his arms around the tree where someone tied his wrists together on the other side. As he held onto the tree, one of the men took a knife and split his shirt all the way down the back. Someone else took the knife and cut his belt and jeans down the back to the bottom of the seat of his pants.

"Hug that tree tight, nigger."

"Make that darkie bleed. I want to see blood running."

"After this you'll be glad to leave town you black son-of-a-bitch."

After they hit him several times with a short bullwhip, his strength waned quickly and he slid down the tree, held up only by the ropes that bound his wrists. As they beat him, they hurled insults, swore at him, and made threats about what would happen to him if he didn't leave town. They also repeatedly asked him questions for which he had no answers. He had no idea what they were asking about. He thought about lying but knew that things could get much worse if they caught him in a lie. Finally the whip stopped and they let him hang on the tree for several minutes.

Someone cut the rope that was holding him to the tree and he crumpled to the ground in a heap, trying to gain any semblance of composure.

"Hey, nigger. You gotta promise us that you're gonna leave Mississippi if we let you go."

"Yeah. If we catch your black ass around here again, we'll whip you to death. You understand, nigger?"

"When we let you go, you have to leave Mississippi and never come back. You have to promise now that you are going to Chicago and we aren't ever gonna see your nigger butt around here again."

"I promise," the young man replied softly. "I promise I'll go to Chicago and never come back to Mississippi. I was plannin' to go there already because that's where the work is."

The men carried him back to where the cars were parked and threw him into the trunk of a car. They drove him back to Meadville and dropped him out onto the shoulder along Highway 84.

"Don't forget your promise nigger." They left him there with the hood still over his head. He woke up later with his family treating the cuts on his back. He could remember almost everything that had happened to him until they dropped him off on the roadside. After that, everything was in a fog. Two days later, after limited treatment and recuperation, he packed up to leave town with the help of a preacher from Roxie and several of the men from his community.

Less than a week later Mississippi was thrown back into the shadows of another scandal when three young civil rights workers disappeared from Neshoba County. On June 21st, the three had gone to Philadelphia to investigate the burning of the Mount Zion Church, a black church and a favorite meeting place for civil rights workers. Earlier in the month, several colored men and women had been beaten as they left a church meeting in which the civil rights workers had been teaching how to register voters and conducting mock elections.

Local authorities did very little to investigate the disappearance of the three men. In fact, there were already rumblings that officers from the highway patrol and from the Neshoba County Sheriff's Department were involved in the disappearances. Since Daddy had no affiliation with the Klans in Neshoba County, we were not privileged to the details of the events surrounding the disappearance of the three men. We had to rely on information that was filtered through the other Klan groups and through the local law enforcement officers, none of which were particularly reliable for separating fact from hearsay.

I was appalled. Did the two Klan groups coordinate these events or were they purely coincidental? Did the young man who had been kidnapped and beaten realize how lucky he was that they had released him on his promise to leave Mississippi? Had the three men who disappeared in Philadelphia been met with the same violence? Would they be found tied to trees somewhere bleeding from wounds inflicted by whips or bean poles? Worse yet, how can you justify such action on Sunday, the sacred Sabbath? Most of these men were church-going Christian men – many of them, like my father, were ministers.

President Johnson's reaction to the violence and disappearance of the three civil rights workers in Mississippi was swift, sharp, and pointed. On the second day of July, he signed the Civil Rights Act of 1964, prohibiting discrimination based on race, color, religion, or national origin. It provided power for the federal government to enforce desegregation in all of the states and, most importantly, it provided power for the FBI to investigate violations of the civil rights guaranteed in the act. Finally, the FBI had teeth with which to tear into the local violence.

Ten days after Johnson signed the Civil Rights Act, the violence hit closer to home, though we weren't aware of it at the time. Joe Edwards, the young colored man I had met two months earlier at the Shamrock Inn, disappeared. I didn't hear about it until two days later when Leroy, the colored man who worked with me at the Texaco Station, told me about it. At first, I didn't know who he was talking about because I had only talked with Joe a couple of times, and I only knew him as Joe Ed. When Leroy told me that Joe Ed was the colored man who worked for the Shamrock Inn, I knew immediately to whom he was referring. I was shocked, but I really wasn't surprised. Running girls between the brothels wasn't the worst thing that Joe had done. Joe was consorting with white women at the Shamrock; something he continued to do even after having been caught one time by some of the men who used to meet at the restaurant. If the woman hadn't intervened, the men would have taken care of him that very day. Even after he had been caught, he continued to see white women.

To the Klans, consorting with white women would have been more than enough reason to have done something awful to him, but it wasn't the only reason. Some of the men in the group also believed that Joe valued his importance too highly because he "knew so much 'bout almost everybody." He probably did know quite a bit about the clientele at the Shamrock and about the payoffs that were being made to the local police by the Shamrock and by the Morville Lounge in Deer Park. When I had seen him at the Shamrock in the past, he always seemed to be just out of earshot of the men that were meeting at the back of the restaurant. Maybe he had also heard too much or said the wrong thing within earshot of the men he was observing.

I didn't even get a chance to come to grips with the news about Joe before more news hit me. Divers looking for the bodies of the three civil rights workers who disappeared from Philadelphia, Mississippi, found the bodies of the two young men that had disappeared from Meadville eight weeks earlier. The badly decayed bodies had been discovered near a boat ramp in a loop of the old Mississippi River near Tallulah, Louisiana. After they discovered the bodies, they dredged up the chains that had been used to sink the bodies of the two men. One of the men had been chained to the block of a Jeep engine; the other was chained to a length of railroad iron and several loops of chain. They were identified as Henry Dee and Clarence Moore, missing since May. Their identities were revealed by the drivers' licenses still in their pockets.

Immediately after the discovery of the bodies, a new wave of concern and worry overwhelmed some of the Klansmen who met with Daddy at the Natchez meetings. One of them was especially concerned because the murdered men had been found near his boat landing. In addition, he was worried that the FBI would be able to trace the Jeep engine block back to him. Another was worried that the FBI would find his involvement in the dual murder through informants that had infiltrated the Klan group. None of them were comfortable with the exposure of the murders or with the possibility that they would somehow be connected to the violence.

Several days later, I was working at the Texaco station in Ferriday when there was a commotion at the Gulf station next to us. I tried to get a glimpse over the short brick wall to see what was going on, but they had moved whatever it was to the work bays on the other side of the station, away from the view of the traffic that moved on the main street. Leroy said something about a car, but he ducked away so quickly that I didn't hear what he had said. I followed him, yelling, "What car?"

"They found that car that belongs to Joe Ed. You know. That boy that disappeared from Vidalia a few days ago."

"Dang. I've gotta go over there and see that. One of my friends just told me that he heard about some kind of commotion out on the levy across from the Mimosa subdivision a couple of nights ago. I bet that's where they found the car."

I finished up a lube and oil change on a car then parked it at the side of the station near the office. Just as I got out of the car, another of our regular customers pulled up to the gas pumps so I trotted out and grabbed the nozzle out of the premium pump, popped his gas cap, and started filling when I noticed how curious he was about the commotion over at the Gulf station. It was then that I saw two of the sheriff's deputies walking around the end of the building.

"I don't really know what is going on over there, Mister Green. I haven't been over there yet."

"They found that nigger's car out on the road by the bowling alley. I guess they found some blood or something, so they're gonna go over it with a fine-toothed comb. I think that jig-a-boo up and went to Chicago or somethin' just to have them chasin' their tails."

"I don't think so. I heard something happened to him, and I think some of those ol' boys over there already know who did it," I said as I pointed my thumb in the direction of the deputies gathered around the Gulf station.

"Boy, if them boys heard you talkin' like that, they'd kick the shit out of you, even if it was truth – which it probably is," he said with a big grin.

After Mister Green paid for his gas, I went into the office and talked for a while with Mister Spruill. I asked if he would mind if I walked over to see the car at the Gulf station. He said OK, so I shuffled off along the back of the station to get next door. When I went around the end of the wall that separated the two stations, one of the deputies barked at me to get back over where I belonged. "Boy, get your ass back over to the Texaco station. You ain't got no business over here. Now, git!"

Before I got a chance to see Joe's car, it was moved to another storage place, but nobody seemed to know where. Someone said that they had taken it to the Buick dealer in Natchez because Joe still owed money for the car. All I ever heard about Joe after that were rumors about how and why he had disappeared. Some of the local law enforcement even tried to blame his disappearance on black civil rights workers new to the area - highly unlikely because they wouldn't have taken the chance of abandoning the car in an all white neighborhood. Others hinted that he was taken to Mississippi and skinned alive.

Later that week I dropped off a pair of shoes at Frank's Shoe Shop because I had worn the heels down pretty badly at the Texaco place. I couldn't afford a new pair and I trusted Frank to repair them well enough to keep them going for a while. I underestimated him again. He not only repaired the heels, he put a thick layer of leather across the toes where I had almost worn them through by crawling around on the concrete drive and floors under the grease and tire racks. When I picked the shoes up, Frank and I struck up a conversation about all the racially motivated violence and bombings in the area.

He said, "That's why I stays down here in this section of town. Y'all folks can stop down here to give me work, but if I moves my business into town, someone ain't gonna like it much. They gonna make trouble. I don't want no trouble."

"Shoot. I don't think anyone around here is likely to give you any trouble, Frank. Not unless you get involved with the civil rights move …"

"Don't y'all git me involved with them folks either," he cut me off. "I likes the thought of being equal, but I don't think we needs to be mixing up things. We sure don't need that kind of trouble here or anywhere."

I took a glance at his back room and started, "But ain't you kinda mixing things up back there."

"No sir. Not me. I ain't never had no white women back there. If they comes down here they stays right out here in the front so everyone can see. I ain't gonna wind up like Joe Ed. Sometimes the white men come down here for some honey, but they always black girls – an' they ain't here to make babies," he said with such emphasis that I had to laugh. "Some of them boys like 'em young and black. Like forbidden fruit. All I do is make 'em a place to gits together."

"Yeah. I've heard about that. I hear we have some mighty lonely deputies here in the parish, Mister Frank," I shot back.

"Yeah, those boys is my friends," he just chuckled nervously as I got my shoes.

"How much do I owe you, Mister Frank?"

"Well, sir. Since you still call me Mister Frank, I guess you owes me three dollars. But you old enough to call me Frank – jus' Frank. If you call me Frank, you owes me just two dollars," he said with a chuckle.

"Well, Mister Frank. I guess I owe you three dollars. Thank you very much for everything." With that, I picked up my shoes and left.

In late 1964 there were increased rumors about the falling out in the Klans, so they were compelled to do something to prove their solidarity. During the latter part of July and early August, Daddy attended meetings in Concordia and Rapides Parishes in Louisiana, then in Adams and Franklin Counties in Mississippi. Even though he was becoming more affiliated with the UKA, he was still very close to some of the klaverns and local groups of the OKA and White Knights. He indicated that something was planned for mid-August but didn't reveal what it would be. "The whole nation is going to see just how powerful the Klan has become in Louisiana, Mississippi and Alabama."

On August 14th, the Southern states were lit by the cross fires burned at prominent civil rights offices, churches, and meeting locations. In addition, churches and businesses friendly to colored people and civil rights workers were set ablaze throughout Louisiana and Mississippi. In Natchez, they set Jake's Place, a colored juke joint, ablaze with the patrons still inside because it was being frequented by white civil rights workers who came to drink. It didn't matter to the Klans that the joint was owned by a respected white man. It only mattered that Jake's was being integrated by the white civil rights workers joining their colored friends for drinks. No arrests were made in any of the arsons around either of the states that night.

The show of force seemed to have backfired. Local and state officials became more resolved in stopping the Klan violence of the area. Additionally, several of the civil rights groups around the states were planning reprisals – marches and demonstrations to show their own organization and power. They were also hinting at the possibility of meeting violence with violence at all of the demonstrations. The mayor in Natchez began to apply more pressure on the Klans to halt the violence in and around Natchez. He also began to apply pressure to local businesses that promoted or supported Klan activities in and around the city.

In late August, I dropped in at the Shell station to visit with Wilbur. I hadn't seen him for more than a month and I wanted to see how he and his family were doing. When I drove up, Wilbur was in the process of closing up the station. I honked to let him know I was there, and then I pulled up to the side of the station, parked by his car, and waited. After he closed the last bay door and turned out the lights, he came out and knelt between the cars and started talking very softly, "Buddy, where you been? I been needin' to talk to you for weeks. Ol' Ben told me somethin' about what he saw down by his place a couple of months back. I'm afraid to tell anyone about it."

"What are you talkin' about? Who is Ol' Ben? Do we need to take this somewhere else to talk about it?" My curiosity was piqued by his secrecy.

"Buddy, would you feel okay to go across the tracks so nobody can see us talkin'? It will be okay over there. If you go just across the tracks and turn off on that little dirt road, the tracks will hide us and nobody can hear what I got to tell you."

"Okay, Wilbur. You go like you are going home, and I'll drive down into Ridgecrest like I'm going home. I'll come back up through Crestview and drive up behind you."

When I left the station, I drove through Ridgecrest, crossed the bridge over to Crestview Drive, drove back to Highway 84, turned on the gravel road toward Wilbur's house, then turned onto the dirt road just behind the tracks. As I turned onto the dirt road, I turned off my lights and pulled up short behind Wilbur. I got out and walked to the front of his car where he was sitting on the front bumper. I took a seat on the other side of the bumper and Wilbur began to speak.

"Ol' Ben lives in the house down where the tracks and the levee come together. You know where that road goes off the highway and goes across the tracks where that little railroad shack is. His house is that little gray shack just under the levee just up from that ol' railroad shack."

"Yeah. I know where you are talking about, Wilbur. That's just down on the other side of Mimosa Drive. It's the road that goes between Highway 84 and the levee road back to Ferriday."

"Well, just before that boy from over in Vadalia disappeared, Ol' Ben heard some stuff out on that cutoff road that night."

"Are you talkin' about the night Joe Edwards disappeared?"

"Yeah. That's the one. Ben said he heard someone yellin' out on that road. He said that someone was yellin,' 'Don't make me run after you, nigger. I'll shoot you in the ass and drag you back to the road behind my car.' He said he looked out on the road and saw a police car parked up there behind that two-tone Buick, but he couldn't see no one. He said that some of the voices ran past his place and back toward the levee. He heard someone up toward the top of the levee road yell back towards the highway, 'Bring the car up here and run that son of a bitch down. If he makes it over to the river, no tellin' what will happen.'"

Wilbur stopped for a moment, rubbed his palms together, then wiped them on the legs of his pants as he collected his thoughts. Soon, he began to speak, "After a minute, someone backed one of them police cars back down the highway, then turned it up the road toward the levee – they was going real fast. The car went up over the top of the levee and stopped with the front of the car going down the other side, toward the river. They wuz gone back there for a long time when he heard some shootin' back there on the Old River. He said he heard three or four shots. He didn't see no one come back from the levee, but he saw someone out there leavin' in all the police cars. They jus' left that other car out there on the highway. They left that Buick out there on the highway for a few days, then they moved it over to the other side of the road, down by the bowlin' alley."

I sat stunned for a couple of minutes. The implications were enormous.

"So, you think they killed Joe Ed back there on the Old River. Dang, Wilbur. If it was the police, we can't do anything about it; there ain't no one else to tell. Did he say if he knew which police it was?"

Wilbur sounded concerned when he answered, "No. His eyes ain't very strong anymore, especially at night. He wuz real scared that they could see him watchin' that night. He wuz worried that they could come back to get him, too."

He said that the first police car didn't look like the rest of the police cars. The other two cars were like the rest of the police cars here.

I thought about it for a minute, then told him, "Don't tell this to anyone else, because I know only one of our police who would do something like this, and he lives right there in Ridgecrest – less than a mile from your house. If he found out that anyone knew about it, he would do somethin' dire for sure. I don't know any of the police that I trust enough to tell."

The heavy summer night made it difficult to breathe. I stopped to think about the story again. I felt complimented and scared at the same time. "Hey, Wilbur. Why did you decide to tell me about this? How did you know you could tell me about it?"

When he looked up at me, I could see his big smile even in the dark. "Because I am still alive, and because James is still alive, an' nothin' ain't happened to neither one of us. I know that you know some of them FBI men that come around the station and at your house some times. Maybe you can tell some of them about this and they can go look over on the other side of the levee for that boy."

I was honored by his trust and frankness. However, I was also sorry for what I was about to tell him. "Wilbur. I think the FBI is giving information to the police and to the Klans. If we tell them anything, I'm afraid that it will come right back at us. I don't think I'm ready to take that chance. When they come by the house, they don't just ask questions – they talk."

"Buddy. You don't be tellin' nobody either, then. I think this could be bad for all of us, no matter what."

We chatted for a while longer and caught up on all of the latest family talk. For a while, I could feel like my old friend was back again and that he trusted me enough to take the risk of telling me his story. After we parted, I drove home and sat in my driveway to think about what had just happened. After I sat there for about 15 minutes, I went into the house. Nobody paid attention to me as I did my homework and got ready for bed. After I crawled into bed, I went to sleep immediately; I had not felt such a deep, peaceful sleep for a long time.

As August was the month of cross burnings, September was to become the month of bombings. Businesses all over Mississippi and Louisiana suffered, especially businesses and churches in McComb, Mississippi, where more than twenty bombs were exploded in August and September.

Natchez had almost as many in the same period. Nobody was exempted from the wrath of the Klan bombs. Someone exploded one at the home of Mayor Nosser in late September. The bomb exploded near the house, just after his daughter passed the area where it had been placed. Shortly after the bombing of the mayor's home, another bomb went off at the home of a black contractor who had been working with the mayor on the construction of a new mall for Natchez. The Klans were sending a message to the mayor and to other Natchez businessmen that it was not safe to do business with colored businessmen; they could get to anyone. They set off several stink bombs and small explosives in some of the mayor's businesses and at the Chevrolet dealership. To quell the violence of the night, the Natchez Chief of Police established roving guards armed with shotguns at key points throughout the city.

To prevent the continued violence in Natchez, the Chief of Police banned gambling and the sale of hard liquor within the city limits. He enforced the ban by sending his officers into juke joints all over the city to check up on them and close down violators. It was effective in reducing the violence in Natchez, but it compounded the situation in Concordia Parish. People who couldn't find what they wanted on the Natchez side of the river simply crossed the bridge to the Louisiana side and found places where they could gamble, drink, or buy liquor that they could take back across the bridge. Business in Vidalia boomed, but it upset the balance of power and money in Concordia Parish, resulting in power struggles in both the Klans and the local businesses.

Since business in Concordia Parish was infused with new markets for alcohol, gambling, and prostitutes, some of the law enforcement officers from Natchez and Concordia Parish decided to take advantage of the situation. One of the police officers, Greg Parsons, met with two men at a property in Deer Park owned by J. G. Robertson. Together they were going to convert the property, which was being used as a sports club, into a lounge where they would feature gambling, slot machines, alcohol, and prostitutes provided by Nellie's Brothel in Natchez. In the future, this would prove to be the doing and undoing of several of the conspirators. It would also provide motive for more violence in Concordia Parish.

In addition to all of the other circumstances that stirred the storm of mistrust and violence around Concordia Parish, the Klans took yet another step. They generated a document accusing white people in the area of associating with "niggers" who were supposedly causing some of the unrest. They even had a list of some of the women around Vidalia and Ferriday that were allegedly consorting with colored men. In some cases, they also listed the names of the colored men supposedly involved. They offered no proof, just allegations. To further inflame readers, they included a picture of a white woman and a colored man in an embrace. I thought it odd that there were no names of white men who were consorting with colored women. Maybe the list of white men was just too long to include, or it just didn't matter.

As the stress built around Concordia Parish, it became overwhelming at my house in late October. Someone, again, accused Frank Morris of getting fresh with one of the white women who visited his shop. I knew it was going to be a rehash of the same charges that had been made a few months earlier. I also knew that Frank was no more guilty this time than he was the time before – he would never do anything that would jeopardize his business.

Right after the accusations were made, the Klans started talking about bringing a wrecking crew down on Frank's shop. The prospect of a wrecking crew being brought down on Frank filled me with dread and fear.

With new charges leveled against Frank, the local klaverns called for another investigation of the charges, as was traditional. For this investigation, they selected Daddy, another local Klansman from the Original Klans, and E. L. McDaniel, the Grand Dragon from the Natchez klavern of the Original Klans. Daddy and Mister Moore were selected because of their personal knowledge of Frank Morris. Mister McDaniel was selected because he was familiar with Frank Morris through the investigation earlier in the year, one in which he had refused to call a wrecking crew hit on Frank Morris.

After I finished work one night, I went over to the King Hotel for coffee and a snack with Daddy before the men met. Mister Moore was already there talking with J. D. Nugent. As the two men sat together, I was struck by the contrast between the two. Mister Moore was about the same age as my father, clean shaven, tousled hair, and in good physical shape. Mister Nugent was less than six feet tall and weighed about 350 pounds. Though I am sure that he tucked his shirt in when he dressed, I never saw it that way - it hung over his gut like a tent. The two of them were in a rather heated discussion about who had brought up the charges against Frank Morris. When Mister McDaniel arrived, he and Daddy joined the other two men at the large table. It became very evident rather quickly that they all believed the charges were made by Deputy Sherriff Frank Delaughter. I could also tell that none of them took the charges very seriously, though they were resolved to getting to the bottom of the matter.

I heard Mister McDaniels say, "I don't know what Delaughter has against that nigger, but he sure hates him. This is the third time that he's tried to charge him with something."

"Probably somethin' he put his wife up to."

"Well, he is in here all the time. I don't know if he has a thing for that colored woman that cleans the rooms or if he wants to keep an eye on the girls that use the rooms."

The men all chuckled, then went back to their conversation. The men met several more times over the next month as they compared their evidence, and considered a possible hit on Frank's shop during the week after Thanksgiving should they find him guilty of any of the accusations. They finally decided that the accusations against Frank were unfounded and there would be no hit.

During the week after Thanksgiving, Frank Delaughter skulked around the parish like a dog with mange; it was apparent that Big Frank was angry about the committee's decision. When the investigation team met for their debriefing, Mister McDaniel confided in the other men that Delaughter had already requested a wrecking crew from the Natchez-Adams klaverns to hit Frank's shop anyway. When Mister McDaniel turned down his request, Delaughter was extremely upset. He warned Mister McDaniel that it might be a good idea to stay out of Concordia Parish for a while, to which Mister McDaniel responded that if anything happened to him, it wouldn't be safe for Delaughter to go outside anywhere.

During the investigation, the Klans had not been not idle. They continued to distribute their periodicals and propaganda slandering good people of both colors. With all of the agitation of the Klan propaganda, the additional strain of competition between the liquor and gambling houses, and the growing animosity between the races, it didn't take long for the violence to strike even closer to home.

After the investigation, Daddy met with Frank Morris to give him the details of the charges and of the results of the investigation. Daddy also warned him about possible reprisals by Frank Delaughter, suggesting that he sleep in the small house that he and Daddy had completed only a few months earlier. Daddy advised him that it was no longer safe for Frank to sleep in the small room behind the shop. During the two weeks after Thanksgiving, Deputy Sheriff Delaughter spent an inordinate amount of time patrolling the area near Frank's shop. He also spent more time parked in the alley way down by Mister Haney's Big House where he could keep an eye on the shop. He was also seen driving around the area with one or two strangers in the car.

Shortly after midnight on Thursday, December 10, Frank Morris was sleeping in the small room at the back of his shoe shop when he was awakened by sound of glass breaking. Startled and alarmed by the noise, he lay in his bed for a moment to collect his thoughts. As he lay there, he heard glass shattering again so he silently slipped out of bed and moved cautiously to the door that opened into the shop. As he stealthily stepped into the dark room, he saw the shapes of three men standing just outside the front window. One was using an axe handle to break out the large plate glass window right behind his shoeshine stand while another was leaning over the window ledge pouring something from a large can. Frank realized that his feet were wet and that he was standing in a pool of some kind of liquid – gasoline!

Frank thought, "How did they do that? How did they get it poured all the way in here?"

Realizing that he was standing in the acrid smelling liquid, he also realized what their intentions were. He bolted toward the front of the shop. Suddenly he saw the two of the men standing closer to the window, the largest of whom pointed a shotgun at his chest and growled, "Get back. You'd be better off back there, nigger."

About a block away, Tee Wee Kelly walked out onto the sidewalk on Fourth Street just in time to hear the breaking glass. The bar on Carolina Avenue where he had been drinking had just closed, so he was making his way to another after-hours club to make the most of his nightlife. He also recognized Deputy Delaughter parked at the service station at the end of town, only two blocks from Frank's shop, in full view of the shop and all of Fourth Street. Tee Wee ducked back into the shadows and watched, frozen in terror, as one of the three men ran into the alley next to the shop and jumped into the back of a dark car parked near the side of the building near the street. He could barely make out the shadow of a man inside the shop as the figure stepped toward the front of the store. Just as Tee Wee realized it was Frank, the big man had shoved the shotgun at the figure and shouted, "Get back. You'd be better off back there, nigger."

Inside the shop, Frank realized that he had to get out quickly so he started backing his way toward the room at the back of his shop. As he went, he saw the smaller man in khakis strike what looked like a large match against something that he was holding in his other hand. It lit with a loud bang and the man tossed it through the broken window. Frank turned and lunged toward his bedroom as everything around him exploded into flames – completely enveloping him. Panic-stricken and temporarily blinded by the explosion, he dashed through the flames and into the small room, grabbed the doorknob, and yanked the door open. After he made his way out the door, he realized he was on fire from head to toe and the only way to extinguish the fire was with the hoses at the Billups station several hundred feet North of his shop. He had to open a small gate to let himself out into the alley beside his shop and saw that the car and the men were gone. He couldn't see well enough to run, so he felt his way across the alley toward the street then turned toward the Billups station looking for help. Before he got there he was overwhelmed by the smoke and flames; he collapsed at the edge of the sidewalk. A trail of burning bed clothes and bloody footprints led back through the gate to the back door of his shop.

From his hiding place, Tee Wee watched as the other two men ran into the alley and jumped into the car after setting the building on fire. He was sure he had seen one of the men before and was filled with fear, knowing that he could never reveal this to anyone; he could trust no one with what he had seen. He started to step forward to help Frank, but decided to stay hidden when he realized that he would be in full view of Deputy Delaughter only a block away from where he was standing. He watched as several people got to Frank to do what little they could as he smoldered at the dirty edge of the alley.

The attendant at the Billups station reeled out the water hose as far as it would reach, then stood spraying water toward Frank, who lay in a pitiful heap. Unfortunately, the hose wasn't long enough, so the stream of water fell woefully short of its mark – none of it reached Frank; none of it brought any kind of relief. As he smoldered at the end of the sidewalk,

Frank repeatedly whimpered, "Help me. Oh, God, Help me. Them boys done burned me bad."

Two Ferriday police officers were returning to town after they made a high speed run to Vidalia to blow the soot out of their patrol car when they saw the commotion in town. "Oh, damn. The Billups staion is on fire. Call the fire department out and let's get our butts down there right now."

As they drove up Fourth Street, the second officer said, "It's not the Billups station; it's the shoe shop."

"Oh, shit. Frank sleeps in the back of that place half the time. Get the fire department here fast."

"Just pull up into the alley when we get there. I'll go check on Frank."

As they drove up in front of the shop, the second officer panicked and screamed, "Up there. Up there. Stop the car! Stop the car there."

The driver pulled in across the end of the station's driveway and stopped across the sidewalk. The passenger jumped out of the car and ran the few steps to the smoldering mass at the edge of the sidewalk. "Oh, my God. It's Frank. We gotta do somethin' quick."

"He is burnt all over. Man, I can't believe this. Frank. Frank! You gonna be alright. We'll get you to the hospital. Call the ambulance down here."

"We don't have time for that. Let's just get him into the back of the car and take him down to the hospital. We can get him there before they even get the ambulance out of the garage."

They started to help Frank up, but when they reached down to lift him, Frank stood himself up and walked the few steps to the car. After the officers opened the back door, Frank rolled himself onto the seat as best he could. Someone else jumped into the back seat with Frank, then the officers slammed the back door, jumped into the car and sped off with the red light flashing and the siren blaring.

They took Frank to the Concordia Parish Hospital in Ferriday where they began treatment. Since he had received third degree burns over most of his body, the medical staff had given him less than a ten percent chance of surviving. Though most of his ramblings were incomprehensible, they could plainly understand when he repeated, "I thought they wuz my friends."

After the police took Frank to the hospital, Tee Wee disappeared into the shadows and spoke to no one about what he had seen. Who would believe him anyway? He was dumbfounded that Deputy Delaughter stood by his car at the Coast station less than two blocks away. While Frank's shop burned to the ground, the deputy stood talking with a stranger while standing in the open door of his car.

Before the sun had risen on that Friday morning, the Ferriday Chief of Police, an FBI agent, and an investigator from the Ferriday Fire Department gathered at Frank's bedside in the intensive care ward of the hospital. Police Chief Robert Warren pulled a chair up next to his bed and started talking, "Frank, this is Mister Bob. We are here to help. Go ahead and talk and don't worry."

"I don't know what happened ... I was layin' there asleep and I heard someone breaking glass out. They broke the glass out. They broke the glass out. I come out into my shop ... it look like one he beat on the window with a axe handle or somethin' and then the two men and another man aroun' there. They wuz pourin' gas all around the place. I said, 'What are you doin' there?' One of them tol' me to 'get back in there nigger. Be better off, nigger.'"

"Did you recognize these men? This is important. Did you recognize them?"

"No, sir. I didn't. I couldn't recognize them."

"Frank, go ahead and tell them if you want to. Me and Mister Noland will leave if you want to talk to him by yourself."

"It's alright, Mister Bob. Only thing is, I just didn't recognize them."

"Just couldn't recognize them?"

"No sir."

"Could you give us any description, Frank? Were they young or old?"

"Young men. One of them wuz kinda white. Real white."

"He was what?"

"Real white."

"Could you tell if he had blonde hair, black hair, red hair, or something? Could you see any of that? Frank?"

During the question, Frank had slipped into unconsciousness. Chief Warren prompted him, "Frank, can you still hear me?"

"Yes sir."

"Frank, do you think you have seen those men before?"

"I think so."

"Do you think they are from here?"

"Yes sir. I think they from here."

"Where do you think they might work here, Frank?"

"I think they might work over at International Paper or something like that over in Natchez," Frank whispered, barely audible.

"Huh?"

"In Natchez, Mississippi, or something like that."

The men looked confused. "The National Food? Do you think they worked over in Natchez? Frank?"

"Yeah, very much."

"Do you think it was a double-barrel or single-barrel shotgun, Frank?"

With that question, Frank groaned and slipped again into unconsciousness. A nurse standing at the side of the room said, "He had a shot a while ago."

"Is that a pain killer?"

"Uh huh."

"How long do you think that might last?"

"Two to three hours," she replied.

The men left the room and had a short discussion in the hall before they decided to resume the interrogation after Frank reawakened. They adjourned to get breakfast at a diner near the hospital. While they were away, the hospital staff moved Frank to a private room where they could care for him and continue the investigation without having an unintended audience. When the investigators reconvened at the hospital, the FBI agent went into the room with the Ferriday Fire Chief Noland Mouelle, and Levi Hewitt, Frank's close friend. Frank was still muttering under his breath, "I thought they wuz my friends."

Levi stood over Frank's bed and started, "Frank, this is Levi."

Frank's response was weak, "What about Peanut?" referring to his grandson who often stayed with him at the shop or in the small house behind the shop.

"Peanut is alright."

"Did he get burned?"

"Uh uh. He didn't get burned."

"Can you identify who they wuz, Frank?"

"I don't know 'xactly who it wuz. Ungh. I don't know 'xactly who they wuz."

They continued asking him questions, hoping to get a hint to the identities of the men who attacked him. They asked him about his position in the shop before the fire started, hoping to jar his memory. He continued to insist that he couldn't identify any of the men, but his answers were incongruous with his continued mumbling, "I thought they wuz my friends."

Frank considered all white people as his friends, so he could have been referring to anyone. I also figured that he would not have said anything even if he had known his attacker, since he didn't know that he was dying. He would have been afraid of reprisals by anyone that might have been involved. He was also very concerned about his family and friends, especially his grandson. "Just take care of yourself and the boy. I don't know whether I will git well or not, 'cause of the bad shape I'm in."

Levi tried to reassure him, "No, you ain't in no bad shape." Then he pressed on, "We worried about it. We want to find out who it is, but you won't tell us."

"I don't know exactly who it wuz. I had to run real fast. See, I come out there a man put a shotgun on me, told me to get back in there."

"Well you must've saw them if he told you to get back in there."

"Uh-huh."

"Did you? Huh?"

"Uh-huh."

"Well why don't you tell us who it is?" he said in frustration, knowing that Frank knew almost anyone of any renown in the town and hardly ever forgot a name.

"Don't 'xactly know."

"Had you ever seem 'em before?"

"Uh-huh. I guess so."

"Had they ever been in the shop before?"

"Uh-huh. I do ... "Frank seemed to get confused for a minute or he possibly scared himself with what he considered a near slip of the tongue.

The men began to discuss Frank's responses, "He did say that they had been in the shop before."

"But he just won't tell who it is."

"No." Levi confirmed, "He won't tell who it is."

With that, Chief Mouelle pulled his chair up to the bedside and began his interrogation, "I'm trying to find something out here. We are trying to get this thing straightened out. Where do these folks come from?"

Frank recognized Chief Mouelle's voice and answered, "I don't know where they come from Mister Law."

"You don't know where they come from?"

"No sir. I don't know exactly."

"Do they live in Ferriday?"

"I imagine they do."

"You imagine they do?"

"The old fellow – the one out there puttin' gasoline on the buildin'. Yes sir."

"You saw them put it around the building?"

"Yes."

"Well, did they put any inside?"

"They must have. I came out … I came out … I don't see how they did it so quick."

"Well something else I want to ask you. Where do they work?"

"I don't know where they work at."

"They work at the paper mill?"

"I think so, but I don't know."

"Or do they work over at Young's in Natchez?"

"Yes. I wasn't 'xactly straight. If I was I could move fast."

"You had to move fast?"

"Yes. What I mean is I coulda gotten to the door."

The chief continued to press for answers about the men, but he evaded direct answers. After Chief Mouelle questioned him for a while, the FBI agent also pressed him for the same information and got the same results. After a while, Doctor Colvin stepped up and leaned over to Frank, "I want you to know you are in real bad condition."

"Yes sir."

Doctor Colvin continued as if he were talking to a very close friend asking for a favor, "And I want you to do something for me. I want you to cooperate with these men. Do all you can to help them find out who burned your place and who burned you. Will you do that for me?"

"Yes. Yes. Alright, Doctor. I don't know exactly who the men wuz. One had on khaki pants and he wuz pourin' gas out and when I got up to see, he hit the window, he did. He hit the window and broke the window pane out and while he was breakin' panes out I come out to catch this joker – he had a shotgun – told me, 'Get back in, nigger.'"

Frank continued to answer questions as best he could. He was becoming more confused as his condition continued to deteriorate and he grew tired. "I can't say who it was. I probably seen them before. The one with the jacket on had a shotgun and I went on back in the house – sure had a time getting' myself out, 'cause man, it's … 'bout gone."

As the FBI agent continued, Frank revealed that there were three or more men, two of them about his size and a larger man who pointed the shotgun at him. He also estimated their ages to be between thirty and thirty-five and that one of the smaller men had gray hair and was wearing khaki trousers. But the most gruesome detail came right at the end of the conversation. "I had to get to the back room to get out."

"I see. And was the place on fire then?"

"Yes sir. Yes." Then after he thought about it, he recanted, "No sir. He struck the match …"

"You saw him strike the match?"

"Yes sir."

"Then he threw it inside?"

"Yes sir."

"Thank you, Frank. Anything else that you can tell me that might help?"

"No sir, that's all. I can't tell no more. I sho can't. How they do it in such a hurry – I ain't had a chance to do nothin'."

After a few more questions, they left so Frank could rest. When he regained consciousness a couple of times, he continued to mumble something about how he thought "they wuz my friends."

When I drove through Ferriday to go to school on Friday morning, I saw the burnt shell of Frank's Shoe Shop but didn't realize yet that Frank had been inside the shop when it burned. Nobody at school knew anything about it, so I didn't learn any of the details of the fire that day. Even when

I went to work after school, I still got no more information about the fire until just before we closed the station. Don Lender came by to fill up his old Ford truck and I struck up a conversation with him about the fire when he started giving more details than I ever expected. I had known Don for a while but never knew he was a fireman. After he told me how badly Frank had been burned, I was glad that I hadn't found out earlier in the day – the knowledge had already become such a burden.

After I left work, I planned to drive by Frank's place to see the damage. As I drove past the Billups station, I slowed to a crawl, then turned left onto Georgia Avenue. As the my headlights swept across the parking lot of the auto dealership that was on the corner, next to Frank's shop, I noticed that there were no cars parked in the lot. I thought, *How strange. There are usually eight to twelve cars parked out here.*

I parked the car about half way up the street, just past the back of the Billups station and parked the car. I got out of the car and walked to the edge of the car lot, wondering if any of the cars had been damaged. I started to walk into the lot, but reconsidered when I noticed one of the policemen that was still at the scene watching me closely. I veered onto the sidewalk and walked toward third street when I caught sight of one of the young men that once worked in Frank's shop. I walked over toward him and asked, "Hey, C. C. Are you here to see what happened the other night?"

"No sah. I lives right over yonder jus' past Third Street. I jus' come by to show my respec' to Mister Frank. He done taught me an awful lot 'bout life an' makin' a hones' livin'. He was a awfully good man."

"Hey, C. C. Were any of the cars burned up from the fire the other night?"

"No sah, Mister Buddy. There wasn't no cars out here for the fire."

"You mean they got them out of the way before the fire could damage any of them?"

"No sah. I means that they weren't no cars out here the other night. They moved all of the cars off the lot on the day before the fire."

Before I even thought about what I was saying, I blurted out, "It's like someone around here knew that there was going to be a fire and they wanted to hedge their bets a little. It certainly doesn't look good."

"Yes sah. It sure looks like someone knew this was going to happen."

When I looked over at the burn site, I realized that the officer was moving my direction, so I told C. C., "We better get out of here before they start asking us questions, too."

As C. C. walked away, I got into my car and drove back toward the center of Ferriday on Third Street, then made a left on Alabama to get back to Fourth. After I turned onto Fourth Street, I drove past Frank's shop again and wondered what they would find as they sifted through the burned shell of the building looking for clues. I thought about stopping, but reconsidered when I saw Deputy Delaughter parked across the street observing the progress of the investigation with interest. Just seeing him there brought out my anger and frustration.

When I got home, Daddy was already at the house and in an absolute panic. I asked him if he knew about Frank and he barked at me as if he thought I had done it. I didn't know that Jimmy, my younger brother, had seen the destruction from the school bus window that morning and had called home and told Mama how upset he was. When she called Daddy at work, he left right away, came home to pick up my younger brothers, and then had started making telephone calls to find out what had happened. If my father was nothing else, he was resourceful. He had made only a few calls before he began to get the gruesome details about the fire.

It wasn't long before I began to understand the depth of his panic – as if he knew who had done it, but he could do nothing about it. It was on this day, also, that I found out how deeply my father cared for Frank – he was angry with his sources because he couldn't get as much information as he felt he needed, and he was livid that anyone from the Klans would have anything to do with an attack in his town without his having been notified. He was enraged because Frank was his friend and this attack had been for no good reason. Most of his evening was spent on the telephone gathering intelligence. Since the telephone was located on the kitchen wall, we could hear almost everything he said, but it was only one side of the conversation. There were several times when the conversation grew heated and very intense.

"I don't give a shit who you are, you don't come over here and shit where we live. You tell him that if he does something like this again he is messin' with the wrong people. He better watch out or he might find hisself face down in the river with that badge shoved up his ass."

"Don't even try to threaten me with that stuff. We have enough on him and the rest of these local yokels to bury him in his own shit. You make all the threats you want to, but if anything wuz to happen to me, these boys will take him and half his officers down the latrine."

"Just how do you think I got involved with all this? I don't have anything to worry about from those boys over in Adams County, or Franklin County, or Jefferson County, or Rankin County, or Rapides Parish, or Catahoula Parish, or LaSalle Parish. You tell him that if he tries anything else, we will bring in enough people to take him and that place around him apart piece by piece – right down around his ears. You tell him and that little short shit that keeps his nose up his butt the same thing. I don't want to hear anything like this again, period." With that he hung the phone up with a bang.

A few minutes later the phone rang again. Daddy had regained his composure when he started talking. "Hey, Gerald. I s'pose you heard what happened over here last night."

"Tell them, 'Don't do anything. We'll take care of things ourselves.' We don't need this thing turned into something it ain't."

"Now you know better than that. Frank Morris ain't, and never wuz, messin' around with no white women. I knew Frank better than anyone around and I know he wuz always set up with a girl in his back room or back in the house, but he ain't never messed around with any white women. Don't try to give me that shit. It ain't gonna wash."

"No, YOU don't understand. They burned a good man out for no reason at all. He had that place there all of his life and I ain't never heard no one complain about anything he ever did. Everybody in town knows Frank. We all know who he is and what he does. There ain't nobody but colored girls in that back room and you know it – you been there, too."

"Well, we ARE going to get to the bottom of this, and it ain't gonna get quiet around here until we know who did it and why."

I walked to the back of the house and sat down on the edge of my bed and buried my face in my hands. I don't know if it was fear, anger, or sorrow that made me break down. I didn't want to cry, I just did. Jimmy and Johnny were both in their beds already so I wasn't sure if they could hear me sobbing; I tried to keep quiet. I knew that if I continued to sit there and think about it, I would only get worse so I walked out into the kitchen to get a glass of tea and try to settle down. Since the phone was on the other side of the kitchen, I could still hear Daddy though he was talking very softly now.

"Hey, Doctor Burns. I'm just trying to find out how Frank is doing. Is he awake enough to talk to me?"

"He's not awake at all anymore? What kind of condition is he in, anyway?"

"Less than ten percent? Ten percent! Is there anything that you can do for him?"

"I understand. Just keep enough painkiller in him so that he doesn't have to suffer any more. There ain't no reason for him to have to suffer like that. Do what you can for him, Doc."

Hearing that piece of conversation didn't help at all. I walked out into the workshop, unable to find peace or understanding. I walked out into the side yard where I leaned up against a playhouse that I had been building for one of Daddy's customers, one like I had built for Frank Morris during the summer, one I had painted white with red trim to match the trim on his shop. As I thought about it, I felt as if my humanity had been drained from me; I could cry no more. As the minutes passed, I felt cold and empty. All I wanted to do was sleep. I returned to my bed and escaped into the comfort of slumber.

After I finished work on Saturday afternoon, I noticed that the investigators were no longer around the shop, so I stopped to examine the damage. I walked up on the sidewalk where there was still glass from the window that had been broken before the fire. When I looked across the charred window seal, I could almost see Frank working at his stitching machine. I was struck by the weight of the smell of the wet remains of the fire, but it was just another fire at that point – something I had seen in the past. However, when I walked around to the alley the fire became different and very personal. I was suddenly overwhelmed by the smell of burnt flesh. When I looked back toward where the back corner of the building would have been, I could see the faint trail of bloody footprints Frank left after having cut his feet on the glass from the broken window; bloody footprints accented by burned, black flesh that tainted the air with the smell of death. Finally I noticed the end of the trail where there was a burned outline where he had collapsed near the sidewalk in front of the auto sales office. Stunned by the whole scene, I tried to put the pieces together.

By the time I got home, Daddy had settled down and seemed satisfied with the information that he had collected, but not with the conclusions he had drawn. He had several of the klaverns and citizens' groups on alert in case something were to happen to him. I was sure that he suspected two of our local deputies of having precipitated the brutal attack on Frank. He had heard that one of the men in the car was a colored man and the other was a local man who worked over at the paper mill, but I was sure he didn't believe either of the stories. Later in the evening I heard him talking to someone on the phone again, "We've got things in hand now. I think we are at about the bottom of this thing. We have a couple of things to wrap up and I need to talk to one more person that I am sure knows what all this is about."

As I did almost every night, I turned the television on and tuned it to the CBS Evening News to see the latest news from Walter Cronkite. As I watched, I was suddenly struck by the irony and sadness of the situation when he announced that Martin Luther King had won the Nobel Peace Prize on December 10th, the day that Frank Morris had been so brutally attacked. Daddy was still sitting near the phone in the kitchen when he heard the news and it sent him into another tirade. "How could they give that agitating nigger the Peace Prize for stirring up all this trouble down here? Someone's gonna kill that nigger sooner or later. If he keeps coming down here and stirring these people up, someone's gonna bomb the shit out of him and his whole family."

I held my tongue because I knew how upset he was already. Something was all wrong with my world! How could so much of the world celebrate what King had done through the civil rights movement while it generated so much hate and violence where I lived? How could an act of peace produce so much venom in my own house? How could someone like my father be a part of an organization that was so bent on violence toward colored people, and yet so upset by violence against one colored man?

Daddy continued his quest to find out all he could about Frank's murder. He spent hours on the phone talking with Klansmen and police all over Louisiana and Mississippi. Our long distance telephone bill was going to be huge. In addition, he made frequent trips out of town to chase down leads about the hit and anyone who might be involved.

After church on Sunday, Daddy and I went to the hospital to see Frank. I thought it would be good to see him, but nothing anyone could have told me would have prepared me for what I was about to see. The man in the hospital bed was swollen and disfigured with tubes in his mouth, nose and in what was left of one of his arms. His skin was split at the top of his chest and on one of his arms. The air in the room was very cool and heavy with the smell of burnt flesh. I always had a weak stomach, so the sight and smell was too much for me. I had to wait in the hall, then down in the lobby while Daddy stayed to say a prayer over Frank. I didn't know how he could stay there; to stand the sight and smell of the terrible apparition that was Frank Morris.

On Monday, four days after he was attacked, Frank succumbed to his injuries. He died quietly in his hospital room. The attendance at his funeral was indicative of his popularity in our area, since there were several white people in attendance; many of them were local dignitaries. I didn't get to attend the funeral because I had to work so Leroy could attend.

Tee Wee Kelly did not get to attend the funeral either. As he was walking down Georgia Avenue on Monday, a police car pulled up on Fifth Street just as he stepped into the street. Another pulled up behind him on Georgia Avenue. The officer in the first car motioned for him to approach the car. As Tee Wee stepped near the car the Deputy said, "Tee Wee, I don't think there is anything left in this town for you. I think you need to leave town as fast as possible. Someone around here thinks you know too much. They said that maybe someone saw you down by Mister Frank's place on the night of the fire. Have you been telling any tall tales in the bars at night?"

While they were burying his friend, Tee Wee was packing to leave town. By Wednesday, he was gone, never to return to the town and friends that he loved. I never saw him in Ferriday again.

The following Thursday, we got news from Aunt Millie that Cora had died in her sleep on Wednesday. Daddy and I went to her funeral on the following Saturday at the Mount Zion Church in Fenwick. We were the only white people in the church, but they took us to the front row to sit with Aunty Luella, Uncle Levi, and Uncle Perry like we were part of the family. It had been a long time since I had attended a service like that one. After Reverend Berry prayed the invocation, the pianist picked up with a rhythm and intensity that would inspire the soul in anyone to sing out and dance, and some did. There were only about 50 people in the church, but they sounded like thousands. They drummed their hands on the backs of the large wooden pews and stomped their feet in rhythm with the music; their vocal course was truly a joyful noise suitable to raise the rafters. I got caught up in the revelry of the moment and started clapping, stomping and singing to the top of my lungs. What a wonderful release. It was almost enough to make me forget why I was there.

After we sang several gospel songs and hymns, Reverend Berry read Cora's eulogy. He told of her life as a slave, then as a freedman after the Civil War. I wished that he could have told the story of her life as she had related it to Roxie and me, but it would have taken days. It wasn't really necessary because most of the people in the church knew Cora's story as well as I did. During the eulogy, I became aware of the importance of Granny Cora's stories – I had been listening to the stories of the life of a slave – a slave! After the eulogy, the reverend delivered a short sermon in which he spoke about the love of God and the peace in heaven where all wrongs would be righted and all souls would be equal. As he asserted each point, the congregation responded with an "Amen" or "Yes, Lord." When he finished his message, he prayed for Cora and then he prayed for the congregation with a special focus to the white folks that had come to honor Cora.

We sang the last song softly and I could hear the quiet sobbing all over the church. Aunty Luella reached down for my hand and held it up with hers as she sang. As the song was trailing into silence, she walked me up to the wooden casket where we stood silently for a moment. I watched Aunty Cora closely as if I expected her to move when I realized that she was wearing a beautiful purple dress with cloth buttons and lace on both sides of the front. The dress smelled of smoke and aromatic cedar from having been stored in the chest for so long. It was then that the reality of the math hit me. I looked up at Aunt Luella, "Is that the dress? It must be a hundred years old."

Aunt Luella assured me that it was the same dress that Master Donny had given Cora when she was so young. Then she leaned right down to my ear and said, "She dressed up real special 'cause she be wearin' her special buryin' stockin's."

I was so glad that she said something about the stockings because I had completely forgotten about the gift that I made to Granny Cora so many years before. She had put those stockings away for years just for this special day. Now she lay there in her finest in a pillow lined wooden box looking like she finally found the peace that she so desperately worked for all of her life.

After each of the members of the congregation stood before the casket to bid her goodbye, the pallbearers picked the casket up and walked it out into the small grave yard behind the church. They set the casket down carefully across three ropes that were spaced evenly at the end of an open grave. As everyone watched, six of the pall bearers, three on each side, grabbed the ends of the ropes and hoisted the casket a couple of inches off the ground. They walked the casket over the open grave and lowered it slowly into the ground. Finally the casket settled at the bottom of the grave and we were all overwhelmed by emotion as we realized that Cora had finally reached her final resting place. I found a special peace when I looked down at the top of the coffin; I was sure that she was in the arms of her Master Donny and in the presence of her beloved Jesus.

On the Sunday before Christmas, I drove Daddy to church at Zion Hill, in Olla, Louisiana. While we were at church, a man that I knew only as Mister Tichenor called Daddy aside and they talked for almost an hour. I called him Mister Tichenor because of his propensity to nip on bottles of Dr. Tichenor's Anteseptic, which I suspected of having been filled with moonshine. He suggested that Daddy needed to talk to an acquaintance of his from Delhi, Louisiana. As they talked, they walked away from me, so I didn't get the details of the conversation.

During the week, we were out of school for the holidays, and I was working only part time, so I was spending more time at home. On Tuesday, Daddy worked only part of the day and returned home shortly after noon. He made a long distance call to the man in Delhi and I could hear the excitement grow in his voice as they talked. After he hung up the phone, Daddy made a quick call to E. L. McDaniel and declared, "I know who called the hit, and we might have a real mess to clean up. I'll call you back later and tell you what I find out."

He walked into the kitchen, dialed another number, and sat down in his chair while the phone was ringing. When someone picked up, he said, "I need to speak to Mister Spencer. Mister Douglas Spencer."

"Mister Spencer, this is Ed Blanche from the Concordia Parish chapters of the OKA and United Klans. I understand you are the Grand Giant of Richland Parish and you handle the crews in your area. I want to know did you send the crew down here to make that hit in Ferriday, and I want to know who sanctioned the hit. We found Frank Morris innocent of those charges and we didn't call for a hit."

I couldn't hear the reply, but it was pretty obvious. Daddy's voice got louder and his excitement grew, "Who does he think he is, anyway. Who do *you* think he is? He holds no rank in any of the Klans in any of the area around here. He has no right to call a hit on anybody. He is the one that called for the hit in the first place, and we turned him down. So who gives him the right to call a hit, and who, or what, gives you the right to send one?!"

The voice on the other end of the line grew loud and angry, inciting Daddy even more. "I don't care who you are or who said it was OK. You do not come down here into my parish and do anything unless WE say it is okay. You send a boy and a bunch of hoodlums down here and they make a mess out of what should have been a simple hit – they made a real mess of things. They went way too far and we won't let that kind of thing happen around here again."

After he listened for a minute, he shot back, "I don't care who calls it. If it doesn't come from one of us, you don't send anyone. I don't care if he is the sheriff, I don't care if he is the mayor, I don't care if he is the governor, or even God – I don't give a shit who it is. You do not send a crew down here for anything unless the order comes from the Grand Titan of the Dominion – and that is me."

"If anything like this ever happens again, some of those boys are not going to make it home. These boys down here have a lot of uncapped wells and they are looking to fill them up. From now on, you keep your boys in line and you keep them up there in Richland Parish. You do not send anyone into our area to do any kind of business. One more thing: that other problem we have. We will deal with him and the other one in our own way. We take care of our own problems."

I can only guess what was going on at the other end of the phone. Whatever it was, it put Daddy into a rage. He continued shouting at the man for several minutes, then after making several more threats, hung the phone up, and slammed the receiver onto the floor beside his chair. He quickly got up from his chair and went into the kitchen to dial another number.

"Hey, Sheriff. This is Ed. I hate to bother you again, but you need to know what is going on. I just spoke to that hoodlum that calls himself the Grand Giant in Richland Parish. He was the one that sent the hit on Frank's shop. It was a some of his boys that came down, and from the sounds of it, one of them might have been his boy – I mean his son or something. The problem that we have is that he said that it was our sheriff that called the hit. I explained to that stupid son-of-a-bitch that Delaughter is only the deputy sheriff here and that he does not have the right or authority to call a hit on anybody in this area."

"Yes sir. I guess he told Spencer that he is the law down here, and that whatever he said goes."

"Yeah, Sheriff. I just wanted you to know and to tell you to watch your back. I don't trust that SOB any further than I can throw him."

I guess the sheriff took over the conversation from there because Daddy listened quietly for a few minutes, then hung the phone up without even saying goodbye. Right after he hung the phone up, he got up and walked into the kitchen to dial another number, then returned to his chair in the living room.

"Hey, RJ. Ed here. How are things with you?"

"Yeah. I want you to put the word out on the street just in case anything happens over here. Those boys that came down here and hit Frank Morris were from the klaverns in Richland Parish. Our boy Frank Delaughter called down that hit, even after we cleared Frank Morris of any charges. He doesn't know that we found out the truth already, but I am sure he is probably finding out right about now. I just spoke to Doug Spencer from Richland Parish, and he gave me some of the details about the hit, though it wasn't what he really wanted to do."

He listened for a minute, then started again, "No. That is why I am talking to you now. That prick threatened me and my family and said that Delaughter would take care of me. If anything happens to any of us,

I want you to go up there and take care of all of them. You know what you have to do."

Daddy got out of his chair for a moment and I thought he was going to put the phone away, when he walked over and looked out the front door and said, "RJ. If either of those men or their people come anywhere around here and start something, you make sure it gets finished – and I mean finish it for good. You and the rest of the boys take care of all of them."

When he said boys, I thought he was talking about my brothers and me, but it quickly became apparent that he was talking about the Klansmen with whom he worked at the tire company. "Yeah. I don't want to start anything else, but I will end it if I have to. I just need for you and the Silver Dollars here to back me up in case something goes wrong. And, RJ. If they get to me even a little bit, I want you boys to put the fear of God into this whole parish and in those yayhoos up in Richland Parish."

"Thanks RJ. Yes. I would do the same for you. You know I trust you with my life. Take care and keep an eye on things over here so we can know if something is coming."

With that, Daddy walked back into the kitchen and dialed another number. I knew he had called the King Hotel because of his response. "Hi Diane. Is Mister Nugent there right now? I need to see if we can get a meeting together pretty quick."

"Thanks, Diane. Yeah. I'll see you when we come down to the hotel."

"OK, I'll wait."

I could tell he was on hold for a couple of minutes, as he paced between his chair and just inside the kitchen door where the phone was mounted. After several minutes, he finally spoke. "Hey, Mister Nugent. We have a problem that we need to deal with in a hurry. We need to get some of our most trusted together with the Silver Dollars and meet at the hotel to see what we need to do about this."

Daddy sat thoughtfully for a couple of moments. As he pondered, he took his cigarettes out of his pocked and tapped the top of the pack against his finger several times to dislodge a cigarette. He put the pack up to his mouth and took the cigarette loosely between his lips, then put the pack back into his shirt pocket. As he flicked his lighter open to light the cigarette, the conversation continued.

"No. Just those on my private list and the Silver Dollars only – and definitely not Delaughter. He IS the problem right now."

"I'll tell you all more about it when we get together, but the important thing right now is what happened to Frank Morris. That hit was done by them boys up in Richland Parish, and I am sure you know one or two of them. The worst part is that that pretender for sheriff, Frank Delaughter, called down the hit. He was the one that caused this thing from the very start. You called it right back in October."

"No. I understand. There was no way for any of us to know what was about to happen. All we knew then was that Delaughter had it in for Frank, and he wanted him hit real hard and fast. We turned him down twice, and I guess he was gonna have his way – one way or another."

"We need to figure out what to do about it now, and what we have to do so this doesn't happen again in our region. We can't have our locals calling down hits just because they want it, and we certainly cannot have anyone coming into our area from the outside and making hits just because someone called one. We have to let them know that nobody just comes into our parish – our region – and does a hit just because someone here has a private vendetta to serve up."

"Okay. You get the boys together and we will talk about it. I am sure that Delaughter knows that we know by now. Spencer would have called him first thing. All we can do now is try to get this thing in hand and let him know that this is as far as it goes. I already called the boys over in Adams County and Franklin County. They will take over if anything happens to any of us over here. I know that Frank don't want any part of those boys. So let's just meet and put an end to this mess before someone else gets hurt real bad. I'll see you when we all get together. Bye."

After he hung the phone up with Mister Nugent, he called someone else in Natchez. I never heard him use a name, but I was sure it was another of the Silver Dollars. The call lasted about forty-five minutes while he told them the whole story, starting with the earliest accusations against Frank Morris. After he explained the connection of Frank Delaughter to the klaverns and wrecking crew from Richland Parish, Daddy invited him to the meeting at the King Hotel, then told him that he would see him there.

After the conversation with the man in Natchez, Daddy hung the phone up and dialed another local number – I could tell because he only dialed seven numbers. When the person answered, Daddy didn't identify himself; he cupped his hand over the mouthpiece of the phone and spoke in a most sinister voice, "The Klans know what you did and the local law knows what you did. You know what the klan can do, and you know that you can't trust the one that calls hisself the law in this parish, so this town ain't safe for you anymore. This is your first and only warning – it would be safer if you left town as soon as you can."

With that, he hung up the phone and went back to his chair in the living room. After he sat in his chair, he whistled, then yelled for my mother, "Mary. Bring me a drink and come turn the TV on."

It always upset me when he treated her like some kind of personal servant. I yelled back to the back of the house, "I got it Mama."

I walked back to the refrigerator and got a beer out for Daddy. I was tempted to shake it a few times, but he would probably have killed me for testing him in the hard times that we were going through. I walked in and handed him the beer, then turned around and pulled the switch to turn on the TV. As I walked out of the room, I said, "Thank you, too."

I went to my room, opened *The Count of Monte Cristo*, and continued reading. Daddy sat in his chair and watched television for another couple of hours.

CHAPTER 6

Winds that Fan the Flames

At the end of December, I got my license back – I could drive again! Still only seventeen years old, I tested for and received a Commercial Driver's License – now I could be a truck driver. With my new license, I took a job at PedCo, a local petroleum distribution warehouse, where I pumped gas on school days and delivered petroleum products to oil drilling locations all over Louisiana and Mississippi when I wasn't in school. The new job was very prestigious and the pay was much better— very impressive for a high school student.

The strain between Daddy and me got another kick in the head when I could no longer spend as much time on his woodwork shop projects as he wanted. He didn't seem to worry about how I should get my homework done; he was concerned about how he was going to deliver all of the gun cabinets, coffee tables, and playhouses he promised. At the same time, we got into terrible arguments when my grades slipped. I didn't think he really cared about how well I did in school, but he was already talking about how he wanted me to go to college. I agreed with him on the college issue because the Selective Services required teenagers to register for the draft at the age of eighteen. If I were not in college, I would be immediately eligible for the draft.

I was still confused about how Daddy reconciled his religious beliefs with his activities in the Klans. He was traveling and attending meetings all over the two states and I could no longer travel with him regularly. We seemed to argue about everything—the way I spent my money, my school work, my contribution to the household finances—everything. He seemed paranoid about the thought that I was going to do something that would get me in trouble and cause dishonor to his name. If I went anywhere and did anything that looked the least bit suspicious, my father knew about it before I got home. I felt like a prisoner. One day while driving home, I weaved to avoid something that had fallen from the back of a pickup truck. When I got home, Daddy accused me of driving drunk—demanding to know if I had been drinking. He then proceeded to let me know, in no uncertain terms, that if he caught me drinking he would "bust my ass." Fortunately, this happened on an evening when I had not stopped at Banty's Rooster Club where I sometimes stopped to have a beer or to play a few hands of blackjack with friends.

Daddy was still bent on some kind of vengeance for the attack on Frank Morris. He continued to make phone calls to get more information and confirm what he already knew. His persistence paid off because someone confirmed a name from his list of suspects. I was frustrated by his increased secrecy regarding people that had been involved with the hit on Frank Morris. When people called the house, some of them resorted to disguising their voices and improved the complexities of the codes they used when talking to one another. I could hear only parts of the conversation again. "We will verify this and if it is right we will take care of it."

Though I didn't always recognize who was calling, I could usually tell what the conversation was about by the way Daddy reacted. Sometimes, the paranoia in what he said made it easier to remember the snippets of conversation.

"No. And don't say those kinds of things on these phones because we don't know who is listenin' in," he said, referring to the FBI. "It is not just the local yokels we are dealing with any more. These boys can listen in on phone calls, they can trace calls made anywhere in the United States, and they can listen through walls."

"They already been here a couple of times. I know they know somethin' and I know they can't prove anythin'. But even if they have all the proof in the world, there ain't no way they gonna convict anyone in this county of killin' a colored man; especially if it has anythin' to do with the local law."

"You just make sure of your facts and we will take care of it our way and don't you go messin' with these yokels over here. One of these boys beat a man to death over here in the jail in Ferriday. It wasn't too long ago when he beat another one almost to death. He is mean and he likes his job."

I knew he was talking about Deputy Sheriff Delaughter. Rumors had been circulating for several years that he had beaten someone to death in jail with his bare hands. The rumors I heard were even more brutal than that, because it involved the use of billy clubs, chairs, night sticks, and lengths of fire hose. Those same rumors included the participation and observation of these beatings by other deputies and local law enforcement officers, including the Louisiana Highway Patrol. I heard that the officers took a couple of suspected civil rights workers into the jail, shackled them with their necks bent over the backs of their chairs in which they were seated, and beat them with a fire hose. After the civil rights workers were beaten, they were held for several days without any charges, taken to another part of the parish and told to leave and never return.

Daddy was still on the phone, "If you come over here and start askin' questions or talkin' to the wrong people, these boys will mess you up real bad. Let the boys that live here get the information we need. They done good so far."

When he hung up the phone, Daddy sat down in his living room chair and started watching the news, something he did more often in those days. I followed behind him, taking my seat on the couch. I tried to start a conversation with him, but he was lost in the television almost immediately. He reached into his shirt pocket for a pack of cigarettes, poked his finger into the pack and found it was empty. He crushed the pack and handed it to me, "Get me another pack of cigarettes, Buddy."

I got him another pack of cigarettes from the cabinet as they played a teaser of an upcoming story about a grain elevator that exploded. After I handed him the cigarettes, I sat down and waited for the story. I listened intently to the details of story of a grain elevator and silo that had exploded, blowing the cone-shaped top of the dome almost a quarter of a mile away. When they explained that the explosion had been caused by grain dust, I was dumbfounded. I really did not believe the story. How could grain dust from wheat or corn cause an explosion large enough to blow the top of a grain silo four hundred yards from the source?

When I was at work the following day, I quickly put away the barrels of oil and other inventory that we received during the day. I went out to the large gas tanks at the back of the warehouse and took inventory of the amount of gasoline and diesel we had in the tanks. While at the back of the warehouse, I saw several empty fifty-five gallon drums stored against the back of the building—I was immediately inspired to prove that grain dust could not explode violently enough to destroy a silo.

I got home that evening and set about collecting the things I needed to debunk the grain dust explosion. I cut eighteen inches of detonation cord from the box in the workshop, then cut an equal length of fuse cord and put it all into a small box. I calculated that the length of fuse would give me about forty-five seconds to get away. I also took two cherry bombs and placed them into the box. After I left school the following day, I stopped by the grocery store on the way to work and bought a two pound bag of flour.

When I got to work, I quickly put away new inventory, and set up two load-outs for delivery to a couple of local drilling companies. After I completed all of my chores, I took one of the fifty-five gallon drums from the back of the building and rolled it about a hundred yards into the middle of the cotton field behind the warehouse. I pulled on the lever to remove the barrel ring that secured the lid to the drum. When I removed the lid, I looked down into the drum and noticed there were a couple of gallons of liquid left in the bottom. I tipped the drum over to remove the remnants and realized it was some kind of solvent or naptha. Though a little concerned, I continued with my project. I cut a small hole into the bag of flour and inserted one of the cherry bombs. I pushed the blade of my pocket knife through the det-cord to make a small slit and slid the cherry bomb fuse through the slit. I pushed the fuse of the second cherry bomb into the long end of the det-cord, then shoved the length of fuse cord into the other end. I wrapped the det-cord one time around the bag of flour, trapping the fuse cord so that it stuck straight up into the air. I placed my contrivance into the bottom of the barrel with care to have the fuse sticking straight up. I placed the lid partially on the drum so that it was balanced on the edge. I was ready.

I struck a match, reached down into the drum and lit the fuse. I slid the lid into place at the top of the barrel, picked up the barrel ring and snapped it onto the top of the barrel as quickly as possible, then started running back to the trees behind the warehouse to seek cover. I didn't quite make it.

Baboom! As I spun around, I heard a rocketing noise as the lid went up, but I never saw it. My eyes were caught by the large mushroom of smoke followed by a perfect smoke ring that climbed into the air. What a sight it was! Then reality hit; I hadn't seen where the lid went and I was still exposed in the field. I sprinted for the cover of the trees where I panicked because I was now faced with the possibility of a smoking hot drum lid falling into the top of one of the gasoline tanks. "Oh, God. Please," I prayed. Mortified, I stood waiting to hear the sound of the lid falling to the ground—nothing. As I watched the smoke dissipate in the light breeze, another wave of panic hit me. Even though the explosion was in an empty field, there were houses and businesses all the way around it. I was sure that someone would call the police and they were sure to come looking for the source of the noise and smoke.

I ran back out to the center of the field to collect the drum. When I saw the damage to the drum, I was shocked. It was split from the top down to the bottom expansion ring—it was split two thirds of the way down the side of the barrel! I grabbed the top edge of the drum and dragged it through the field to the back of the warehouse. I returned to the field to retrieve the lid and the barrel ring but I could find neither of them. I hurried back to the warehouse to answer the phone or greet the police when they arrived; they never did. Nobody called, nobody came by the warehouse, and nobody but my father ever mentioned anything.

When I got home from work that evening, he said, "I heard you had a little explosion behind the warehouse today."

I turned to look at him and saw an amused grin on his face. Then he did something that he did only when he was trying to contain his amusement; he bit his tongue lightly as he stuck it out a bit, disguising the remnant of a grin. It was one of the few times in my life when my father seemed genuinely amused by anything I did. My fears were transformed as I related my misadventure to him. He tried to hide his amusement, but I knew that he would be telling his coworkers at the tire plant about it the next day and have a good laugh. My biggest laugh from the incident was in the consideration of the possibilities—at some time during the spring, the cotton farmer who worked that field would be plowing in preparation for planting and he would run across a large lid. What was he going to think? I still smile about it each time I entertain the thought of the farmer finding the mysterious hardware in his field.

After Frank Morris was killed, the FBI presence was more pronounced in Ferriday. They were also more visible at my house. They came by to talk to Daddy about once every two weeks; more often right before or after any marches, demonstrations, or cross burnings. They were also driving new cars—1965 Chevrolet Caprice 396s. When they came to the house, the conversations and interviews were usually very cordial and polite, though there were several times through January where things got heated. I think the FBI insinuated that some of Daddy's Klan friends were responsible for Frank Morris' death, possibly someone very close to him. Daddy was not one to back down very easily when he had the bit between his teeth. During one of the interviews in January, Daddy went nose-to-nose with one of the agents in a very heated debate.

"I don't give a shit who you are. You don't come over here and tell us we have to do anything for these outside agitators, and you definitely don't come into my house and make accusations about these patriots that are looking out for our country. Most of them fought in the war for this country. One of these old boys you just talked about is walking around with only one testicle because he lost one to a mine in the war. About half of these men fought in Korea, the Pacific, or in Europe to fight this kind of oppression."

The agent countered with, "You don't know who you have in your groups anymore. You have dens of thugs running around over here in sheets, hiding under hoods that are destroying the country you fought for."

"You don't know what you are talkin' about. These men were, and are, patriots and they are still fightin' for what is right. Besides, if you revenuers knew what you were talkin' about you'd be out makin' arrests right now instead of rootin' around here tryin' to dig up shit on these boys over here. I know somethin' about what is goin' on over here, and you ain't even close."

The agent shot back, "We're pretty sure we know who did it and we are pretty sure you know all of them very well. You better watch it before you find yourself tangled up with the wrong people over here. We'll bring this whole thing down around your ears."

Then he made a mistake; he pointed his finger in Daddy's face and made a veiled threat, "We will tie you to this mess and we may find out that you helped to burn out Frank."

Daddy lurched forward and yelled, "Get out! Get out now and bring someone who knows what he is talkin' about next time you come into my house. You don't come in here and disrespect me and my friends; you don't come in here and threaten me in front of my family. Not you and not anyone else." With that he reached out and collared the agent, shoving him backward very hard. The agent stumbled, hit the screen door, tripped down the step, and rolled out into the yard.

Without another word, the agent picked himself up and walked to his car as his partner stood and walked out of the house. As the second agent was leaving, he turned and offered Daddy his outstretched hand and said, "Mister Blanche, we will be in contact with you. But be careful who you run with over here and over at the plant. You got some things going on right now that I am sure you don't want to be involved with."

At that time, I don't think Daddy had figured out the true sources of some of his information. I also don't think he was aware of the growing influence of the FBI on the local law enforcement groups in Adams, Jefferson, and Franklin Counties. He seemed even less aware of how the FBI was able to get such accurate information on the Klan operations throughout Louisiana - especially in Rapides, LaSalle, Catahoula, and Concordia Parishes – those parishes that were closer to home.

From what I had seen and heard, information was flowing both ways through members of the local law enforcement and through the FBI. There were those within the Klans that fed information to the FBI and to the local law enforcement regarding Klan activities, including meetings, rallies, and cross burnings. One Klan informant led the FBI and the Mississippi Highway Safety Patrol to numerous caches of bombs, grenades, and explosives that were ready for distribution for Klan projects in Lincoln, Franklin, and Pike Counties.

Information came from the FBI also. They had special units in the North that were investigating the civil rights workers they considered to be agitators or anarchists. If any of the suspected anarchists were scheduled to come into the Concordia Parish or Adams County area, the FBI would alert the local police of the impending arrival of the outside agitators.

However, some of the local officers were feeding information about the civil rights workers back to the Klans so they could also be prepared. In addition, the Klans were getting information about some of the civil rights activities that weren't coming through any of the local law enforcement groups or FBI.

After the FBI moved into Mississippi in greater numbers, Klan activity became sporadic. It was more difficult for them to meet in secrecy in large numbers. Because they were being watched so closely, bombing activities were greatly reduced. Since the Klans were doing less, civil rights groups and outside agitators were being blamed for many of the bombings and burnings. With so many civil rights groups forming and moving into Mississippi, they were beginning to fight amongst themselves as badly as the Klans were infighting. The Klans were doing as much as they could to stir up problems between the competing factions.

In January, Sheriff Cross approached Daddy and said, "Ed, I like the way you handled this Frank Morris thing and I may need your help on a few things. It seems I have a bull in a china shop here and I need all the help I can get to keep a couple of these boys in line." He was referring to his self-proclaimed senior deputy and two of the others that had been rumored to be present at meetings and beatings. "I don't even feel safe around some of those boys anymore. When we have to go somewhere, I take my own car so I don't have to ride with him. I need someone I can trust. So I am making you my "special deputy." You won't be getting' no uniform and such, but I'll call on you when I need you."

While things seemed to be going crazy around Concordia Parish, they were equally crazy through the rest of the United States. In February, 1965, Malcolm X was killed in New York and the Klans were elated with the possibility that he was probably "killed by his own kind." I was with Daddy and several of his plant coworkers—also Klansmen—when they got into an animated discussion about Malcolm X's life and death.

"That nigger never did get straightened out after he was in prison. It was probably one of his old prison buddies that didn't like somethin' he said after he got out."

"No. It didn't have nothin' to do with his prison buddies. Them Black Muslims are real extreme; that's what he wuz, you know."

"Well, he done dropped out of the Black Muslims and started up another group. It's just like it is down here. One of his own kind got him for dropping out of the Black Muslim."

Their venomous speculation was, ironically, accurate. The news broadcasts verified that Malcolm X had indeed been assassinated by members of the Nation of Islam, Black Muslims. Oh, how the Klans gloated over this irony. That was the favored topic of choice when any of them got together for the next two weeks. To me, this was just one more example of the kind of violence that I did not understand. I didn't even want to try to understand it because it would only lend itself to some justification of another senseless act of violence.

The Klans didn't stay focused on the assassination very long. They were busy printing another document for distribution around Natchez, this time with a list of white women who were allegedly consorting with colored men. It also listed several businesses in Natchez and Vidalia that should be boycotted because they were catering to a predominately colored clientele. I knew some of the people and businesses that were listed in the document. I was concerned. "How can they get away with this? Daddy couldn't have anything to do with this because he knows better."

I was convinced that Daddy could not have had any part in the generation and printing of the paper. This scandalous document would hurt many and help no one. I could think of no reason to put something like this in print except to cause more hate and discontent.

In early March, word was out that there was going to be a march from Selma, Alabama to the state capital in Montgomery as some kind of protest and demonstration. The demonstration was to go to the capital to demand some answers from Governor Wallace for the sabotage of a nighttime demonstration in Marion County the week before. The lights were turned off and the demonstrators were attacked by the Alabama State Troopers. During the event, one of the young demonstrators was shot and killed by a State Trooper as he hid in a café trying to protect his parents from the violence.

Some of the Klansmen from Mississippi were anxious to go do what they could to observe and harass the marchers. While some of the Klansmen prepared to go to Selma to confront the demonstrators, others were preparing to counteract any of the civil rights activists that might try to form an impromptu demonstration in Natchez to coincide with the one in Selma. They were collecting then distributing small grenades, smoke bombs, hand weapons, and irritants that could be deployed against the marchers if they were confronted.

R. J. Glover provided several squirt bottles of high life, the ammonium-based irritant that that he had provided for earlier events. It was now more refined, it smelled foul, burned the skin, and could temporarily blind a target if it hit them right. He even demonstrated to some of the other men how to deploy the irritant without being seen. Using one of the squirt bottles filled with water, he held the bottle in his right hand, then stood with his arms crossed so that the bottle peeked from under his left armpit. When someone walked past him, he would give the bottle a sharp squeeze to squirt them on the back of the head. If someone turned around at the wrong time, he squirted them in the face, demonstrating how the victim could be blinded. He told them to move away quickly if they got the victim in the face, then told them not to run because it would draw attention.

After everything was distributed, the men continued to plan their strategies for the different areas of Natchez where the civil rights workers may plan to demonstrate. For each of the possible areas, each Klansman had a designated role and a designated area of confrontation. They also had a stack of pamphlets for distribution to passersby. Early Saturday morning, some of the men met at the Natchez Hunt Club, loaded into a couple of cars, and headed off to Selma, Alabama. The men that stayed behind braced for the impact of what they expected—or hoped—would happen in Natchez.

Sunday passed without incident in Natchez, but not so in Selma. Alabama's Governor Wallace declared the march a public safety threat and sent his state troopers in to prevent it from leaving Selma. The CBS Evening News announced that the marchers had clashed with the State Troopers at the foot of the bridge leaving Selma. The video footage that followed revealed the melee to the world. The officers of the law, those sworn to keep the peace, used tear gas against the defenseless parade of marchers, then waded into them with clubs and whips. It was a brutal attack that left many of the marchers injured and bloody, some requiring hospitalization.

That night, I drove Daddy over to the Natchez Hunt Club so he could get a nap as we drove. When we got to the club, things were rather chaotic. The men that returned from Selma were elated with what had happened to the marchers. "We didn't have to do nothin'. Those niggers came off that bridge from Selma and there wuz police everywhere!"

"Yeah. As soon as the front of the march got past the first police line all hell broke loose."

"Them coloreds didn't have a chance. I heard the cops yell somethin' at the lead marchers then they just waded into them like they wuz pissed about something. They wuz whippin' 'em and beatin' 'em with them clubs they carry, then they threw tear gas cans into the middle of the crowd."

"Even before the teargas they wuz ridin' horses up into the middle of 'em while they hit 'em with them big whips. One of them horses got skitterish from all the ruckus and he wuz rarin' up and jumpin' around all over while the police wuz hangin' on for dear life. I think he trampled three or four niggers before they settled him down. Funniest damn thing I ever saw in my life."

"Boy, I tell you. When they started beatin' on them coloreds, they started beatin' on everybody. It didn't matter how old, or if they wuz women, or whatever. They wuz just beatin' on everybody."

"Those ol' boys came prepared, too. All the police that wuz waitin' over at the bottom of the bridge wuz wearin' army helmets. Some of them were wearin' jackets with some kind of protection underneath. They wuz wearin' pads and protective vests so they wouldn't get hurt if they got hit by something."

"Yeah. That turned out to be a big nothin'. They had all these big plans about marchin' from Selma all the way to Montgomery. Shit, they didn't even make it ten blocks."

"I'm all pissed off now. I drove all the way to Selma and I didn't get to hit one nigger. What a waste!" The men giggled like a bunch of kids at a sleepover. Each new comment brought a wave of laughter and grunts of agreement. "Yeah. Why should those police have all the fun?"

"Well, I think it will be a while before they try that again. They must have put twenty or thirty of them in the hospital and just beat the shit out of a whole bunch of them."

I was shocked at the very idea that the police, or even the Klansmen, would beat up a woman, regardless of her color. I had always been taught that a man did NOT hit women unless it was a life or death situation. I had also been taught that I should respect my elders, even if they were colored. Now here are some of the very people that helped teach these values to me, and they were talking about how exciting and funny it was to see colored women and old people get beat and whipped just like men.

After the meeting, I drove Daddy back to the house. I asked if anything had happened in Natchez during the day.

"No. These colored people over here and around home ain't gonna give us no problems. We take care of them so they don't need to do this stuff. If we get outside agitators in here trying to stir up trouble, we get them out of here before they even know what hit them."

"You know you are just delaying the inevitable." I said. "Those guys at the hunt club and over in Selma are just making matters worse. Every time that kind of stuff hits the news, they get a new surge of people from all over America signing up to come down here to march and demonstrate."

"White people all over the South—all over America—believe the races should be kept apart. We do not want a gray society. This Great Society stuff is all wrong and we have people everywhere that are ready to fight to keep it like it is. Today was just an example of what we are ready to do."

"Daddy, they were beating women down there so badly that they had to be sent to the hospital. How can we justify that in any society? That is like the kind of stuff you were telling us you saw overseas during the war. What were you fighting for then?"

"When women start acting like men, they get treated like men. If they are gonna get out and march with the men, then they better damn well be ready to take a beating like a man."

"So if they get out and act like white people, we should treat them like white people?" I wasn't sure how he would take my point.

"You treat them like people, colored or white. We just don't do it together. We are not going to let that happen down here. If they want to bastardize the white race in the rest of America, we can't do anything about that, but we are not going to let it happen here."

"What if that had been Frank Morris that got beat down there?"

"Frank would never be there. Frank Morris was colored; he knew he was colored and he knew his place. He didn't believe in this nonsense. He was a good man."

"So he was a good man as long as he knew his place? Well someone didn't think so. That's why they sent a goon squad to take care of him before he could stir up any trouble."

My sarcasm went unacknowledged. I was sure he was going to unload on me for giving a flippant answer, especially for including Frank in the remark.

He didn't unload, but he gave the most unbelievable answer that I had ever heard. "They are saying now that Frank was burned out by his own people. Someone said that some outside agitators came in and burned him out just to stir up with the colored people in the area."

"Daddy, you know that isn't true. You know that Frank would have told them if he had been attacked by colored people. He knew everybody in town. The only reason he didn't tell who attacked him was because he didn't recognize them or he was afraid of what would happen if he talked. When he talked to those people, he didn't know he was going to die. You know and I know who attacked Frank, and it wasn't any outside agitators."

"Boy, you don't know what you are talking about now. And that kind of talk can get you beat or killed. Those boys don't mess around."

"You can't tell anyone who killed Frank for the same reason Frank couldn't tell because at least one of those goons wears a star on his chest. And no one is going to do anything because there are only the two of us in this car, and I sure as hell ain't gonna tell anyone. You know more about it than I do."

"Just keep your mouth shut about Frank around here. You only know a part of it. You don't want to know the rest of it. There is no way for you to protect yourself against some of these men. They run this whole area — power and money."

"Don't worry. I plan to live a long life. I want to drive trucks all over this country."

By the time we hit the Natchez-Vidalia Bridge, he had fallen asleep, so I drove the next twelve miles in silence, mulling over the things that we had talked about. I knew the dangers of living in this area; I heard the stories of the violence every day. Some of the people responsible for the violence didn't try to hide it at all; in fact, they flaunted it. Who would ever have the audacity to challenge them?

The men at the Natchez Hunt Club were wrong about scaring the marchers so badly that they wouldn't try it again. The following Tuesday, Doctor Martin Luther King and about three thousand demonstrators duplicated Sunday's march to the end of the bridge where they held a prayer service to honor those that had fallen there. Though the march was conducted without incident, three white ministers that had come to participate in the march were beaten at a restaurant in Selma later in the evening. One of them, Reverend James Reeb from Boston, was refused treatment at the hospital in Selma because he was considered an outside agitator. Though he was near death, he was taken to a hospital in Birmingham almost two hours away. Two days later Reverend Reeb died from the injuries received during his beating.

The march from Selma to Montgomery was scheduled to begin again on March 21st, when the governor's ban was overturned by a judge after Reverend Reeb's death. The Klansmen met several times during the week before the march to plan strategies and distribute their assets. During the meeting in Natchez, they decided that three of the men would go and shadow the entire march, sabotaging as much as they could. They would meet some of the Alabama Klansmen to find places to stay and learn how best to infiltrate any security perimeters around the marchers during their overnight stops.

The march started at a chapel in Selma. Almost nine thousand participants chanted and sang as they marched down the road and across the bridge which led them out of town and toward Montgomery. The marchers were protected by several thousand members of the US Army and National Guard. The FBI was there in force to take pictures and monitor the goings on of the event. During part of the march, the number of demonstrators had to be reduced to three hundred because they were marching along a very busy two-lane road. On Wednesday night, the march took on a party atmosphere when several entertainers performed for them at a rally. When the march reached Montgomery on Thursday, their numbers had swollen to more than twenty-five thousand people. When they arrived at the capitol building, Doctor Martin Luther King addressed them with a speech in which he predicted that it would not be long until we all lived in a world of peace, although peace would not come on that night.

During the following weeks, the Klansmen met several times to discuss the marches and examine the evidence that they collected from the campsites along the road from the march. At one of the meetings, several of the men had photos of men and women that had to have been taken in the camps when they were still in use. The monochrome pictures were grainy and some of them were poorly focused, as if shot in poor light or taken with cameras that had poor lens quality.

I couldn't believe my eyes as I looked at some of the pictures. One of the pictures revealed a couple fornicating, while another, even more scandalous, had a colored man in a very close embrace with a white woman. I was impressed that the Klansmen could get into the camp close enough to get the pictures. I asked, "Which one of you took these pictures? They are pretty impressive."

"None of us took these pictures. We couldn't get near this place until after the people were gone."

"How did you get them then? Did you have a spy in the camp?"

"No. We got them from the police."

"Selma or Montgomery police or from one of the county sheriffs?"

"Boy, you ask way too many questions about stuff you don't need to know."

Then one of the other Klansmen whom I had known most of my life chided, "Well if you really have to know, we got them from the Natchez Police Department."

"How could they get over there to get pictures? They don't have any jurisdiction in Alabama. So how did they get them?"

"They got them from the FBI who had to stay out there to protect them niggers and their whores. Just look at that white whore makin' out with that black bastard. No shame. No dignity. No discretion."

"How could they get this kind of stuff from the FBI? Did they steal it some way? The FBI ain't gonna give this kind of stuff to you guys."

"Boy, you got a lot to learn kid. The FBI can do anything they want to. How do you think we find out when those outside agitators are coming in here? They have those people under surveillance so they know where they are almost all the time. We even got word that one of those boys from the

FBI even gave the local law the license number of the car that wuz carryin' those three boys over in Philadelphia. That's how those boys knew who to go after, because the FBI told them that those boys were comin' and where they would be."

"Yeah. Just like they have all of you under surveillance so they can keep an eye on what you are up to. I wouldn't doubt that they gave this stuff to you guys just to see what you would do with it. Next thing you know, you'll have these things posted in your on the bathroom walls so you'll have something to look at while you …"

"Boy. I'll knock the shit out of you. Mind your manners and your business. You ain't earned the right to make those kinds of remarks about any of us."

"I still can't believe you got this stuff from the FBI. Why would they give this stuff to anybody?"

I was shocked by the contents of the pictures and by the idea that the FBI would have anything to do with taking them, much less distributing this kind of smut to the local police or making it available to the Klans by any means. At the end of the month I found out how they were going to use the pictures. They compiled the photos into a periodical called *The Fiery Cross*, a document intended to reveal the poor behavior and sinfulness of the people involved with the march. They captioned each of the pictures.

For the picture with the white woman and colored man in an embrace they wrote, "White whore with nigger buck." For the colored couple caught in flagrante, "Niggers fornicating in a public area." They had one that showed the contents of a refuse heap left behind in one of the camps. In the heap were several beer bottles, a couple of whiskey bottles, and a couple of used condoms. The caption read, "This is the garbage they leave behind for our children to find." The document was nothing more than two pages of revealing and disturbing pictures, each with an equally inflammatory caption.

Even worse than the pictures was the story slandering the white woman who had been killed by Klansmen as she was transporting demonstrators back to Selma. It stated that she was the mother of five who abandoned her children in Chicago so she could come down to Selma to have sex with the young nigger boys that would be there for the march. Though I had seen women abandon their children for less reason, I could not make myself believe that this woman would have done such a thing. I made the mistake of asking Daddy about the story and the pictures again.

"We got the story and the pictures from the FBI. They have a special division just for keeping track of the agitators from the North. They have records of some of those agitators that have attended special training in Cuba, just so they could come back here and stir up trouble. They are all anarchists. That woman in the story is a whore who got just what she deserved. She had no right to abandon her children to come down here just to consort with these colored boys."

"Do you really believe that is what she did? She came down here just to have sex with colored men? I'll bet they don't have anything on her at all. It is something they just made up to justify the senseless killing of a woman. Do you really believe the FBI gave them the story about the woman?"

"I know exactly where the story came from and it was the FBI—the same place where we got the pictures from."

I don't know which possibility bothered me more. Was my father really so gullible that he would buy into such a story or was the very agency that I held in such high esteem really culpable in the distribution of such slanderous pictures and stories? Both possibilities made me sick to the pit of my stomach.

In addition to the work they were doing on the new edition of *The Fiery Cross*, they also used some of the pictures for another document for mass distribution. This document would tell the "true story" of the debauchery and immorality of the marchers in the camps. It also had another inflammatory and scandalous list of names of Natchez white people that were too closely associated with colored people—people who threatened our society through their alleged indiscretions, or people we should no longer trust because their allegiances were suspect. I sat and bit my tongue as I read the list of names. I tried to imagine how it would feel to read the list and find the name of one of my relatives or one of my high school teachers on the list. Fortunately, it was unimaginable. The document was so far afield, it was difficult to even accept it as real.

Just as I finished reading through the documents, one of the Adams County Klansmen came by and threw what looked like a small folded newspaper onto the table. Daddy picked the paper up and started reading through the article on the first page. All I could read was the banner on the front page: *Miss-Lou Observer*. I finally caught a glimpse of the title of the article Daddy was reading; *To the Grand Dragon*. I could hardly wait to get my hands on the paper. Here was a man who had the nerve to stand up to the state leader of the Klans in the great state of Mississippi – the Grand Dragon.

After Daddy finished the article, he perused the rest of the paper then threw it down on the table in disgust. "I knew he was gonna try to stir up some trouble. This man is a traitor to every white person in all of Mississippi. We need to shut him down. Nobody is going to read this shit and take it serious, but we can show him that this stuff ain't gonna be tolerated. Make sure we put a line on him in the document and start spreading the word to boycott his law office. We can starve him out of town.

I picked the paper up and started reading the letter to the Grand Dragon. He really railed at the Grand Dragon and the Klans for publishing the previous documents bearing the lists of the names of white people in the area accused of consorting with colored people. He didn't mince words when he addressed the Klans as cowards hiding behind their robes and hoods, nor did he make any apologies for the way he attacked and convicted them of the beatings and bombings that had become their signatures of terror and dominance in the area. In fact, he finished the article with a disclaimer of apology; no remorse whatsoever.

I had a new hero. I only wished I had the pure gall and nerve of this man. He struck out at the Klans with impunity. After asking a couple of questions, I found out that the paper was printed by a Natchez lawyer by the name of Forest Johnson. This was a man I hoped I would someday meet.

On the way home I challenged Daddy about the documents and about the rumored FBI participation as a resource, "If Frank Morris knew about these operations by the FBI and their free exchange with the local law enforcement, it is no wonder he could not reveal the identity of his attackers. Who do I trust if I ever find myself in trouble with any of these people? Who do you trust? Do you really trust any of these people any more? I don't."

He lit another cigarette as he thought about it for a minute. "No, not really. Not for a long time now."

I felt Daddy's admission was an opening for my recent thoughts. "Daddy, I don't want to live the rest of my life like this. I am going to be graduating this year. I am supposed to be making decisions about what I am going to do with the rest of my life and I don't even understand what is going on in my life right now. I am supposed to love my neighbor, but I don't even know who my neighbor is any more."

"You'll go to college next year and you'll figure it out when you get there. Your cousin Jeff is in college now and he is doing well. You'll do the same."

"Daddy, I don't know if I'm ready for college. I don't know what I want to do."

"You just go to college and you'll figure it out just like Jeff."

I really had no idea what I was going to do with my future. I wasn't doing that well in school and I didn't know what direction to take. All I knew was that I could drive anything with wheels. I could take any truck that came to the warehouse and put the trailer doors square against the loading dock first time, every time. I could work the butts off of two other men. Working at the warehouse, I had developed skills and strength that were unique for a boy my size. I hardly ever used a hand truck to move barrels around the warehouse. Though I only weighed about 130 pounds, I could tilt the 475 pound oil drums over on the rims and spin them as if they were empty. Routinely I loaded 55 gallon drums of oil into the three-quarter ton pickup from the loading dock, a drop of about two feet. I could also load the drums into the back of the truck from the ground, a lift of about thirty inches. When new drivers made deliveries, John Pugh, the warehouse manager, showed me off like a proud farmer showing off his prize bull. "Here. Buddy will put the truck on the dock for you. Watch the way this skinny kid gets those barrels in and out of the warehouse." I never disappointed him.

C H A P T E R 7

Higher Education

During the year after my prom night auto accident, I hadn't gone on a date nor had I attended any school functions other than an occasional football game. I was very self-conscious about my broken teeth, scrawny frame, and an occasional bout with acne. Katherine and Candice continued to try to coach me on social skills and to encourage me to date. "There are sophomore and freshman girls out there just dying to go out with a senior boy like you." I tried to ask several girls for dates, but my shyness was overwhelming.

I still did not have a date when prom night arrived. I went stag and sat at a table with several other guys who had come without dates. The music was great because it was the latest rock and top forty tunes played by a live band. Though I enjoyed the music, I didn't get up and dance a single dance. It was embarrassing.

One month after the prom—graduation! I didn't graduate with honors, but I did graduate with many more credits than I needed because I had been attending Radio and Television Electronics Training at the Concordia Parish Trade School. I don't know how I did it sometimes: high school, trade school, working at PedCo, and in Daddy's cabinet shop. I did them all and graduated.

After I graduated from high school in 1965, I continued to attend the trade school as I worked through the summer. Almost all of my work at PedCo was delivery of petroleum products to the many wildcat drilling rigs around Louisiana and Mississippi. Each week my delivery runs took me further and further into the unimproved country roads in Mississippi. Some of the roads were nothing more than dirt paths made by scraping through the forest with the blade of a Caterpillar D9 bulldozer. When they made the roads, they would push the smaller trees over and push dirt into the hole left by the root ball. If the tree was too large, they would simply go around it in an arc large enough to accommodate the long semi-trailers that held the drilling platforms and machinery. These were roads that would test the skills of the most experienced of drivers, especially during rainy weather.

Because I was spending more time driving on isolated roads and there were increasing incidents of violence in those areas, I decided I needed to have some form of protection with me. I started searching for a small caliber pistol that would tuck easily into the armrests of the trucks or in my car. Before June I was the proud owner of a nickel plated Smith & Wesson .44 Magnum revolver. This thing was huge!

Although I had owned my .22 rifle most of my life, I had never owned or fired a gun this formidable. After I bought two boxes of ammunition and made up a couple of cardboard targets, I took the pistol down to the levee along the Old River for target practice. I set the targets up along the steep side of the levee then counted off thirty paces and gouged a line through the soft ground to mark my firing line. Though I had held and dry-fired the gun several times, it felt oversized in my hands; the grip felt as if it had been fitted for a giant with hands twice my size—and my hands were already large. To aim, I held my left hand out in front of me to cradle the bottom of the grip which I held tight in my right hand. I pulled the gun up, pulled the hammer back, set the sights on the first target, and squeezed the trigger …

BLAM! The gun jumped completely out of my hand!

I picked the gun up and went to inspect the target. I was expecting a huge hole because of the blast, but only found a hole about half the size of the diameter of the bullet right through the bull's-eye. However, the bank behind the target had a huge hole blasted out where the bullet struck. That was impressive; however, it was my last bull's-eye of the day. Since the pistol had jumped out of my hand on the first shot, I tried to hold it tighter to control it on the subsequent shots. I was hitting the targets and

I was not losing the gun, but I also wasn't getting bull's-eyes. I had won several awards for my shooting prowess, so I was a little disappointed with my effectiveness.

That night, Daddy started asking me questions about the gun, so I told him about my experience on the levee. He said, "I taught small arms fire in the navy. I will show you how to shoot that thing."

On Saturday, Daddy and I took the targets and a couple of boxes of ammo down to the levee again. I set the targets up in the same place so I had the same firing line marked in the dirt. Daddy took the gun in his right hand and stepped up to the firing line. He crossed his forearms so that his left hand cupped his right elbow and his right hand crossed his left elbow. As he stood with his left side to the target, he sighted the target and slowly squeezed the trigger. He fired several shots from that position, hitting the bull's eye each time.

I thought, *Marvelous. Maybe I'll be able to hit what I'm supposed to be hitting with this thing.*

I took the gun and duplicated what Daddy had just illustrated so well. I crossed my forearms, cupped my left hand over my right elbow, cradled my right hand and gun in the crook of my left elbow, and took careful aim at the target. Just as I started to squeeze the trigger, Daddy said, "Relax. You need to be relaxed when you pull the trigger or else you won't be able to hit shit."

I relaxed and pulled the hammer back as I took a deep breath. I squeezed the trigger slowly.

Blam. The gun jumped back and the hammer struck me at the top of my nose, just inside my left eye socket. I stood stunned for a moment before I realized that Daddy was talking to me. He gave me his patented Ed Blanche smile as he said, "I think you relaxed too much."

I was still seeing stars when I realized that I had blood running down the left side of my nose and down my face. I felt pretty lucky that the hammer hit me where it did; had it hit me about one inch to the left it would have knocked my eye out. Though my eye stung like crazy, we continued our target practice, but I hooked the ring finger of my shooting hand into my left sleeve to keep the gun from hitting me again. When we got home, I cleaned my new injury and examined it closely. I knew it would leave a permanent scar. I thought to myself, "Nice! One more scar for my face."

In August, I turned 18 and had to register with the Selective Service within 30 days to avoid prosecution. Now I was eligible for the draft. Since the war in Vietnam was escalating, I was sure to be conscripted to fight those communists that were trying to overrun our South Vietnamese allies. Having been raised in the ignorance and influences of the Joseph McCarthy era, I would kill or die to keep anyone from becoming a communist. I was ready to go, but life had yet more lessons for me.

On August 13, we were watching the evening news when they showed some rather graphic footage of the riots that were going in Watts, the negro section of Los Angeles, California. They reported that the looters were running pell mell through the city, breaking out storefront windows, taking everything that wasn't tied down. After taking the merchandise, they were setting the buildings afire. Once the fires were lit, the firefighters couldn't do their jobs because snipers were shooting at them from rooftops. Even where there were no snipers, the rioters were bombing the firefighters and police with bricks, roofing material, and pieces torn off of the buildings. Grocery supplies within the riot district were already reaching critical levels; essential supplies were not available unless the residents could get out of the district to shop.

The Klans had a heyday with the information they were getting from the news and other sources. Daddy and I went to the King Hotel in Ferriday that night where he met with several of the Concordia Parish Deputies and some of the local Klansmen. Doug Nugent, the owner of the hotel, came in and sat with them while they discussed the possibilities. They were trying to figure out how to get copies of as many of the photos coming out of the Watts area as they could. Since some were connected to law enforcement and news media, they were going to start calling in all favors to get these pictures that depicted the rioters in the worst possible light.

"You know what I think. I think they should just put a big fence around that whole area and let them niggers kill each other off. At the rate they're goin' now, they'll be stealin' food from each other just to get by before that thing is ended."

"Shit. I think they should just roll the army in there and shoot anyone caught looting right on the spot."

"Yeah. And they should shoot any of the snipers that they find right on the spot. Better yet, since the firefighters can't get in to save them, just burn the buildin' right out from under anyone caught snipin'."

"What started all that shit anyway? Do they just feel like they can take over the city any time they want?"

"I don't know. Does it matter? They have a nice city there and they decide they want to tear it to the ground and steal whatever they can. It's alright by me. Let 'em tear the place down around their ears. Let 'em steal and loot everything they can. Let 'em eat cake. Let 'em starve theirselfs to kingdom come. I don't care if the whole bunch of them niggers kills theirselfs off. It just means less problems for this country in the future."

"I wish they wuz some way we could get some of that film that they showed on the news tonight. They wuz people runnin' all over takin' stuff, stores wuz burned to the ground, and there wuz smoke jest fillin' the air."

"Well this ain't never gonna happen here. We ain't gonna put up with it like them Californians. Why do they put up with it anyway? You'd think they don't know how to deal with their niggers out there."

They all had a big laugh over the last remark. That is finally when I piped in, "Do you realize that there are as many colored people in Watts as there are people in all of Mississippi? If the entire population of Mississippi were to come over here and start rioting in the middle of this town, you guys would be camping out in Clayton or Jonesville just like me. If that many people start rioting anywhere, I'm gonna be in the next state. That's crazy."

"Watch your mouth, boy. You don't know what we would do. Besides, who taught you to call these niggers colored people?"

"Daddy."

"Your daddy taught you that? Ed, what are you teachin' your boys anyway?"

Mister Bill chimed in, "Ed's got five of the finest boys in this parish. Ain't none of them ever been in any kind of trouble. And that boy sittin' right there can work the boots off of any of you boys any day of the week."

"No sir. Not on Sunday. I don't work on Sunday."

They all chuckled. "Yeah. You don't work on Sunday, but I've heard that you know how to blow up a cotton field on Saturday."

I got pretty nervous with that statement. How did they even know about it? Then I remembered that I had told the story to Daddy, so I shot him a glance to let him know what I was thinking. He shot back, "I didn't tell them, so it must have been someone you told."

"But I haven't told anyone. I haven't even told my brothers."

Deputy Frank Delaughter spoke up, "Boy. Do you really think any explosion that big would go un-noticed? I was out there looking around the minute after you left that day. I found that split barrel at the back of the warehouse. I ain't never seen a barrel blowed up that bad. What did you use for the explosion, anyway?"

"A two-pound bag of general purpose flour, two cherry bombs, and about a pint of naphtha that was left in the bottom of the barrel."

"Boy. Don't lie to me. You ain't gonna blow up a barrel that bad with just flour and a couple of cherry bombs."

"Oh, I forgot about the eighteen inches of det-cord."

"I don't believe your scrawny lyin' little ass."

"I didn't believe it either; that's why I tried it. I saw on the news where that grain silo blew up down in south Louisiana, so I tried to prove that grain dust couldn't blow up like that. I was wrong. Way wrong." Then I added, "Did anyone ever find the lid to that barrel? I looked all over that field and didn't see it at all."

"No, but if it blew that lid as far as it did the top of that silo, it is probably in Russia. Boy, you could have started an international incident."

For some reason, I felt proud of my accomplishment. I had some kind of acclaim now, a certain notoriety with the local police. It made me smile.

On Friday, I delivered several loads of diesel and other petroleum products to pumping stations around the Lake Saint John oil field and to wildcat rigs drilling in Mississippi. When I delivered a tank of diesel to one of the drilling rigs, the riot in Watts was the topic of the day, like it was everywhere else that day. "They need to call out the army and send 'em in to start shooting those nigger thiefs. I don't care what you call it; niggers is niggers and stealin' is stealin'.'"

"You ever wonder why we don't have no niggers workin' out here on the drilling platforms? 'Cause them lazy bastards would get killed on their first day out here 'cause they don't know how to work, and they don't know how to pay attention. Shit, can you imagine havin' one of them darkies up on the monkey boards?"

"Yeah. I can. Hangin' from the safety rail with about ten feet of rope; and I don't mean safety line."

Everyone on the drilling platform laughed. "It will be a cold day in hell before niggers work in the oil field. Hell, the work is too hard for them. I don't even know any niggers that want to do this kind of work."

"Hey, boy. Are you old enough to be driving that truck? What are you; about 13? You want to work with a bunch of niggers?"

He was right about one thing; I didn't look my eighteen years. "I've been driving that truck for almost two years now and I'm 18. I have been working with colored people ever since I started working more than four years ago and I ain't never had any problems with any of them."

One of the roustabouts who worked "second tongs" was busy slinging the chains while adding a new length of pipe. "Don't tell me you're one of them nigger lovers. We don't like niggers, and we don't like nigger lovers." As he was talking, he started toward me in a menacing stance.

The tool pusher stepped up on the platform just in time. "Bart, get your hardhat on," he yelled at the roustabout.

"OK, Mister West. I'll get it just as soon as we get this pipe tightened and I kick that squirt's ass."

"Get that hard hat on now or get off my rig."

The roustabout reached over and hooked the chain on the end of the tongs and positioned them on the pipe while the driller took the slack out of the chain. The driller tightened the tongs by releasing the clutch for a moment, then he bumped the clutch a couple of times to make the tongs yank on the pipe enough to tighten it securely. On the second bump, one of the chain's links split and the chain released from the tongs with a bang, snapping the bitter end around like the tail of a whip. The split link whipped through the air and caught the young roustabout in the head just above his right ear—he went down with a thud.

Since everyone else on the deck was ducking to avoid the chain, none of them saw the roustabout go down. As soon as the chain settled, I jumped over the driller's outstretched legs to get to the roustabout. I grabbed the red oil rag out of my back pocket and pressed it against the side of his head. The driller reached over and grabbed me by the back of my shirt, lifting me back over the downed man. "What are you doing boy?"

"The chain hit him. I think it split his skull."

Mister West grabbed my oil rag from my hands and went over to the roustabout and pressed it hard against his head. "Dan, go get the company truck and bring it to the bottom of the ladder."

The men picked up the roustabout's limp body and took it over to the edge of the deck, near the ladder. Mister West took a towel and wrapped it around the man's head to hold the rag in place. After a couple of minutes, the man's eyes fluttered open and looked around in confused bewilderment. "What happened?"

"The chain snapped and got you pretty good. You're gonna need stitches. You're split open pretty good."

"Damn!" When he looked up and saw me, he reached out toward me and slurred, "This is your fault you little nigger lover. I won't forget this."

Mister West reprimanded him, "You did this to yourself. I had just told you to put your hardhat on. If you had your hardhat on, all you'd have got was a dent in it. That boy was the first person to help you when you were down."

"But he's a nigger lover."

"He ain't no such thing. Do you even know who that boy is? His daddy is one of the biggest kluckers in the state of Louisiana. I've known that boy and his family for ten years and they are some of the best people I know. Now lay still till we get you in the truck so we can get you to the doctor."

As they took the man down the ladder to the truck, Mister West turned to me and said, "He's harmless and is full of hot air. He's been with me for about a year now and the only thing wrong with him is that he is one of the most hardheaded individuals I know." Then he added, "I guess it is a good thing he is hard headed this time. That thing opened his head up pretty good."

"Yeah, I know. I've been working around the men enough to know how they like to pick at me."

As he went down the ladder, he turned and said, "I gotta go now. You say hello to your family."

While I put the hose back onto the truck and put my invoices away, the driller walked up to me, "Sorry I roughed you up in there. I actually thought you were startin' to beat up on him for callin' you a nigger lover. Not that he didn't deserve it. When you come out to these rigs, be careful about what you say to these boys. After they've been on site for a few days, they start gettin' a little antsy. Everything gets to be a bone of contention."

"Yes sir. I know that. It didn't bother me none. I've been called worse things by my own daddy."

As I drove back to the warehouse, I found it especially relaxing. Again, I found a certain satisfaction in having been referred to as a "nigger lover" but I couldn't understand the man's animosity toward me for having said anything positive about having worked with colored people. I just reminded myself that I had to be more careful because of the sensitivity over the racial issues, even when they weren't that close to home. After that, I got distracted by the low, pleasant whine that the tires made on the Mississippi concrete highway.

I got back to the warehouse, finished my paperwork, and turned in my log book so I could get home quickly. When I got home, I told my younger brothers that I wanted to go to the Natchez Skating Rink and asked if they were interested in going. After we got dressed, Billy and I jumped into his new 1960 Chevrolet and headed toward Natchez. The skating rink was one of those places we could go without getting an interrogation from Daddy. Going to the skating rink was like going to an oversized family reunion. Daddy knew and trusted the owner of the skating rink and knew most of the parents who had been bringing their children to the skating rink for years.

At the rink, we discovered they were throwing a party for two of the regulars, Dan Moore and Steve Hebert, who had just joined the Army and were going to boot camp the following week. When either of them skated, they were the focus of all attention. They moved with ease through the other skaters, skating backward, doing spins and loops, and occasional jumps that were worthy of Olympic medals. Many times when they skated, the rink would empty so that everyone could watch them skate their routines. When the lights dropped and they announced that the next dance would be for partners only, girls lined up six deep to skate with either of the boys.

After we skated most of the night, we said goodbye to Pat and Steve and wished them good luck on their new careers. When Billy and I left, we decided we would get something to eat and take several other kids home when we left. With one other boy and four girls, we piled into his car and drove away. I was riding shotgun as we drove past the tire plant and turned down Concord Avenue as we always did. We liked leaving that way because the railway crossing on Concord was raised and we could catch a little air in the car if we hit the tracks at the right speed. Billy had never driven over the tracks before, so he was going twice the speed we needed to catch air. I yelled at him, "Billy, slow down. We are going way too fast for the tracks, especially from this side."

"We're okay. We've been doing this for years."

"Not at this speed, you're doing almost fifty."

I didn't have time to give another warning. We hit the tracks and the car lurched into the air with a crunch of metal as both ends of the car scraped the pavement. As we sailed through the air, we went partially over a car that was parked along the roadside with someone standing at the passenger window chatting with the passengers. As we flew down the hill, the car filled with a course of screams as the nose dipped and headed toward the pavement. The car landed very hard; first the nose, then the tail with a terrible crunching of metal at both ends. I started yelling, "Hit the brakes! Hit the brakes!"

We slid to a stop just short of Saint Catherine Street at the bottom of the hill. "What the heck were you thinking? We could have all been hurt! Is everyone okay?"

Comments from our passengers were overlapped. "My butt hurts."

"I think I sprained every joint in my body. That hurt like hell."

"I thought we were gonna go right over on the top."

"Billy, we better get out and check the car over. That was a really hard landing." I said.

When I got out to inspect the car, I noticed the scrape marks on the bottom of the front bumper and the deep dents in the air dam under the bumper. I ran my hands around the tires to check for cuts or bumps then tried to check the shocks and springs, but there was not enough light to see damage. We drove very carefully as we delivered our other passengers, then limped the car home. On Saturday morning we inspected his car again and found that all of the shocks were damaged, one of the springs was bent, and two of his headlights were cracked, in addition to all the bent metal on the underside of the car.

During the week that followed, our attention was diverted to more important things. The riot in Watts became the hot topic everywhere I went. The images and news coming out of the riot area only increased the resentment and hostility toward the rioters. After having seen more of the television images and news pictures, I was quickly losing my empathy for the colored people caught up in the riot. It seemed totally senseless. Why would people in a bad situation do such things to make it even worse? After I saw one newsreel of the rubble of a destroyed building and heard the news commentator explaining that most of the shelves from the stores were empty because the looters had taken everything, I felt my own hostilities swell. For a while, I felt no empathy or sympathy; it had been replaced by hostility over the brutality and senselessness of the riot.

The men that Daddy met at the King Hotel literally cheered when they saw that the police had opened fire on the rioters and saw news where the National Guard had been called to quell the violence. They were elated that the police were firing on the rioters and that one of them had been killed.

"If they'd have done that on the first day, they wouldn't have had a second day. If they'd have dropped a couple of those niggers in the street for everyone to see, the rest of them would still be in hiding."

"I heard they burned down the entire business section of the town and they done more than one hundred million dollars worth of damage."

"I wouldn't care if they burned the whole town to the ground with everyone in it; every man, woman, and child."

"Well they durn near did, except they didn't throw enough niggers on the fire."

"They have more than ten thousand Army National Guard in there with those niggers to keep 'em from killin' each other. They shoulda sent them in there to help them kill each other."

"They done set up a curfew so that none of them darkies can go out after dark. What good is that gonna do, since they done shot out all of the streetlights how they gonna see the niggers in the dark unless they can make 'em smile some way."

After the curfew comment, they laughed for a while before the conversation turned into a series of bad jokes and ugly chuckles. I sat and drank my coffee in silence as I tried to avoid the intrusion of the racial epithets. I could hardly wait to get home; I was bored with the conversation. Since Frank's death, Daddy was spending more time at the hotel than at any of his other meeting locations, even when I knew he was not meeting with his group of Klansmen. I also understood that there were more women practicing the world's oldest profession at the hotel.

The men from the Concordia Klans never seemed to have the news that found its way out of the Klan groups in Adams county. On Monday, I went with Daddy to a meeting at the Natchez Hunt Club and was as bored with the conversation there as I had been a few nights earlier until one of the men mentioned a name that I knew from Franklin County. "Did you hear that they found the body of Sam Trent over in Eddiceton? They found out that he was informin' to the FBI. Those boys over in Bunkley and Meadville took care of him fast. He ..."

Daddy cut him off before he could utter another word, "Sam Trent is not and never was an informant. Who told you that shit, anyway?"

"That's what some of those boys over in Franklin County told us. They said that Sam was going to a meeting over there to try to convince them that he wasn't talkin' to the law about anything."

"You know the real reason that he was killed? He had the gall to piss off old man Banner. I don't know what started it all, but I know that old man Tom Banner has been talking all over the county that Sam had opened his mouth one too many times. But I can tell you right now, it had nothing to do with talking to the FBI."

"That old man's word is law over in Franklin. What he says goes. He done had so many people beat for not givin' in to him some way that it ain't even funny."

"Well a big part of the problem is those two sons of his. They believe everything he tells them; and when he says jump, they jump. They don't even stop to ask how high."

Daddy emphasized his point. "Sam Trent couldn't have been informin' to the FBI. First of all, he was too afraid to even talk to the FBI. If he spotted an FBI agent in Franklin County, he'd be in Adams County before you could count to twenty. He was afraid of his own shadow and that is why he was tryin' to set up a meetin' with the klavern over there. Second, everybody in that county knew Sam. You wouldn't be able to find a person in that county or this one that has ever seen him say one word to ANY law enforcement. He was always afraid that they were gonna come after him for something, even if he hadn't done anything. Third, I've know Sam Trent since 1954, and he was as loyal to the Klans as any man I've ever known. I think that was the whole problem with him and old man Banner. Sam was the one that helped organize those boys out in Bunkley to form their own group and get out of the Meadville klaverns."

"You're probably right, Ed. But there ain't no way they're ever gonna prove that. That bunch over there is tighter than ever. I ain't so sure about some of the men we got workin' with us around here. I'm sure we got someone over here talkin' to the law."

"I know that they do a lot of tradin' of information over here and in Franklin County. Here in Adams, we're tight with the local law, and they are tight with the FBI. How do you think we got all those pictures from down in Selma and get warnings about when some of those agitators are gonna be in the area? Sometimes you gotta give a little to get a little."

"Well things are getting' too scary around here anymore. When klukkers start killin' klukkers for nothin' then it just ain't right. How can we last if we can't even trust each other no more?"

"It ain't all of them. There's always a few bad apples in every barrel. We have two families that are causin' most of the problems around here. It is the same way with the niggers. Almost all of the problems are caused by just a few families. If we can control the few, we can control all of them."

"Well, Ed. That is what we are workin' on right now. We know that we got a couple of NAACP activist here in Natchez now, and they have been warned. I think it is high time we made the warnin's a little stronger and a lot louder."

I knew they were planning for something to happen soon because R. J. Glover came by the house several times to meet with Daddy. Each time he came by, he brought in more assets. I was growing increasingly concerned about the safety of my family since I knew some of the assets that he delivered were small explosives, detonation cord, and blasting caps, all of which could be very dangerous in small hands. My youngest brothers were only six and eight. They had seen the explosives being used and tested before, so they had no real fear of the contents of the small boxes, coils, cans, and jugs.

IN THE CROSSFIRE OF THE KLANS

Daddy made it clear in one of the meetings with Dean that he wanted nothing to do with what the Natchez group was planning. Dean assured Daddy that there was no way he would be connected with anything they did. What they had to do was something that one man could handle with a little help. When he left, Dean reminded him to stay out of sight for the next few days. We didn't have to wait long to find out what the Natchez group had been working on.

George Metcalfe worked for more than twenty years at Armstrong Tire and Rubber in Natchez where he knew almost all of the other tire builders and was considered a friend by many. One of those tire builders was Wharlest Jackson with whom Metcalfe had worked for ten years. The two men had become friends almost immediately. In March, the two became charter members of the NAACP chapter in Natchez when Charles Evers had come to help get them organized. During that first meeting, George Metcalfe became president of the Natchez chapter of the NAACP.

On Friday, August 27, 1965, George Metcalfe was leaving work early because he had worked double shifts twice during the week. He walked through the Armstrong parking lot and climbed into his immaculate two-tone 1955 Chevrolet Two-Ten. When he turned the ignition key to start the engine, the explosion from under the firewall almost blew his feet off. The blast knocked him out for a moment. Though he was semi-conscious, he was afraid of fire, and got himself out of his car and into the parking lot. He could hardly move because his right ankle was shattered and his arm broken by the blast. Both of his feet were damaged and shrapnel from the firewall had cut him from head to toe. His neck and face had been burned; his right eye was bleeding profusely. The bomb blast was so violent that several of the cars parked nearby were badly damaged.

He was taken to the hospital where they tended his wounds and tried to comfort him. After tending him, they moved him to a private room where several FBI agents and two Natchez Police officers questioned him. They already knew why he had been attacked. Now they had to deduce who had attacked him. They questioned the gate guards and everyone else who had been in or around the parking lot. They also came to our house and spent more than an hour talking with Daddy about what he might know. He gave the appearance of being cooperative, but provided no useful information. I was sure that the FBI thought he knew more than he was revealing.

Immediately after Metcalfe was bombed at Armstrong, the FBI doubled the number of agents in Natchez. In addition, the Mississippi Highway and Safety Patrol dispatched another ten officers into the area to aid in the investigation and to quell the violence that was expected in reprisal. Fortunately, they managed to keep things from boiling over one more time.

Because of the increased presence of the FBI and MHSP around Natchez after the Metcalfe bombing, Klan activities decreased. Most of the civil rights groups in the area took advantage of the conditions by conducting demonstrations at several of the larger businesses in the area. The day after the bombing, the Natchez NAACP group presented the city council with a list of 12 demands, including the need for colored police on the Natchez Police Department and making jobs for colored people in the stores where they did so much of their shopping. If their demands were not met, they were going to march in protest on September 2.

The mayor was concerned about the possibility of a riot if any of the civil rights groups conducted a demonstration downtown. Emotions were running very high within the colored community, the law enforcement groups, and the Klan groups all around the city. To keep order, the Mississippi governor sent 650 National Guard troops into Natchez at the request of the Natchez Chief of Police. Charles Evers, the leader of the Mississippi NAACP, halted the march because he was sure that there would be violence and bloodshed in a clash with the guardsmen. He also called for a boycott of the entire downtown area of Natchez. To maintain control throughout the city, Natchez imposed a ten o'clock curfew. After a few days, the Guard was withdrawn from the city.

On September 9, about 250 people marched peacefully to city hall under the scrutiny of the Natchez Police and the MHSP as Hurricane Betsy charged into the mouth of the Mississippi River toward Natchez. The weather and the presence of such a great number of law enforcement officers intimidated many of those that had intended to march, so the number of demonstrators was not really considered newsworthy. It garnered very little attention from the local news and none at all from the national media. Committed to their cause, the NAACP and their supporters immediately planned another march for September 17. Before they could get the march fully organized, the Natchez City Council and mayor got a court order to prevent any more marches within the city limits. When the demonstrators prepared to march as scheduled, the police were there to meet them. When told that they would be arrested if they marched, the demonstrators simply replied, "Get the cells ready, 'cause we are gonna march."

When the demonstrators walked through the streets, the police arrested them by the dozens. With each arrest, the demonstrators went peacefully. By the time the demonstrators reached city hall, half of them had been arrested and taken to jail. They stopped the arrests because the jails were overflowing their designed capacity; more than one hundred people were in the small cells.

To protest the arrests, the NAACP staged another march on the 27th. They were incensed by the arrest and treatment of the demonstrators from the earlier marches. With the renewed spirit of the cause and publicity won by the arrest in the previous march, they started with more than 700 protesters. Just as before, law enforcement started arresting them immediately. Since the jails were again filled to capacity, the police started incarcerating the protesters in the Natchez City Auditorium. Since they could only hold them in the auditorium for a short time, because of the limited toilet facilities and lack of bedding, they started moving them to the state penitentiary in Parchmen, Mississippi more than two hundred miles away. Soon, the state of Mississippi was detaining more than two hundred peaceful protesters at the Parchmen Farm, its most notorious, all male, maximum security prison.

After the first civil rights march at the beginning of September, the Klans thought it important that they made their presence felt. Daddy was pretty busy for the next couple of weeks because they were preparing to conduct a Klan rally in the Liberty Park area of Natchez. When Daddy was busy preparing for these kinds of events, that meant that my brothers and I were also busy. I lost track of the protestors that were jailed in Natchez and heard nothing more about the plight of those that were taken to Parchman.

During October the Klans were very busy getting *The Fiery Cross* printed in sufficient quantities for full distribution to all of the rally participants and anyone else that showed any interest at the park. *The Fiery Cross* periodical that they developed was a super edition of the April creation, including all of the pictures of the Selma march, the captions, and the story of Viola Liuzzo, the mother of five from Chicago who had been killed by the Klansmen while she ferried some of the marchers back to Selma. Of course, the story that they told about Viola was that which had been conjured up by the FBI and local press.

It was during the preparation for the upcoming rally in Natchez that I recognized my father's exceptional organizational talents. He attended meetings at the Natchez Hunt Club where they were coordinating the creation and duplication of the documents that were needed to conduct the rally, and for distribution to the participants. In Vidalia they met at the Shamrock Inn to plan and coordinate the security for the event. They were going to have an army of undercover agents guarding the entrances to the park, stationed at strategic points around the rally location, and milling about in the crowds to spot and isolate anyone they felt was there to stir up trouble. In Ferriday, they met at the King Hotel with Klansmen and law enforcement officers to coordinate the traffic control of the large number of people that they expected for the rally. He held meetings in several of the towns north and west of Ferriday to recruit more men to help with security and traffic control. They even planned to set up an area for incident command to handle everything from dispensing first aid to riot control.

On the day of the rally, the NAACP stole part of the Klan's thunder by marching more than five hundred demonstrators from a local church to the Adams County Courthouse where the Klans were scheduled to appear later in the day. After they arrived at the courthouse steps, Charles Evers addressed the demonstrators about the need to keep the faith and stay the course. He offered them encouragement in the work that they were doing and thanked them for the sacrifices they had made and for those that they were prepared to make. During the address, the number of demonstrators had grown to more than eight hundred. After the demonstration, the crowd dispersed in peace long before the Klans arrived.

That cool fall morning, Daddy had asked me and one of my younger brothers to go with him to run errands and help with the distribution of the Klan material on which he had worked so diligently. With Jimmy in tow, we drove directly to the Adams County Courthouse where we stopped long enough for Daddy to change, and to join the others on the courthouse lawn. When we pulled up to the curb, he stood at the side of the car and put his robes on, then his hood. I had never seen these robes before. They were no longer white. Instead, his robes were crimson red with a bright green satin trim around the lapel area, with two green stripes and one gold at the bottom of each sleeve. Part of the green was obscured by the shoulder flaps, almost like epaulettes, of a cape that hung from his back. The UKA Klan logo, a white cross with a blood drop in the center in a red circle, was stitched into the left breast of the robe. The matching helmet was pointed at the top in mockery of the Catholic diocese. He did not don the hood portion of the helmet that would have obscured his face. He was easy to spot even after he moved into the large crowd that had already gathered in anticipation of the Klan parade. Jimmy and I parked the car then returned to watch the parade arrive. When we arrived at the courthouse, Daddy had disappeared. We found a high spot under the porch of the annex where we had a good view of the courthouse grounds and of State Street. The porch afforded us a great shade to observe the parade as the day heated up.

After we sat on the rail for a while, we saw the crowd which had swelled into State Street in front of the courthouse turn to watch the approaching Klansmen. Jimmy and I leaned out around a large post to see them approaching. Before we could see the parade, we could hear the heavy cadence and echoes of horseshoes on the concrete surface of State Street. When they came into our view, we saw several Klansmen with their robes flowing in the breeze, led on prancing horses. E. L. McDaniel, the Grand Dragon of Mississippi, led the parade of uniformed Klansmen in the green satin robes that marked his state rank. A short distance behind, I could see Daddy marching at the front of the ranks with his bright red robes in sharp contrast to the white robes that surrounded him. There were almost six hundred people in the parade; more than a hundred of them robed in their Klan regalia.

When the parade reached the front of the courthouse, they did a right face and marched up the steps from the street. The Grand Dragon and several of his entourage marched up to the top of the stairs that led to the courthouse doors. He stood between the stately white pillars and addressed the large crowd assembled on the lawn, sidewalks, and street. Many of the marchers had joined us on the annex porch, blocking our view of the proceedings. We could see nothing and could only hear part of his speech as Grand Dragon McDaniel made his address to the crowd. Much of his address focused on keeping the white race pure by resisting the efforts of the Jewish-backed civil rights workers that were infiltrating the state daily. "As white people, it is our duty to prevent the mongrelization of the white race and to protect our children from the outside agitators that are here to change our whole way of life. Let all those niggers and outside agitators out there know that the Klans are alive and the South shall rise again."

After the rally on the steps of the courthouse, Daddy, Jimmy and I drove to Liberty Park where they had a large field set up as a parking lot, though there was already a small paved parking lot available. We drove past the parking area to one of the booths that they had set up at the back of the field where we unloaded the literature and materials. After we dropped the material, I parked the car in a spot that was reserved for Daddy. I sat in the car for a while as arriving Klansmen walked into the field at the front of the car and disappeared behind a stand of trees. There was nothing on the radio, so I thought I would get out and take in a bit of the park where it would be cooler.

I walked back toward the road to the entrance of the parking area. As I stood there trying to decide which way to go, I became curious about all of the cars driving into the area. I looked at the people arriving in the cars to see if I recognized any of them. I relaxed a bit too much as I sat on an old stump and read aloud the counties stamped on the car tags from Mississippi. I also saw cars with Louisiana, Arkansas, Texas, Alabama, and Tennessee.

"Hey. What are you doing over there?"

I barely heard the question and never thought it was directed at me, so I continued to watch the cars turn into the parking area. Suddenly I felt someone grab my shoulder and pull me around on the stump. "Hey, boy. What are you doing here?"

"Take your hands off of me. I drove my daddy over here so I could run errands if he needs something."

"Boy, don't you bark at me like that. I'll wring your scrawny little neck. I don't know you or your daddy, so how are you going to prove that you aren't in here spying for the FBI?"

I don't know why that struck me so funny, but I started laughing hysterically. Perhaps it was because I had been told that the FBI had provided them with the pictures for their periodical. Perhaps it was because I suspected a couple of the men that I had seen arriving to have been FBI informants. I also thought a couple of the other men to have been agents that I recognized from the station where I once worked and from their visits to my house. I blurted out, "Nice job. You already let two cars with FBI agents go through already and you accuse me of being an FBI spy?"

"Are you parked in here, too?"

"Yes, right up there in the first row in the reserved spots."

"Those spots are reserved for Klan officials, so I think it's time for you to get in your car and leave."

"Sure. I'll be glad to, but can I get your name first?"

"Why do you need my name?"

"Because Daddy is going to go berserk when he comes out here and finds out I left without him. And I am NOT going to get my butt kicked for leaving him here until I get the name of the man that made me do it."

The large man grabbed me by my collars and yanked me off the stump. "You little turd, you don't back talk me and you don't get smart. I'll kick your ass right here and ..."

"We got a problem over here?"

I recognized the voice, so I turned my head to address him, "Hey Mister Glover. This guy thinks I'm some kind of FBI spy."

"You know this boy Mister Glover? I caught him out here watchin' everyone drive in and readin' their license plates."

"Shit. That boy ought to have your job, Jackson. He probably knows about half the people that are drivin' in here and where they are from. Hell, he is the only one besides the law that can spot the FBI agents that will probably show up here. That is Ed Blanche's boy."

"Hell. I didn't know who he was. He never told me he was Ed's boy."

"You never gave me a chance and you never asked. You're too bent on turning me into some kind of spy." Then I turned to Mister Glover and said, "Oh, by the way. Your FBI agents are already here; one car from Louisiana and one from Mississippi. There's probably more by now, since he's had my feet dangling off the ground for the last five minutes."

RJ chuckled and said, "You better come with me."

As I started to walk away, the big man spun me around and sneered, "You better watch you back, boy. I feed shit like you to my pigs."

I jumped in the car with RJ and rode back to the reserved parking section. As we got out of the car, he turned to me and said, "You watch your back with that man, Buddy. That is Jackson Smith, and he's part of that rogue bunch over in Franklin County. They are part of those bunches from Franklin, Lincoln, and Pike Counties that's been causin' so much trouble. Watch your back. That man and his bunch are just mean."

That was a rather ominous warning. R. J. Glover was one of those men that didn't seem to fear anything and from whom you had to earn respect; nothing was given. I had always been a little bit afraid of RJ, so it really disturbed me to hear him talking that way about someone else.

He continued, "He doesn't know it yet, but him and his bunch have the FBI all over them. He's got a fox in the hen house over there because someone out of that bunch has been informin' to the FBI. They gave up explosives and ammo all over those counties because the FBI knew exactly where to look. He is really mad that more and more of his boys are jumpin' out of his band and joinin' up with the UKA and White Knights. He ain't one of your daddy's biggest admirers either. He blames your daddy for stealin' members from some of the older groups over here."

It was still odd to think that my father had that kind of influence anywhere, with any kind of group. I had never seen him in that light before. I did know firsthand about his skills to pick things apart.

I still didn't feel like waiting in the car, so I walked back out to the edge of the field where the large cross stood out against the dark sky. I had never seen so many people gathered into one location before, so I sat mesmerized by the throngs of people, many of whom were robed, milling about between the tents and tables. It wasn't long before the attention of the crowd was focused to the stage area by the blaring of loudspeakers from the public announcement system. I moved closer along the edge of the tree line to get a better view of the rally program. Several people stepped up to the microphone to address the large crowd, but I could not identify most of them because I was so far away. I did recognize E.L. McDaniel when he stepped to the microphone because he was still in his distinctive robes. After he made a short speech and introduction, someone came to the microphone to lead the crowd in an invocation. I stood silent and bowed my head as they prayed, but wondered if God heard prayers of petition and protection when they were delivered from such groups and individuals that weren't really gathered in His name. After the prayer, I was again entertained by the people in the crowd. There were men, women, and children dressed in their Klan robes milling about in the area of the twenty-five-foot cross erected in the middle of the field. After the invocation, Robert Shelton, the Grand Imperial Wizard of the United Klans of America, stepped up to the microphone and gave a long and rather enthusiastic speech. Throughout the speech he would occasionally break his speech with, "The South shall rise again." Each time, the large crowd would echo the chant with such enthusiasm that it seemed to echo like a shot through the forest. I was sure they could hear it in Natchez. Like the other Klan speeches I had heard, this one was also salted with the standard Klan rhetoric, spewing Klan propaganda about what was going to happen if our children had to go to school with niggers, the mongrelization of the white race by breeding with non-whites, the deterioration of our society by the influence of outside agitators from the North, and what we needed to do to keep the South segregated. He denounced the federal government, the President of the United States, and the civil rights movement. Like McDaniel had done in the earlier rally, he blamed the problems of our society on the influence of the communists and the agitators that were being coordinated and financed by the rich Jews in the North. It was his contention that the racial strife of the South was part of a Jewish-backed communist plan.

After the Grand Imperial Wizard completed his address, some of the robed Klansmen marched out to the cross and organized themselves around it, each one picking up a three-foot torch as he took his place in a large circle. Because of their distinctively colorful uniforms, I recognized Daddy, EL McDaniel, and Robert Shelton. After they had taken their places within the circle, they all held their torches high for a moment then, as in a salute, held them pointed directly at the cross. The Grand Dragon turned with his torch held in front of the man to his left, who struck a lighter and lit the torch. After his torch was lit, the Grand Dragon turned and lit the torch of the man on his right, who did the same; each man passing the flame to the man on his right until it passed completely around the circle. After the last torch was lit, the Klansmen all raised their torches overhead in a salute, then slowly lowered them as they marched toward the cross. As they approached the cross, they lowered the torches to contact the base of the cross in unison. The cross burst into flames so intensely, the Klansmen had to step back a couple of steps to avoid being set afire. After they reformed the circle, they tossed their torches into a heap at the base of the cross then stepped back into their original positions and held their arms out to their sides, each one making his own cross. Because the torches added to the fuel at the base of the cross, they caused a flare of flames that licked right to the top of it. With so much of the flames concentrated at the bottom, it didn't take long for the cross to burn through about halfway up. Without warning, the top of the cross came crashing down, sending up a shower of sparks and flames as the Klansmen scattered in all directions. Though I was a little concerned about the safety of the men, I had to laugh at the sight of robed Klansmen scurrying about in a panic with their skirts lifted to avoid tripping.

As things settled a bit, I noticed a uniformed Mississippi Highway and Safety Patrol Officer walking through the crowd. He wasn't strolling as if he were on patrol like I had seen several of them do through the evening. He had a determined gait and a purpose to his direction. In the light of the cross, he stepped up to one of the Klansmen and demanded, "Is your name Paul Banner?"

"Yes. Why do you need to know?"

"Paul G. Banner?"

"That's me."

He handed him an envelope and says, "This is for you. You have been subpoenaed to appear before the House Un-American Activities Committee in Washington, D.C. You have a safe trip now, ya hear?"

"You chicken-shit son of a bitch. Where were you this morning when that band of niggers was gatherin' on the courthouse steps, mockin' us right in front of the bunch of you?"

"Oh, that is when we were over at Steve Books' house to serve him up one of them things also. Y'all can drive up there together."

I stood in shocked admiration. That patrolman had walked into the midst of the Klansmen without flinching. He had just given a subpoena to one of the most notorious Klansmen in all of Mississippi, one who was suspected of having been involved with several murders in Franklin and Adams Counties.

I found Daddy and told him where I had parked the car, then helped Jimmy pick up the remaining material left in the merchandise booth. I took the stuff back out to the car and waited while Jimmy stayed behind with Daddy. I watched as people began passing in front of the car as they walked to their own cars. As a challenge to myself regarding the comment that R. J. Glover made earlier about my knowing half of the people here, I started counting the people that I could recognize in the dim light. I didn't know half of them, but I did count one hundred twenty-three men, women, and children that I recognized well enough to know their home towns. I also spotted two Concordia Parish sheriff's deputies, three Natchez police officers, two Mississippi Highway Safety Patrol officers, and at least four FBI agents.

When we drove home that night, Daddy asked me about what kind of trouble I caused at the parking lot entrance. I tried to explain it to him, but to no avail. He was convinced that I had done something to initiate the fracas and there was no way I was going to convince him otherwise. It wasn't the first time I felt as if there was no way to please him. In fact, I felt that way about almost everything that I did. The only thing that earned his praise was my driving. Most of the time, I felt it wasn't even worth the effort to try to satisfy him. I just gave up and didn't even try to defend myself. I drove home in silence, hoping that he would fall asleep and let the issue die, but Daddy didn't sleep when he was this agitated, and I know that issues only die of old age.

After the Klan rally, the United Klans grew very inactive around Concordia Parish and Adams County for several months. FBI and Mississippi Highway Safety Patrol presences were maintained at a high concentration in Natchez, keeping things quiet for a while. During their hiatus, some of the Klansmen must have become bored, so they decided to focus their attention on white people they thought had too much contact with colored people. Rusty Toliver soon became one of their victims.

The Tolivers had attended church with us many years ago when Daddy had been pastoring Calvary Baptist Church, a country church near Union Church, Mississippi. They had two boys, Rayford and Rusty, who were only about a year apart in age, were in Sunday school and church every Sunday. Like most of the people in that area, the Tolivers led a meager existence hauling pulpwood and working odd jobs where they could find them in Franklin County. After the boys had grown, Rusty, the younger of the two, moved to Natchez where he got a job delivering goods for a food distribution center. As far as I knew, Rusty was a hardworking, honest man who was trying to climb out of the poverty he had known all of his life.

One afternoon after Rusty completed his routes, which included deliveries to several stores and a pharmacy owned by colored people, he returned to the distribution center to clock out. After he clocked out, he walked through the parking lot toward his car when several hooded men attacked him, forcing him into the back seat of a blue Oldsmobile. In the car, they threw a hood over his head and drove him to a farm near Washington, Mississippi. There they tied him between two trees with his arms stretched out and his feet barely touching the ground. As they cut away his clothes with a large Bowie knife, they taunted him, "Boy, what makes you think you can go out there and treat those niggers like they're so important and ignore the white people right down the street?"

"What are y'all talkin' about?"

"Some of them boys over on Pine Street said they saw you takin' groceries into that nigger's store before you delivered to Hainey's. You gonna serve the niggers before you serve the white people? That ain't gonna work."

"That's the way they come up on my route. I'm supposed to take the most direct route from one delivery to the next. They told me in the center that's the way I'm s'posed to do it, so that's the way I do it."

After they cut his pants away, they ripped at his shirt to bare his back. "Ain't none of them other drivers hittin' the nigger stores first. They make 'em wait until after all the whites is served. We been hearin' that you been real friendly with some of them niggers, 'specially the ones down here that have money. You think we don't see this stuff; we are the United Klans of America; the Invisible Empire. We see everything. We gonna teach you to know your place. We ain't gonna have you turnin' into no nigger lover,"

They took a short whip and started beating him across his bare back and legs. "You take care of your family first. You don't go takin' food out of your family's mouth to feed no niggers."

With each lash, Rusty sagged lower and lower until his legs could no longer support him. He was literally suspended by his outstretched arms. After they beat him into unconsciousness, they cut him down, letting him fall into a heap where one of them walked up and kicked him in the ribs. They let him lie there until he regained consciousness, then they picked him up and threw him back into the car with a warning, "Boy, don't you bleed on my upholstery."

They drove him back to the distribution center where they tossed him out of the car unceremoniously. As he lay on the concrete lot, one of them threw the remnants of his clothes out on him and sneered, "Get yourself dressed boy. Nobody around here wants to see your naked ass."

One of them stepped out of the car and held Rusty's hooded head up triumphantly and yelled, "Let this be a lesson to all you would-be nigger lovers out there. We will not tolerate you puttin' niggers before whites. You learn to take care of your own." The lone Klansman got back into the car and they disappeared in a haze of smoke and squealing tires.

Rusty managed to pull the hood off his head and tried to stand but his legs were still too weak. He crawled up to the small door beside the loading docks, pulled himself up on the guard rail, and pushed the button at the side of the door to get the attention of the workers on the inside. One of the loading doors opened, but when the worker saw no truck at the dock, he pulled the door back down. Rusty managed to press the button one more time before he collapsed and fell back down the steps into the parking lot. Fortunately, when the dock worker opened up the large door, he looked out and saw the heap that was Rusty. The workers didn't know what had happened so they called the police who rushed him to the hospital.

Later, the police questioned him, but he couldn't remember any of the details of the attack. He could not tell them who the attackers were, how many there were, or what they were driving. He said, "I only know they were klukkers. At least they said they were part of the United Klans, but I couldn't tell."

Klan groups continued to intimidate white individuals and families that they considered to be helping colored people in any way at all. They threw incendiaries and explosives at homes, broke windows from cars and homes, and brandished weapons as they drove past suspect homes. The Klans also continued to print and distribute leaflets accusing whites in the area of consorting with colored people and naming those they considered to be involved with the civil rights movement.

Meanwhile, Daddy was continuing to meet with Klansmen and sympathizers at the King Hotel and at the Shamrock Inn. At the King Hotel, he had begun keeping company with a woman, Mandy Perkins, and her companion, Jill Mason. Mandy was a coarse, big-breasted olive-skinned woman with dark eyes that reflected her hard life. Jill was a scrawny girl with light skin, dark eyes, and hardly any kind of figure. Both of the women were down on their luck, so Daddy had taken them into hand in his benevolence. At the time, Mandy wasn't capable of caring for her one-year-old daughter so we had taken her in as a part of our family. It wasn't the first time we had a foster child in the house. From my earliest memories we had occasional children fostered in our house when aunts and uncles separated, church members needed help, or someone just fell on bad times. However, this time was different. I could tell that Mama was feeling threatened by the presence of the other women, and felt put upon by the added responsibility of the toddler. Even so, she was compliant with the additional demands on her time and our resources.

Recently, Daddy acquired access and permission to use a large "camp house" out on Robins Island out on Lake Saint John. He arranged for the two women to live in the lake house for a while so they could get back on their feet, but that added another problem because neither of the women had a car. He would occasionally shuttle them to and from the King Hotel or take supplies out to the lake house. When he couldn't make the trip, he sent me out to shuttle the women around. Mandy delighted in teasing me when Daddy wasn't around, trying to seduce me on several occasions when I picked her up at the lake house. Jill played along with her teasing, though she was more reserved and sympathetic about my position. I found neither of the women attractive and thought of both of them as trashy, lowlife prostitutes. I had more romantic fantasies about how I would lose my virginity. After having been accosted in the lake house a number of times, I wouldn't even go in if the women were there.

Right after Thanksgiving, Daddy asked me to take Mandy and Jill to Natchez on the following Monday. After having worked all day shifts on Saturday and Sunday, I really didn't feel like getting up early on Monday; I wanted to sleep in. I managed to get myself up and drove out to the lake house where the women were waiting. The drive from the lake back to Ferriday was pleasant enough, so I was a bit more relaxed. Mandy told me that they would be at the doctor's office for a while and asked if I minded waiting. What choice did I really have? I couldn't just go off and leave them there; Daddy would have a fit. I decided I needed some reading material for my wait, so stopped by the house to pick up my book, *Rifles for Watie*.

With book in hand, I hopped back into the car, backed out onto Crestview Drive and headed toward the highway. As we drove away from the house I noticed a Chevrolet pickup truck pull off of Bea Street right after we passed. I didn't think anything about the pickup at first. When we reached the highway, Mandy asked to stop at the Quick Mart to get a pack of cigarettes. When I pulled into the Quick Mart parking lot from the highway, I noticed that the pickup truck pulled off onto the shoulder just short of the entrance.

After Mandy got her cigarettes, we started toward Natchez again and the Chevy pickup picked up the tail again. At first, they tailed us from a distance, but after we drove past the bowling alley, they pulled up close enough behind that I could clearly see the three men sitting in the cab of the truck. I did not recognize the truck or any of the three men. I asked the two women to look to see if they recognized any of the men. When neither of them recognized any of the men, I became afraid. They were still far enough behind that I could see the license plate was from Mississippi; as they came closer I could read the county stamp, Franklin. I made a note of the license number as the driver pulled right up to my rear bumper. I sped up past the speed limit for a short time to see what he would do. When he got right behind me again, I lifted on the accelerator until we slowed to about fifty miles per hour. They immediately pulled along side where the passenger riding shotgun said, "Pull it over boy, we're gonna kick your ass."

I tromped the accelerator and pulled ahead just enough for them to fall in behind again. As soon as they were completely in the right lane, I started slowing until I was again doing about fifty. Instead of passing, the driver came up behind me and nudged me with his large front bumper, unsettling the car. Both of the women started screaming, "Do something. Do something."

I didn't know what to do, but I did know I had to do something. In fear, I reached down and pulled the .44 magnum from its holster. Mandy recoiled in horror. I rolled my window down all the way, pulled the hammer back on the gun, stuck the gun out the window, and pointed it out over the levee so I wouldn't be hitting anything by accident. I leaned the barrel of the gun back toward the truck just slightly and squeezed the trigger. As I watched in the mirror, I could see the sheer terror on the faces of the men as the gun fired. The driver slammed the brakes so hard, he almost wrecked the truck. The man in the center of the truck had both hands up on the windshield while the one riding shotgun was almost thrown from the vehicle.

When I got to Vidalia, I drove directly to the police station to report the incident, leaving out the part about firing the gun. As soon as I told the sheriff what had happened, he immediately put a call out to the local law enforcement describing the truck and its occupants. After getting the bulletin out, he turned to me and said, "Boy, what have you done that might have made these boys upset with you?"

"Nothing. I don't even know who they were. All I know is that they were in a truck from over in Franklin County."

"Well, those boys over there are upset about everything these days. They think everyone is out to get them and they are out to get back at everybody that ain't them. Hell, I think they are even over there getting back at each other."

"Well I know quite a few people over there, but I don't know why anyone of them would have a reason to do something like this."

"Well. You watch it boy. With all that is going on around here, and with all the stuff your daddy is mixed up in, it could be any number of things that has them boys upset. You watch your back, especially out here on these country roads and long stretches of road."

"Yes sir. I'll do that. We still have to go over to Natchez to get these women over to Doctor Provail."

We made it to Natchez and back to the house without any further incident, but Mandy started her teasing in earnest. "I can't believe you protected us like that. You are a brave boy, and I could make a brave man out of you if you would let me."

"I was protecting all of us. I ain't about to let those guys run me off the road and beat me up. We already had one person disappear along that stretch of road. I am not about to be the second."

"Who else disappeared there?"

"Joe Edwards did more than a year ago. They still haven't found hide nor hair of him. They probably tied him to a link of railroad iron and dropped him in that slough under the levee on the other side of that road that cuts off down past Mimosa Drive."

"You mean that little nigger boy that used to work over at the Shamrock. I knew him. He was a nice boy. I used to talk to him all the time. Whatever happened to him?"

"Nobody knows. He disappeared last July and they found his car down by the bowling alley; almost the same place those men in the pickup hit us this morning."

I could hardly wait to get home. Since it was almost time for Daddy to get home, I knew that there would be fresh coffee on the stove, so I could sit with a cup and relax. Mama knew something was wrong as soon as I walked through the door. "Are you alright? You're as white as a ghost. What happened?"

I didn't have to answer; Mandy and Jill filled the air with an unintelligible explanation as they both tried to talk at the same time. They hadn't completed their story before Daddy got home. The two women could hardly wait to tell him the whole story, telling him how brave I had been to scare the men off and still get to Natchez. What none of them understood was that I had been scared out of my wits. I did the only thing I could think of doing and it was all done out of raw fear.

I don't think I had ever seen that kind of fear on my father's face before. The fear quickly turned to anger, but he didn't know where to direct his anger. "What were you thinking boy, those men could have beat you to death?"

"That is what I was afraid of. They threatened me. I wasn't about to let them stop me. Three of them against one of me and all of them were bigger than me. It was down there in the same place where they found Joe Edwards' car. That's all I could think about."

Then he turned his attention to the two women, "What were you two doing while all this is going on?"

Though I didn't care for either of the women, I had to stop this misguided interrogation, "There wasn't anything they could do. I was driving; I was the one that had the gun. All they could do was watch ... and scream."

"What were you thinking? What did you think they would do if you started shootin' at them?"

"Daddy, I don't know! They threatened me then they hit my car. What was I supposed to do? Pull over and let them beat the hell out of me?"

"Son, you have to watch yourself out there and watch what you do. You go around shootin' at people, some of those old boys will start shootin back."

He wasn't telling me anything I didn't already know. I lived in a parish where every other white man seemed to own a pickup and every pickup had a gun rack in the back window, usually stocked with one or two rifles and a fishing pole. Mississippi was no different; they had just as many pickups, with the same numbers of gun racks, rifles, and fishing poles.

Christmas of 1965 went by too quickly, and I didn't get enrolled in college, so I missed the winter semester at Northeast Louisiana State College. Initially I was concerned because the Selective Service was drafting every available male over eighteen years old to fight in Vietnam. Fortunately, I was still enrolled at the Concordia Parish Trade School which qualified me for a deferment from the draft. I had a 4-S classification and they were only calling up those classified 1-A.

The new year was uneventful for the first couple of months, though the Klans still managed to spread a small amount of terror, with a few poorly placed explosives and Molotov cocktails. The civil rights groups managed several successful demonstrations and marches in Natchez, but had no success in organizing events in Concordia Parish. I was relieved that things seemed to be settling down. I was so tired of the violence and unrest. Winter turned into spring with few incidents.

In early June of 1966, James Meredith started the March Against Fear in which he vowed to march from Memphis, Tennessee to Jackson, Mississippi, convincing the colored people of the South that they had more to gain than they had reasons to fear if they stood up and demonstrated for their rights. On the second day of the march, James Meredith was struck by a bullet fired by a sniper hiding along the roadside. After he was taken to the hospital, Martin Luther King and Stokely Carmichael took his place to continue the march toward Jackson.

The local Klansmen believed the sniping was a setup when they found out that he had been shot with a rifle loaded with bird shot. "If that old boy was serious about killin' that nigger, he'd have shot him with a real bullet."

"Yeah, and he wouldn't have stopped at one shot. Why didn't he shoot that nigger more than once? He wasn't trying to kill that boy. That whole thing was just for show, to get more attention focused on that little march of his."

For a while, conversations between the Klansmen became redundant: the subject invariably turned to the march and staged sniping. Those in our area were quite frustrated that they were unable to do anything at all about the march; they felt upstaged and helpless to do anything about it.

On June 10th, while the marchers made their way south, several of the Klansmen in Natchez schemed to assassinate Martin Luther King. They set into action a plan sure to bring Doctor King to their doorstep—a vile, despicable plan without compassion or regard to human dignity. They were going to lure him to Natchez and reel him in like a fish. All they needed was an unwitting victim they could use as a lure.

Ben White was working on the grounds at the Cooper Hill Plantation in Natchez where he had worked all of his sixty-seven years, following in the footsteps of his father and his grandfather, who had worked there as slaves. Three white men in their thirties pulled up to the curb on Liberty Road adjacent to the plantation. "Hey, you want to make a couple of bucks?" the shouted out to him.

"Yes sir. I guess it 'pends on what it is."

"We just need to have a couple of bushes trimmed and we like the way you got these here looking. These are looking pretty and strong."

"I can do that if they not too tall, but I'm still not done here."

"You look like you could use a break, anyway. Hop in and you can have a Coke; we'll get you back here before they even know you are gone. We got all the tools you need. It won't take very long."

As Ben walked over to the car, a man in the back seat opened the door and Ben approached cautiously. He slid onto the seat, closed the door and started to give direction when the man sitting opposite him in the back seat, Cecil Breeding, pointed a pistol at him, "Shut up, you ol' nigger."

Ben's first impulse was to open the door and step out quickly, but when he touched the door handle Cecil shoved the gun at him menacingly and said, "I don't want to shoot you right here nigger, but I will. Now sit still; we're goin' for a ride."

When the old man tried again to open the back door, Cecil hit him several times with the butt of the pistol. Blood splattered all over the back seat and sprayed against the back window of the car. With the old man slumped over in the seat, Cecil quickly took a handkerchief and wiped the blood off the window so it could not be seen from the outside of the car. The driver, Earl Thompson, looked up in the rear view mirror and blurted, "God damn it all. You done got blood all over the back of the car. You know how hard it is to clean that out of cloth. Shit; do somethin' quick, 'cause he is bleedin' like a stuck pig."

Cecil pulled Ben's shirt up over his head so his blood wouldn't get on the upholstery. After having driven down Liberty Road for a short distance, Earl asked, "Hey Gene, where you want to take this nigger?"

"Just head down this road til we get to the Homochitto Forest. There's places in there where nobody will find him 'til we want them to."

They drove down Liberty Road through the outskirts of Natchez and into the rural area south of the city. Soon they were driving through the Homochitto National Forest where the lush, green of the trees painted a scene of peace and serenity. When they reached Garden City Road, Gene yelled out, "Earl, turn right here."

After a short drive, Earl turned right onto another road that took them into a more secluded area of the forest. They followed the narrow road until they came to a bridge. "Stop here."

They stopped on the bridge where Gene Knight got out and walked around the car with Earl, who opened the trunk to reveal a small arsenal. Gene reached into the trunk and took a rifle out, then made sure it was fully loaded before he walked around to the passenger side of the car where Ben was still seated in the back seat. He yanked the old man's door open and commanded him to get out of the car. Ben could not, or would not comply, so Gene backed up a couple of steps and opened fire on the old man while he was still seated. Gene screamed and raged as he shot round after round into the old man's body. Earl stood in silent shock as some of the rounds tore through the trunk and rear fender of his car. They weren't through yet. Cecil walked around the car and stood beside Gene and asked, "Where you want me to shoot this nigger?"

"Shoot him in the head."

Though Ben was already dead, Cecil Breeding took a step toward the body and fired two shotgun blasts at the old man's face, almost removing his head.

After they stood and looked at the body for a while, Gene reached into the car and grabbed the old man's arm and yanked him out onto the surface of the bridge where he dragged him to the edge of the bridge. After they removed it from the car, they kicked and prodded the old man's body until it was partially leaning against the bridge rail.

Gene looked over at the holes in the upholstery and blood that had splattered and sprayed all over the car. He mused, "Damn, Earl. I sure am sorry about your car. It's a mess."

"Yeah. I don't know what we're gonna do about that."

When the police found Ben White's body, they were shocked at its condition. Ben's head was barely attached to his torso, which was full of bullet holes. Spread around the bridge was a myriad of evidence; shotgun and rifle shells, a trail of blood, paint flakes, and pieces of clothing and upholstery that the investigators thought they were sure to match quickly.

The next day the police were called to investigate an incident in which a car had been abandoned and was fully aflame. After the flames were doused, the fire investigators found several bullet holes through the left rear fender and trunk of the car. They were sure that the car had been set ablaze to hide evidence of a crime. When they traced the vehicle identification number, they traced it back to Earl Thompson, one of the men who had attacked and killed Ben White. Though they seemed to have a staggering amount of evidence, no arrests were made during 1966.

I was enraged when I heard about the murder. If I had anti-KKK sentiment before, it was kicked into overdrive. I heard several rumors concerning the motive for killing the old man, but each one was as ludicrous as the next. There was no excuse and no reason that could ever justify the murder and mutilation of an old man who should be enjoying his retirement–if colored people had such a luxury. Daddy walked into one of my rants and tried to justify the actions of the Klansmen, though I knew he didn't believe a word of what he was saying. I knew that he had been just as shocked as I was when we heard about Ben White's murder and mutilation a few days before. I could only think, "How senseless. They killed that old man for no more a reason than to lure another man to his death. I don't even think King will really show up for the march into Jackson."

After the Ben White murder, our attention turned back to the march to Jackson. It was still progressing toward Jackson, as planned, and Daddy was not pleased about it. While he was ranting about it, I baited Daddy into another argument about the assassination attempt on James Meredith. I don't remember what his defense of the sniper shot on Meredith had been, but I remember my retort which drew his immediate ire, "Yeah. If I ever decide to kill anyone, I'll make sure to use some of those high-powered bird shot rounds that I know so well. To get myself ready, I'll go out and snipe twenty or thirty blackbirds to make sure my ability to kill is at its peak."

"You don't even know the circumstances." Daddy responded. "Someone in his family might have loaded up his gun with bird shot just to keep him from becoming a murderer."

"Yeah. Most likely he spent too much time with his Klan buddies talkin' on the CB Radio and his IQ fell below its normal genius level. I heard that if you move into Tennessee from any other state, you have to lose twenty IQ points just to join the Klans."

"Boy, why do you do that? You say things just to irritate me. You know how mad that makes me. Why do you do it?"

"Maybe I'm tryin' to make you see how ridiculous it all is. People like that ain't helpin' your cause; they're hurtin' it. By shootin' Meredith, he got the march on the national evening news AND now they got Charmichael and King marching with that group. Now what do you think is gonna happen when the whole nation gets wind of what is happening over there in Mississippi? That march is already twice as big as it would have been if that asshole pseudo-sniper had just stayed home."

"Well, the Mississippi State Police is ready for them. They have plans to stop them before they reach Jackson."

"Do you really think it will work? If they stop two thousand of the marchers, six thousand will take their places. Do you really think that anything they do can stop the will of those people? If you go over to Jackson next week, they will be arriving at about the same time you do. They will be there. If I had the time to take off, I think I'd go over just to see it."

That sent him into a rage. He threatened to kick my butt so I eased my way out of the conversation and out of the room. My prediction came true on June 26th, when James Meredith, wounded the week before, led more than twelve thousand demonstrators into Jackson to complete his March Against Fear—twelve thousand demonstrators. The attention of most of America was focused on the event—and I wasn't there to see it.

Three days later, my fears for my future grew when the US Air Force started dropping bombs on Hanoi. With the escalations of the fighting in Vietnam, they were calling up more young men to fight. I knew I had to get into college during the next semester or I would be headed to Southeast Asia with a gun strapped to my back.

The events of July sent half the good Klansmen in Concordia Parish and Adams County into tears. The Louisiana State Police moved in to close the Morville Lounge in Deer Park. During the past year, lounge business had swelled enough to require the addition of several new bedrooms to take care of their swell in clientele. Somehow, the State Police connected the operations of the Morville Lounge with the local operation of the KKK, specifically the United Klans of America. In their investigation, they also uncovered evidence implicating the Concordia Parish Sheriff and several of his deputies who were taking payments from the manager of the lounge for protection—keeping their attention diverted from the goings-on at the establishment.

During the same period of time, Daddy became more visible amongst the Klans, again rising in rank and prestige. He attended weekly meetings in which they were trying to generate more klaverns and recruit more members for the existing klaverns. He also became less tolerant of my views about the Klans and civil rights. The rift between us was turning into a wide chasm; there was no room for tolerance in our divergent views.

In August, I drove to Monroe to start my enrollment for the fall semester of college. I was excited, but I knew I wasn't ready for this. I had never been away from home for more than a couple of days at a time and I still had no idea what direction I should take with my education; I was already doing the kind of work I enjoyed and it paid well, especially for a young man with no other commitments. I enrolled into a full schedule of pre-engineering courses, arranged rental in one of the college dormitories, and got a student assistance job where I would be working part-time in the cafeteria to pay for my food and dorm.

When the college term started, I checked into the dorm and set up life as I knew it, but immediately found out how short my attention span was and how many distractions there were around a college campus of this size. The entire city of Monroe was a distraction for a boy who graduated from a high school with only eighty-six graduating seniors in a town of fewer than three thousand people. In all of Concordia Parish there were fewer than twenty thousand people. Natchez was a city of only twenty thousand people. Now I was living on the outskirts of a city of almost fifty thousand people, not counting the thousands of students living on the Northeast Louisiana State College. Good Lord. There were more students in my college than there were in my entire home town!

My first, and biggest, distraction was my roommate. I was living in a two-man dorm room by myself. I don't remember my roommate having spent more than one night in the dorm. The quiet was deafening. The solitude was something I had never experienced, so I spent very little time in my room. When I had to study, I often went to the student union or the commons where there would be multitudes of other students.

My second distraction was a group of Yankees that had come to Northeast Louisiana State College because the academic requirements were more lax than those in New York and this school was not yet integrated. The four Yanks were from the upstate area around Lake Placid, an area they referred to as the Adirondacks. I found the whole group of them very interesting because their speech and experiences were so different from my own. They were all more worldly than I, but at the same time, they were more naïve and ignorant about life in the South. I didn't know if they were trying to impress me or if it was really so much a part of their vernacular, but they used the words "nigger" and "spooks" more than I had ever expected. It gave me a warped view of people from the North. When we were not in class, I often spent more time with the Yanks than I did in my own room.

One of the boys from New York had a hi-fi stereo, so we listened to the latest records as we sat and talked about theological, philosophical, and political issues. It was during these discussions that I was introduced to groups like Jan and Dean, The Beach Boys, and The Lettermen, an entire genre of music that I never knew existed. It was an experience that whetted my appetite for new music and knowledge about the world around me. I was also introduced to the martial arts by an ex-army soldier who had just returned from Korea. He wore a denim jacket with a unique symbol sewn into the back; that which looked like a spinning swastika with a half white, half black logo in the middle. He told me it was the logo for a new, aggressive Korean form of martial art called Oh Do Kwan. He agreed to teach me the basic arts and katas, though he admitted he was no master.

At the end of the fall semester I went home for the Christmas break to spend time with the family. It was good to be home where there were always people around and the noise level more pleasing to me as everyone competed for talk time. I arrived home early in the morning, so I had time to spend with Mama for a while before everyone else got home. I was standing in the door beside the tall wall heater in the living room when Jimmy got home and attacked me, jumping on my back with his arm around my neck. As soon as I saw his arm come across my face, I grabbed his arm, reached back for his shoulder and bent at the waist, tossing him over my head, through the door, and into the opposite wall in the hallway where he stuck upside down. He let out a loud yelp then started laughing hysterically, kicking his feet above his head—he was really stuck.

We carefully pulled him free of the wall so he wouldn't fall on his head when he was released. After we saw that he was alright, we were panicked by the size of the hole in the wall. Someone said, "Daddy is going to be real mad about that."

I replied, "Let's fix it then."

I called the lumber company in Vidalia to see what kind of paneling they had, then I quickly measured the hallway to see how many panels I would need. It was a perfect opportunity to drive the truck that I had purchased when I was home last; a 1949 Ford with a Mercury engine and transmission. It had a great sound at full throttle. I drove the distance to Vidalia in a hurry, got the material I needed and returned home as quickly as possible. Before Daddy got home from work that afternoon, we had completely paneled the hall; installing new base and header boards to trim our work. After Daddy got home, we all waited with bated breath to see what his reaction to the new hallway would be. He never noticed it. It was life as usual.

Daddy immediately put me to work building coffee tables for all the orders he had received for Christmas gifts. He also had several orders for playhouses, which I knew would keep me busy for the entire holiday period. PedCo also called and wanted me to make several deliveries for them to some of the wildcat rigs now working and drilling throughout Mississippi and Louisiana. I knew this was not going to be a very relaxing holiday.

Those were probably the busiest two weeks of my life. I made several deliveries for PedCo, carrying diesel to the drilling rigs. My brothers and I built several coffee table sets and I finishing two playhouses. I also completed two paintings of magnolias on black velvet; one which I gave to Roxie and the other which I sold for fifty dollars. It was the first painting I ever sold. By the end of the second week, I was ready to go back to college.

For the new term, I elected to take two courses which made my father crazy: art and social dancing. He considered both of them a waste of time and money, but he accepted my choices after I explained to him that I had to have at least one elective per semester, and art would help me with my drawing skills for my engineering degree. My elective choices were going to cause me more than one embarrassing moment during my second semester as a freshman.

Toward midterm, during art class we were using pastels to do still life drawings. My pastels were square, chalky sticks arranged in a fold-back box made to lean back on the lid, making easy access to the pastels. I stood the box of pastels on a tabletop and placed my sketch pad up on the easel to my right. After I started my sketch, I leaned my head onto my left hand with my elbow resting on the table to relax a little. The next thing I remembered was someone tapping me on the shoulder, "Hey, Buddy, wake up. You need to finish up. Class will be over soon."

I realized that I was facedown on the table with my head resting against the box of opened pastels. I lifted my head lazily and turned to tell the boy thanks for waking me. When I turned to face him, he broke into a wide smile and said, "Think nothing of it."

While I finished my drawing I noticed several of the students looking at me and smiling. I had to walk to another building for my next class and each student I passed smiled and bade me hello. When I got to the science building, I decided I needed to go to the restroom before going into chemistry. After using the urinal, I went back to the sinks to wash my hands before walking out. I quickly washed my hands and was about to splash a little water on my face to revive a bit when I looked up in the mirror; I was both shocked and amused. I had a rainbow painted on my forehead—a perfect rainbow. When I had fallen asleep in class, my face slid down the box of pastels, painting a colorful rainbow from my eyebrows right up to my hairline.

My second embarrassment was even worse. I had enrolled in the social dance class hoping to gain a survival set of social skills. There were twice as many girls in the class as there were boys, so I got to participate with a partner in every dance number that we learned. The instructor, Vicki Lane, was a petite beauty who moved about the dance floor with the grace and beauty of a swan. Watching her sashay around the floor was like watching an eagle fly—mesmerizing. I was spellbound.

We were about mid-semester, having already learned the foxtrot, waltz, rumba, and cha-cha. It was time to learn the very romantic and sensual tango. After we learned the history of the dance, our beautiful dance instructor demonstrated the proper technique and narrated, "Since this dance had a saucy Argentina origin, it is performed in a close embrace with either the upper body or the lower body in close contact. In South America and Europe, they dance with the upper body held in a tight embrace with several open moves, like spins and dips. In the American Tango, we dance with a close embrace with the lower body, keeping the pelvis and legs in contact except when performing spins, dips, and other special moves. With the pelvis and legs in contact, the woman leans back across her partner's arm, turns her head and watches over her right shoulder. Men, you lean back only far enough to support your partner's weight. Almost all moves are done with the woman going backward, the man always advancing. Both partners bend just enough at the waist so that the legs are slightly intertwined. The count goes slow, slow, quick, quick, close. Now watch this."

She walked us through the steps first from the man's perspective, then from the woman's. After the demonstration, she had us form two lines with the men in one facing the women in the other, then coached us carefully as we performed the steps without partners. When it looked as if we had the basic beat and step, she said, "Okay. It looks like you are ready to put this to practical application. Ed, will you help me out here?"

At first I didn't think she was speaking to me—then I remembered my real name was Ed, not Buddy. I was shocked but delighted to help out. I admired her for her beautiful figure, her gliding steps that made her flow from move to move, and her gentle way of talking us through the technical parts of the lessons. I walked out to the dance floor with her, put my right arm just above the small of her back, and my left hand into position to receive her hand to take the proper position for the dance. When the music started, I tightened my right arm around her and pressed forward with my right shoulder to lead her backward, but I was not prepared for the intimacy of this dance. As she leaned back, her pelvis pressed against mine and as I stepped forward, my right leg slipped between her legs far enough for our thighs to touch. As we glided through the first minute of steps, she encouraged me in a soft, assured voice and our legs continued to rub. It was all too much for me and I began to panic, *I'm getting excited and she is going to know how I feel!*

I had never held a woman so intimately, especially a woman that I found so attractive and admired so much. I was so sure she could feel my physical interest because our tight dance hold caused me to rub against the right side of her pelvis. Undeterred, she continued to follow my leads to glide to and fro across the dance floor, but I began to feel anxious because I knew the music would be ending soon. It was then that she acknowledged my condition and showed great mercy as she took the lead, dancing me toward the door and turning me away from the class that was watching so carefully. When we reached the edge of the dance floor, she squeezed my hand and, with a wink, she said, "Thank you, Ed. That was a marvelous demonstration. For your wonderful assistance you are dismissed for the rest of the class."

I was never so grateful to anyone in all my life. She had spared me the embarrassment of the revelation of my condition to the entire class. There had been previous classes in which I had felt the yearnings, but this had been the first time where it had become so overwhelming. She had my admiration from the beginning of the class; but for her mercy and discretion, she had my deepest devotion and loyalty. Hers was one class for which I was never late and which I never cut. However, the air always held a special tension when we danced together after that.

C H A P T E R   8

I Get Caught in the Crossfire

While I was away at college, another civil rights worker was killed in Natchez. On February 27th, Wharlest Jackson, a thirty-six year old Korean War veteran got into his 1958 pickup truck in front of Armstrong Tire and Rubber Company. Things had been going well for Jackson during his tenure at the tire plant where only a few days earlier he had accepted a promotion and a substantial pay raise. The position he had taken had always been held by white men, and he had been warned, under threat of his life, that he should not take the job; this position was only for white men. As secretary/treasurer of the NAACP and a friend of George Metcalfe, he felt it was an opportunity that he could not pass up because it was the right thing to do for his career, his family, and his color. When his overtime shift ended at eight o'clock that Monday, he was anxious to get home to spend time with his wife and children before they went to bed.

After starting his truck, he pulled out onto Kelly Avenue immediately, without allowing the truck to warm up. It was cold and wet, and he just wanted to get home. He drove west on Kelly where it turned into Brenham Avenue. He turned the truck onto Minor Street and headed north for several blocks until he had to stop at the junction at Pine Street. As he was going over the rise toward the end of the street, he flipped the signal on for a left turn. As he coasted down toward Pine Street, he touched the brakes and the truck exploded, tearing off the top of the truck, blowing all the glass out of it, and mortally wounding Wharlest Jackson—the blast blew him completely out of the vehicle. Only a few blocks away, his wife and children heard the powerful blast and turned their attention and concerns immediately in that direction.

I heard that one of the children, seeing the concern on his mother's face, ran into the yard, grabbed his wet bicycle, and peddled down the hill toward where the explosion had occurred. The nine-year old peddled down Woodlawn Avenue toward Pine Street as fast as he could go. When he turned the corner onto Pine Street, he saw people gathering around the familiar looking pickup truck one block away. He continued to peddle toward the scene as the rain intensified. When he reached the site of the explosion, he could hardly see what was going on because it was raining and the electricity had been knocked out when the force of the explosion destroyed a power transformer. There were truck parts and glass all over the streets and in the yards of the two houses on Pine Street opposite Minor. The small parking lot on the corner was littered with debris. He stood transfixed by the noise and confusion on the street, where police and fire department vehicles were arriving with great commotion to secure the scene and attend the injured man lying in the street.

After they put the man in the ambulance and took him away, the young boy rode his bicycle back home to find his mother in tears. "Someone called. It's your daddy." She told him. "They done took him to the hospital." She tried to hold her composure, but was quickly overwhelmed by her deep grief and the pain she saw in her children. When they arrived at the hospital, they were told that Wharlest Jackson had been pronounced dead on arrival.

The next day, after the FBI and police had scoured the scene around the intersection looking for evidence, they removed the truck and debris from the scene. I was told that the young boy again returned to the scene, where he rode his bicycle up and down Minor Street, retracing his father's last moments of life. As he passed in front of one of the houses at the top of the rise on Minor, he saw something in the front yard that looked out of place. He dropped his bike at the edge of the street and timidly approached the yard. There he picked up a shoe and returned to his bicycle, mounted it, and peddled home as quickly as possible. When he got home, he found his mother sitting in the living room, still in shock, and mourning deeply over the loss of her husband. He walked to her timidly, handed her the shoe then stood by her as they wept together.

While I was at college, I heard nothing about the bombing in Natchez. I went home for a weekend right after I finished my mid-term exams: I was glad for the opportunity to spend time with the family. When Daddy got home, he came into my room where he caught me smoking as I sat on the edge of my bed. "Picked up another habit while you were at college, huh? Is that what they are teaching you up there these days? What did you start smoking for anyway?"

"I don't know why. I just felt like I had to smoke. Something was missing and I didn't feel right unless I was around other people that were smoking."

"Well, I'll let you know right now that once you get hooked it is a hard habit to break. I'm really disappointed that you think you're man enough to smoke."

"Sorry, Daddy. I just couldn't help it." That was probably the weakest apology or excuse I'd ever made. Smoking was something that just seemed natural to me. Mama and Daddy had both smoked all my life. Besides, even Superman smoked, so how could it be so wrong?

Since it was Friday night, I wondered how many of our old gang was still at the Natchez Skating Rink. I walked into the back bedroom where my younger brothers were gathered and asked if any of them were interested in going to Natchez to visit Roxie and go skating. Suddenly, I had an enthusiastic entourage. For a moment, I thought that Mama and Daddy were going to go with us, but they decided to stay home with the two youngest boys.

Billy, Jimmy and I loaded into the car and we drove to Natchez. As we passed in front of the tire plant, I noticed that only a few of the cars were parked on their usual spots along the street. Most of the cars were parked inside the guarded gate and there was an armed guard patrolling the area just outside the fence where a few cars were parked near the gate. I thought it was unusual, so I asked Roxie about it when I got to her house. She said, "They been doing that ever since that colored man got blown up over there."

"You mean Metcalfe. That was two years ago. I've been over here a dozen times since then and I ain't never seen that much security over at the gate."

"No. I mean that other colored man. I don't know his name. He took a job that belongs to one of the white men. They warned him and they warned Armstrong, but nobody listened, so they blew him up."

"Where did they bomb him this time? How did they do it?"

"I don't know. It wasn't over at Armstrong like it was last time. It was way down the road somewhere on Pine Street because we couldn't go through there for a couple of days; we had to go out Saint Catherine. We also lost our electricity for most of the night."

"Was it the Klans?"

"I don't know. Jerry and me got away from that stuff when they started all of the bombings around here. We got little ones to take care of now. We can't be doin' any of that no more."

I could feel that she was uncomfortable so I changed the subject and started playing with my two nieces who were always delighted with the rough play and attention of their uncles. After we played for a while, Billy, Jimmy and I walked down to the skating rink where it sounded like things were really hopping. When we walked in, we found out what the celebration was about; Steve Hebert was back from the Army. It was exciting news—he looked so distinguished and grown up in his uniform. Even in his short time in the military, he had earned what looked like a chest full of medals.

After I got a soft drink, I walked over to where Steve was sitting and began to listen. I thought it was strange that he didn't have his skates on. He said, "We were on patrol near the Saigon River. We went down to a region near Phu Hoa Dong and were on our way back when someone tripped a "Bouncing Betty." We could hear it jump, but there wasn't any time to do anything about it. It blew up between me and Pat. It blew me right off my feet. All I could do was wait for someone to help me, because I couldn't move and I couldn't see Pat anymore. When that thing blew up, he was only about six feet away from it. They brought us out of the bush then landed a couple of helicopters to get us all the hell out of there. Pat didn't make it back to base alive. They tried to take care of us at the medical facility at the base camp then they evacuated a bunch of us to the Third Field Hospital in Saigon. After they got us out of Saigon, they sent some of us on to Germany then they brought us back to the good ol' US to the Brooke Army Medical Center where they gave me these." He reached down and knocked on his left calf then on his right thigh, just above his knee. With each knock came a hollow resonance that sent a chill down my spine—my blood suddenly felt cold.

I couldn't even talk to Steve after he knocked on his legs. All I could do was move away from him as quickly as possible because I was so empty of something to say or do to comfort him. Somehow I felt responsible. After I watched him from a distance for a while, I saw how well he was handling his new handicap and it encouraged me to say something to him. I walked over and he said, "Hi, Buddy. I saw you sitting over here while ago. I thought you were going to leave without saying hello."

"I just didn't know what to say, Steve. When you and Pat left, I never thought something like this would happen. I didn't even know about it until I came in tonight. I've been in Monroe going to college, so I haven't been keeping up with things around here. I feel really, really bad about this. I still don't know what to say. It's awful."

"It ain't so bad. I saw a lot worse than this over there. If you are going to college, stay in it and get all you can, then you can go over there with a commission instead of bein' a grunt like we were." He stopped for a moment and stared off in the distant corner of the skating rink. For a minute, I thought he was going to cry, then he spoke softly, "You don't want to go over there, Buddy. Nothing good happens to anyone over there."

"I'm ready to go when they call me. I just hope it isn't anytime soon. We should be kickin' their butts over there."

"Yeah, but we don't know who we are fighting. We wind up fighting women and kids because they send them at us with guns and grenades. Someone who is your ally during the daytime becomes your enemy at night. You can't really trust anyone except the guy who lives in the same hooch with you. That was the worst part of being over there. You just don't know who to trust."

When I said goodbye and walked away from Steve, I felt revived on one hand and emptied on the other. It was good to see him back again, but I wish it weren't under such sad and perplexing circumstances. In talking with Steve, I had not come to grips with the reality of Pat's absence. He was so young; how could he be dead already? How was Steve going to make it without his legs? He was a great skater; now he could hardly stand.

When the skating rink closed, Billy, Jimmy and I walked the short distance to the top of the hill. Neither of them seemed to be fazed by what had happened to Pat and Steve, but I felt as if I were right on the edge of reality. *Is this what my future is going to be? What kind of future is this for my brothers? No one deserves to have his life ripped away at such a young age.* I likened it to World War II; *someone is trying to take someone else's freedom away. Someone is being oppressed, and it is our duty as free people to make sure that others remained free.* As I walked along, the irony of growing up in the South hit me. *We are fighting in Vietnam for someone's freedom, and here in Mississippi and Louisiana fighting is going on to make sure that certain people didn't have those freedoms.* Then I had to ask myself another question, *"Are colored men being drafted to go fight in Vietnam also?"* I honestly didn't know the answer.

When my brothers and I returned home on Saturday, I asked Daddy if he had known the man from Armstrong that had been killed by the bomb. His answer shocked me, "I knew him. He deserved what he got because he took a job that should have gone to a white man. That job should've never gone to a nigger."

"Didn't he have the qualifications for the job; the same as the other men? Who was he anyway?"

"It was Wharlest Jackson. He was warned that the job was a white man's job; white men like me and Jerry and Link. He was warned. He got talked to, he got telephone calls, and he got a letter tellin' him that he better not take that job. Nobody can say that he wasn't warned. His managers also got the same kind of warnings. He was not supposed to get that job. There were lots of us tire builders that had more seniority than him. What does he know that makes him better for the job than me?"

I was stunned. I had to think about it for a while before I responded, "I don't know. I didn't even know the man. You're the one who knew him and I thought you told me one time that Jackson was a good man; a good tire builder."

"That doesn't give him the right to hold that job. That job was supposed to go to a white man. Probably someone you know. Now there IS a white man in the job."

I shot back before I thought about it, "Anyone I know?"

"Boy, you don't know what it is like to have to work for a living. You don't know what it means to someone to be passed over for a nigger. You don't know how bad it can get for some of those ol' boys that have worked there for their whole lives and they are still doin' the same job year after year. We are the men who made that company. We are the ones who set up the union over there so everyone would have protected jobs. We are the ones who fought for it for all those years and we are not going to let some uppity nigger come along and take food out of our mouths. We know it and he knew it, too. That ain't gonna happen in my lifetime."

I couldn't stop what I said next, "Daddy, it is gonna happen in my lifetime, and in yours. Change is coming. It is already that way all over the United States, and we are only delaying the inevitable. Do you think this little town and this little state can stand up to the US Government? It ain't like this all over."

"Yeah, and look at the problems they're havin' in all those other places. The niggers have tore up their section of Los Angeles, they are tearing up good businesses and cities all over. They don't know how good they got it. They don't appreciate what they got and they ain't willing to work to make it better for themselves."

"That sounds exactly like what Jackson was trying to do. He was tryin' to make it better for himself until someone decided he didn't' deserve to make it better for himself."

With that, I thought I should leave the room while I was still standing upright. I went back into the shop and put together a couple of table tops for a coffee table and the matching end tables. Sometimes I hated that workshop, but at other times I could lose myself in a project—especially if it were an upright gun cabinet with glass doors.

I returned to college and settled into my usual routine of class, work, study, distractions and more distractions. I gained more confidence in my art and dancing skills. I had become Vicki's favored partner for instructional purposes and demonstrations. At last, I was a teacher's pet! At the end of the semester, she told me that she had never seen such improvement in any of her dancers and that she was hoping that I would return for the fall semester. I yelped at the prospect of returning for this. It was the first time I heard her giggle.

I didn't do as well in my other classes. I hadn't turned in all of the required projects for chemistry and art, so I got incompletes. I hadn't understood the requirements or procedures for making up missed assignments. My ignorance and procrastination would prove to be my undoing.

When I returned home for the summer session, I knew I was going to be busy. I needed to earn enough money to get me through a couple of semesters of college. I knew that Daddy would want me to help out with the workshop also, something I wasn't really looking forward to. Jimmy, John and Larry were all very glad to see me home for another reason; they were hoping I would do more Klan related traveling with Daddy and they could take a rest. Billy surprised everyone and joined the US Navy on his eighteenth birthday during the second week of June. He had gone to the recruiters and filled out all of the necessary paperwork in May, but his signature hadn't been legal yet. When he met with the recruiters on his birthday, he signed all the paperwork and received his tickets for travel to San Diego for boot camp. When he got home, Daddy was furious with him for what he had done. Billy made it very clear that there was nothing that Daddy could do about it because he was now eighteen and Daddy had no say in the matter. He showed us his tickets. He would be taking a bus to Monroe, then he would fly to San Diego on a midnight flight through Dallas. Daddy took him to the bus station in Ferriday the following day and he was gone.

While I had been away at college, Daddy kept my brothers busy working on Klan materials, attending Klan rallies, and driving with him as he traveled about the state organizing and recruiting. They were right; I had hardly settled in when Daddy asked me to drive with him to a rally they were conducting in Lincoln Parish, near Ruston, Louisiana. I told him that I would be glad to drive for him, but I would not "robe up," sell souvenirs, nor distribute material, and I really didn't care to attend the lighting of the cross. He said, "Since you've been living in Monroe for the past year, you know the area better than any of us, and we don't know where this place is yet. We are doing a rally there to recruit and make those people up there understand that we are still around."

Before the rally I took as many deliveries as I could for PedCo, running diesel, gasoline, and other petroleum products to oil rigs all over Louisiana and Mississippi. They also sent me down to Grande Isle, Louisiana to help set up delivery vessels for servicing offshore drilling rigs. After I returned from Grande Isle, I found out that the Klan rally was going to be conducted during the fourth week of June to coincide with the peach festival which would be celebrated in Lincoln Parish during the same period. Daddy had us all busy during the last couple of weeks preceding the rally.

In the week prior to the rally, Daddy met with local Klan members at the King Hotel in Ferriday and the Shamrock Inn in Vidalia. He was also recruiting help from Jonesville, Clayton and Waterproof. He had me pick up the latest edition of *The Fiery Cross* from the printer in Vidalia and some new souvenirs, like Klan insignias and medallions, from the supplier in Natchez. I felt we were being watched wherever we went. Maybe I was feeling a bit paranoid, but I was sure I had been followed by at least one vehicle when I went from Vidalia to Natchez, then by another when I returned home. I didn't recognize either of the vehicles as those of the FBI, but they could have changed the vehicles they were using while I had been away. One of the cars had Adams County tags and was a little older than any of the cars I had seen the FBI use, so I was somewhat concerned that they were members of one of the other Klan factions looking for a chance to sabotage the rally.

On Saturday, June 24, we drove to Winnfield and turned north on Highway 167 toward Ruston. Just before we got to Ruston, we reached a sign with a Klan insignia directing us into a field at the left of the highway. I carefully pulled off of the road and onto a dirt road leading us to a large gate in a four strand barbed wire fence. When we drove up to the gate, a large man opened it and waved us through, pointing us to an area at the back of the field. I drove up to an open tent and unloaded the printed material and souvenirs onto a couple of tables that they had set up. I also unloaded a cooler full of soft drinks and water, then sat around watching everyone making preparations for the big event. When everything else was ready, Daddy put his robe and helmet on; I took the car back to the front of the field and parked it just outside the gate.

The temperature had dropped to a very comfortable level so I got out of the car and climbed onto the top of the large gate. After having to jump off it twice so that people could go through, I climbed up on the large wooden post at the end of the gate and watched the activity in the field and in the parking lot. As I watched the parking lot, I noticed two men wandering around with cameras and clipboards. Occasionally they snapped a picture of a car then recorded the license number of the other cars. They occasionally peered into the windows of the vehicles and snapped pictures or made notes of what they observed. I was surprised that there were no Klansmen posted in the parking lot to act as some sort of security.

I maintained my seat atop the post until the men worked their way over to where I waited. One of the men, curious about my observation post, walked over and said, "What are you doing out here? Why aren't you out there parading around like everyone else?"

"It's not my thing. This is my daddy's way of jousting with windmills. I drive for him and help with odd jobs and errands, but I am not interested in any of that stuff. Most of the men I know that are in some of these groups are not much more than thugs. I don't want anything to do with them."

The other man was looking into the windows of Daddy's black Barracuda when I spotted him writing notes, "The car is open, go ahead and take a look. There is nothing in there illegal or interesting." Then I said jokingly, "I took all the bombs, guns, and dirty pictures out and put them in the tent at the other end of the field. I am sure I can get you some samples if you are interested."

"I'll bet you could. So this Barracuda belongs to you?"

"No. I wouldn't own that piece of doo-doo. I own a '59 Chevy that will blow that piece of crap into the weeds."

"Is this what you drove here today?"

"Yes sir. It's Daddy's car."

"Who is your daddy? What is his interest in all this?"

"Ed Blanche. He is the man standing up there at the other end of the field with the red robes and green trim. He's the Grand Titan."

"I know your daddy. Hell, I've even been to your house – a couple of times. I thought I'd met all his kids. How come I haven't seen you before?"

"I go to college over at NLSC in Monroe, so I've been gone most of the last year. When I'm not in college, I'm working so I'm just not at home much."

"So you don't have anything to do with all this KKK stuff? Why not?"

I thought the man was probably an FBI agent. Even though I wasn't sure who was questioning me, I couldn't help but be honest. "I don't think it is right. I don't know what is right, but I know this is not it."

He walked closer to the fence and looked up at me, "Have you ever thought about joining the KKK so you could keep track of what's going on?"

"Why would I want to do that? I get more than enough information from Daddy and all his cronies. We hear them talkin' all the time. I've gone to meetings, I've helped with printing and mimeographing, and I've heard more little Klan secrets than I really care to know."

"You could really help us out here. You could be collecting information about all these Klan activities and feeding that back to us so we could keep a better eye on things."

I shot back a very sarcastic, "Yeah. Why don't I just stick a gun to my head and pull the trigger. It would be quicker and less painful. Heck, if those boys were to catch me telling you ANYTHING, they'd take me out and beat me to death, especially if I was in the Klans."

"Well, what could you tell us now? You don't really have to be part of the Klans, just let us know what is going on now and then. There ain't no way they would ever know. We would keep the information secret. Nobody would ever know."

I jumped down from the post, walked over to the car, and reached into one of the stacks of paper in a box behind the rear seat. After I found the edition of *The Fiery Cross* that had the pictures from the Selma march, I handed it to him defiantly and said, "Yeah, like you did with these?"

"You mean the pictures? We didn't have anything to do with that. That was all the Klan's doing."

"No sir. The FBI gave those pictures to the police or sheriffs over in Natchez, and they gave it to the Klans. They also gave them the story that goes along with the picture of Viola, or that's what they say."

"Where did you hear that? Nobody in the FBI would ever do anything like that. They'd get fired for leaking any of that stuff."

It was then that a new voice joined our conversation—another agent. "Agent Reese, he's not talking about us. What he's talkin' about could be out of Counter Intelligence. They were down there and they did bring back a lot of pictures. They were tracking a number of the activists from the north that were headed down here for demonstrations and marches."

The agent who had been talking to me turned to the others and said, "That was not us. That was a different organization. FBI investigators would never do anything like that."

I was unimpressed with his protests, "Yeah, and the United Klans of America, and the Original KKK, and the White Knights of the KKK, and the KKK are all different organizations, too. They would never think of doing anything like that either; they NEVER share information, or talk to the police, or the FBI."

Agent Reese looked up from the paper and said, "I think we've attracted someone's attention; he's headed this way."

I quickly took the paper and put it back into the box. I got out and stood next to the car where the agents were waiting when I recognized the man walking toward us. "Oh, shit. It's Jackson Smith. I had a run-in with him at the Liberty Park rally. He is a real prick. He's already threatened to kick my butt; this should do the trick."

I had no sooner got the words out of my mouth when the big man started, "What are you doing out here, you little turd-tapper? You oughta be in there where we can keep an eye on you. You ain't nothin' but a little snoopin' stool pigeon. I'm gonna kick you ass yet. And who the hell are you people?"

Agent Reese was thinking quickly, "Well, Mister Smith, that's what we were just thinking. We are here for the FBI and this boy took exception to our taking pictures of his daddy's car. If you can believe it, this runt was trying to get our film, even after we were kind enough to give him back some papers we found out here in one of the cars."

The other agent piped up, "We were about to kick his butt ourselves. I don't need some upstart to come out here and interrupt me while I am doing my job."

The agents turned as if they were leaving when Agent Reese turned and said, "Mister Blanch, we WILL be in contact with you. We'll probably be seeing you in the future too, Mister Smith."

"Hey, you little shit, how did they know your name?"

"I told them my name, Mister Smith. Now the question is, how did they know YOUR name? You're not the one they've been talkin' to over in Franklin County are you? If they find it as easy to get information from those boys over there as the Adams County and Concordia Parish members do, you got someone over there talkin' big time."

"If you weren't Ed's boy, I'd kick the shit out of you right here and now. You better know your place, boy."

I was scared to death, but I wasn't about to let him know it. Besides, I was still emboldened by the presence of the two FBI agents and the sight of two familiar faces coming across the field. "Don't let that stop you. The only witnesses you have are the other two guys that want to kick my butt already and those two coming across the field, and you already heard two of them say they wanted to kick my butt too. The two comin' across the field would probably back you up too; they're both policemen. Neither one of them like me very much."

Jackson's scowl deepened. "One of these days you're gonna open your mouth to the wrong person at the wrong time and git your ass kicked so bad. I might just be the man to do it."

I'd had enough. I turned to walk toward the two men coming through the field when I shot back at him, "Yeah, I know. I'll get my butt kicked, and you'll eat shit and die."

He reached out and grabbed my shoulder. "I got my eye on you. I can get you almost any time I want, you little piece of shit. And I heard about what you did to those other boys that were keeping track of you. I know you carry a gun with you. Where is it now?"

"It's close enough, but I really don't need it right now. I have a feelin' you're fixin' to leave anyway."

One of the men coming through the gate greeted me, "Hey, Buddy. What's goin' on out here?"

"I'm just tryin' to get my butt kicked tonight, but I don't know who is gonna do it; this honorable Franklin County White Knight or one of those FBI agents out there. They've both threatened to do it in the last five minutes."

"I don't really blame any of them; sometimes I want to kick your butt, too. But I don't think anyone is going to get their butts kicked tonight. Everyone knows the Klans don't like violence, especially at our rallies where we are recruiting." He turned to his companion. "Ain't that right, Jim?"

"Yes sir, Mister B. I don't think we need this kind of rabble around here. So, Mister Smith, you and your FBI friends over there can leave any time you feel like it. I can't believe you Franklin County boys would come over here and try to stir up trouble at one of our rallies. What ever will the Grand Dragon think of this? Jackson, do us all a favor and take off before we make a fuss big enough to bring that whole group out here."

After Smith and the two agents drove off, and Mister B was sure they were gone, he turned to me and gave me a warning, "Buddy, you watch your back out here. Those are some very dangerous characters you were getting tangled up with. I've seen some of Jackson's work before; it wasn't pretty. Why don't you just climb back up on your perch where we can keep an eye on you and we'll go back in for the lighting."

"Yes sir. Thanks, Mister B. I'll do that. I'll just keep an eye on things out here like I was doin' before."

"You do that."

I climbed back up on the gate then slid off onto the post to assume my watch over the field. Everything went much like the rally in Natchez went a year and a half earlier, except this time the cross didn't burn in two and fall over.

Finally, after the evening's cross fire was put out and most of the participants had gone, I drove the car back into the field to pick up Daddy and the materials that were left over. After we were loaded up, I drove us out of the field and onto the highway with a parade of other cars headed south. I was first to break the silence, "How many people were there tonight? It looked like a three or four hundred."

"There were four hundred twenty-three signed up on the sheet, and we got about thirty new member prospects tonight. One of the sheriff's boys said you stood up to Jackson Smith out at the gate tonight. Boy, I don't want you to go within a hundred feet of that man again; he is dangerous."

"I didn't start any of that, Daddy. He came out there while I was trying to find out what the two FBI agents were up to."

"Jim didn't mention the FBI. What were they doing out here?"

"They were taking pictures and writing down license numbers of all the cars in the parking area. They were also looking into the cars to see what they could see inside them. When they came over and started looking in the Barracuda, I started talkin' to 'em. They were tryin' to recruit me to join the Klans for them, but I told 'em I didn't trust them any more than I trusted some of the men over in the Franklin County klaverns. I gave them a copy of *The Fiery Cross* with all the Selma pictures in it then asked them where they thought the pictures came from. They acted like they didn't know anything about that stuff."

"How did Jackson get involved with all that?"

"While I was talkin' to the FBI, he came out and interjected himself into the discussion. He took it upon himself to accuse me of being a stool pigeon for the FBI. The FBI agents helped me out there and pretended that they were also upset with me for meddlin' in their investigations. I wasn't really afraid because the FBI agents hung around until after Mister Smith left."

"Well that's good, but just be careful when you decide to stand up against someone like Jackson. You watch your back all the time from now on. His kind are just as likely to knife you in the back as not. He and that group that he belongs to are one of the roughest bunches around."

"Yes sir. I will be careful. I think it was some of his bunch that bumped me on the highway that day. He knew something about it, because he mentioned it during the fray."

Daddy lit another cigarette and sat silent for a while. I could feel him looking at me through the darkness. "Just watch your back. Hey, when you get to Winfield, stop at the café there so we can get something to eat."

We stopped and got something to eat, joining several other groups of Klansmen that had pulled off at the same stop. It seems that they all knew about the confrontation with Jackson Smith. They didn't know the whole truth about the FBI agents that were present. They really did think I had also tangled with the agents. "Damn, boy. I didn't know you had it in you; taking on the FBI and Jackson Smith in one night. I wouldn't even take on either one of them."

I spent the rest of the meal reveling in my new acclaim and laughing to myself about the irony of the situation. If they knew the truth, they'd probably be a bit more concerned about how they talked around me. I really could be an FBI informant if I wanted to, but how could I do that? These were people that I had grown up with; people I had known most of my life. These were people I loved.

CHAPTER 9

The Greeting

After my confrontation with Jackson, I was afraid to go to Natchez anymore, and there was nowhere in Concordia Parish where I could entertain myself without being under the scrutiny of Deputies Delaughter and Peele, so I spent most of my time working at PedCo. When they didn't have enough work to keep me busy, I stayed at home and worked in the woodshop making coffee tables, gun cabinets, and playhouses. I was housebound and went stir crazy very quickly. At one of the homes where I delivered a gun cabinet for Daddy, I was delighted for the chance to talk to a girl I knew from high school. Diane had auburn hair and big, beautiful brown eyes that smiled when she talked. She was only a junior in high school, so I was a little concerned about asking her out for a date. She opened the door for me when she walked me back to my truck. When we got to the truck, she stepped up onto the running board and looked in the window, "I heard about your truck. This is groovy. Can I sit in it?"

"Sure." I helped her down then opened the door.

She stepped back onto the running board and launched herself up onto the seat with a giggle. "Take me for a spin. I like it. It feels so big. C'mon, take me for a spin."

"OK."

I hopped up into the truck, turned the ignition on, and pressed the starter button.

The V8 sputtered to a start and settled into a romping idle. I backed us out of the driveway and headed up the street toward the highway. When I turned onto Highway 84, she said, "Git on it a little."

I jumped onto the accelerator just hard enough to haze the rear tires then power shifted it into second hard enough to chirp the tires. She giggled and I eased up on the throttle and let the roar of the engine settle into a soft rumble. She grabbed my arm and hugged it, leaned her head on my shoulder and said, "I love it."

As I took her home, we talked freely. She was so delightful I asked her for a date without even flinching. She accepted. When I dropped her off at her driveway, I got out and walked her to her door where she leaned into me and gave me a long, soft hug that warmed me right to my core. I was certainly looking forward to spending time with her!

When Saturday came, I rushed home from work and got dressed quickly, brushing my teeth and then combing my hair, careful to use the required amount of Vitalis brand hair tonic to make a perfect part. I ran out of the house in a haze of goodbyes and have funs. I started to get into my '59 Chevy, then I remembered her reaction to the truck – truck it was. I threaded my way through the back streets of Ridgecrest until I reached her house. When I pulled into her driveway, I killed the engine, jumped out and listened as I walked to her door. It made me feel good to hear her excited voice on the other side of the door as she put on her final touches. I rang the doorbell, and I heard at least three voices ring out in excitement, "He's here!"

When she came to the door, I almost jumped out of my shoes. She looked ravishing in her flowered summer dress that hugged her tiny waist and accented her busty figure. The family members all introduced themselves as I stood nervously in the doorway. After the introductions, she grabbed my hand and walked me out the door and to the truck. As we drove down her street toward the highway, she asked, "Where are we going?"

"The new James Bond movie is showing in Natchez, so I thought it would be fun to see. Do you like James Bond?"

"I don't know. I've never seen any James Bond movies. I've never heard of him."

"This will be a real treat. The movie is *You Only Live Twice*. Bond is a British super spy created by Ian Fleming. I've only seen one of his movies and it was great. I really like what he does with the names of the women in the books, but I don't know if they will do that in the movies"

"What's that?"

"He gives them great …" I realized that there was no way for me to complete the sentence or explain the name game without making sexually expletive remarks. I tried anyway, "He names the women using innuendos; making names out of the names of… uh… women's private parts."

"Like what?"

"Uh…" I realized there was no way for me to get around it, so I blurted out a few of the names, "Sylvia Trench, Pussy Galore, Octopussy. I've read them all. You know, Fleming was a real spy in World War II." I tried to distract her with some trivial information.

"Pussy Galore! That's funny. Sylvia Trench; what does that mean?"

I was fighting my embarrassment and kicking myself for bringing up the subject, but she seemed perfectly at ease. "You know … Trench, like a woman's …"

"Oh, I get it," she cut me off. "Octopussy? That's punny."

She made a pun and I was in love. How silly! It felt good to have a girl be so engaging to take the pressure off. The rest of the evening went very well. During the movie, she giggled with glee at some of the antics and stunts; she held my hand and rubbed my arm. After the movie we drove back to Ferriday to The Sandwich Bar where most of the kids from the high school hung out. It was a circular building with a gravel parking lot all the way around it. When you pulled into any of the parking spots, a waitress would come out to take your order, then return later with your food and drink. I started around the parking lot when I saw a spot near the front door of the building. I pulled in and parked when I spotted Daddy's car parked around the other side of the building. He was sitting with his back to the door, and it looked as if his feet were up in Mandy's lap. I didn't notice Jill sitting in the back seat until she lit a cigarette. I made some remark to Diane about Mandy and Jill but she didn't respond. When the waitress came to the window, I was in the process of ordering when I noticed Daddy get out of his car and start walking toward my door. When he got to my door, he was in a rage about something. "What are you doing here? Don't you know the reputation this place has?"

"I just took Diane to the movies and we were getting something to eat. I didn't get to eat dinner tonight."

"Well if I ever catch you around here again, I'll whup your ass. You don't need to be around this kind of place. People come around here to get drugs and drink. Is that why you are here?"

He actually climbed up on the running board of the truck and had his head stuck through my window as he made accusations and screamed threats at me. I could only sit in stunned silence as he ranted and raged at me through the window. I had no idea why he was so jacked up and angry. I could feel Diane's hands tighten around my arm, so I turned toward her just enough to try to comfort her. As I turned away, Daddy reached in and grabbed my arm, "Don't you turn your back on me while I'm talking' to you."

He continued to rant until I was almost to the point of tears. I didn't know how I kept it together. I simply said, "I'll see you at home Daddy," then I started the truck and put it in reverse. He jumped off the running board and backed away from the truck. As I drove out of the parking lot I could still hear him yelling at me.

I drove Diane home in silence. When we got to her home, I got out and walked her to her door where she grabbed both of my hands and held them together for a moment. "I sure am glad you aren't like that. My daddy and mama both get like that sometimes. I feel like I could just run away."

"I am so very, very sorry about that. I don't have any idea what set him off, unless he was worried that I caught him sitting out there playing footsies with that whore. I've seen him blow up before, but not like that. I really apologize for that. You shouldn't ever have to see anything like that. I'm sorry I didn't say anything back there; I just couldn't." It was all I could do to make that apology without breaking into tears. After I said it, I stood still for a moment and shook uncontrollably.

"Don't worry about it. You did the right thing. He didn't look like he was ready to do anything but fight." She stepped up to me and wrapped her arms around me very tight and just held me for a moment; the shaking subsided. It was then that I realized how short she was; as I stood there, her head only came up to my chest. We started gently rocking side to side as if we were performing a slow dance. Finally, I felt I was going to cry, so I kissed her on the forehead and turned to my truck.

I drove home along the back streets of Ridgecrest, backtracking my drive over. When I reached the bridge between Ridgecrest and Crestview, I stopped and sat for a minute to try to compose myself. It was a futile attempt; I only shook harder and started crying. I drove home, parked my truck, and went directly to bed trying to figure out what I should do about what had happened. I fell asleep before I had any ideas. I was emotionally spent.

For several days after the conflict, Daddy and I avoided each other. I stayed at PedCo as much as possible. I called and talked to Diane several times over the next couple of weeks, but couldn't bring myself to go see her; I felt completely humiliated.

The letter that I got on the following Monday didn't help matters for me. It stated that I had been put on academic suspension because I had failed two courses and my grades were not high enough to carry me. I would have to appeal the suspension before registration for the fall semester began.

During the first week of July, the Klans were busy collecting information and spreading propaganda regarding the riots that had been occurring in Tampa Bay, Florida and Buffalo, New York. With the information from the earlier riots through the year, they were having a field day. They had pictures from each riot, each intended to accent the violence, senseless looting, and destruction of the area around and within the riots. Daddy tried to enlist me to help out with some of the documentation, but I declined, letting him know my work schedule at PedCo and at the shop; we had orders to get out. I also told him that I had to go to school on Monday, July 11th, to appeal my suspension and get my eligibility reinstated so I could attend fall semester. In reality, I could hardly wait to get back to college. Now I realized why I liked being away from home so much and why I did so poorly when I was away. It was a heavy burden to bear.

When he realized I had to go to Monroe anyway he said, "Hey Buddy. I need you to go by Standard Lumber Company when you go to Monroe. They have some table legs on sale up there and I need you to pick up a bunch of those like we have for the coffee table sets, and I need for you to pick me up some for kitchen tables. I have several orders coming up for the tables for Christmas. I also need you to pick up a roll of that felt stuff to line the gun cabinets with. Just talk to Mister Payne and tell him to put it all on my account. I'll give you the numbers for how many of each kind of leg after I figure it out."

I agreed to go to the lumber company, though I really didn't want to. The lumber company was a big Klan hangout and a front for the distribution of Klan material. I had been there many times with Daddy as he made his rounds during the organization of klaverns in the area and when we helped out with recruiting drives. We stopped at the lumber company any time we were in the Monroe area, dropping off, picking up, or just catching up on the latest news. When there were any Klan activities in the area, they used the lumber company as a staging area for material that would be needed. They always had several crosses lashed together, wrapped in burlap and ready to be burned.

Mister Payne, who owned and managed the lumber yard, smoked and chewed tobacco so he always smelled of stale smoke and carried a disgusting spit cup into which he would occasionally drool from a wad of tobacco in his mouth. He was very good about remembering the names of the Klansmen who, like Daddy, would stop by when they traveled through the area. He was also an enigma to me because he seemed to have a keen sense of justice, dealing fairly with both black and white customers, but he believed fervently in the separation of the races and he was ready to do anything to keep things status quo. I usually enjoyed my visits with Mister Payne, but I did not enjoy the company of some of the men that stopped by while I was there. They always seemed to be on a mission of hate or bent on putting someone back in their place.

The Monday morning I was to go to Monroe, Daddy stopped by my room to awaken me. He handed me a sheet of paper with list of table legs and other supplies that he wanted me to bring back from Monroe. "He has couple of other things he is sending down here to us also. He'll have it ready for you by the time you get there."

I drove to school with what felt like a lead weight in my stomach. When I got there I really didn't know where I should start. After having met with the registrar's office and the dean's assistant, I filled out a couple of reams of paperwork to formalize my appeal and re-establish my financial aid. When I turned the paperwork in, they told me to come back after three o'clock to present my appeal to the dean.

Since I had several hours to spare, I decided to take care of the business that was awaiting me at Standard Lumber. On my way across town, I stopped and got something to eat and enjoyed a cold soft drink. When I got to the lumberyard, I parked at the far end of the building near the load out gate. When I got out of the car, I saw Mister Payne standing at the service counter toward the middle of the store. When he saw me coming toward the door, he came outside to meet me, "Hey, Buddy. What are you doin' up here? College classes don't start for another month."

"I messed up last semester, Mister Payne, so I have to appeal my suspension from college. I really messed up bad. I hope they let me back in because you know what is gonna happen if I don't get back in."

"Yeah. They'll have you over there killin' those little slope-headed gooks in Vietnam. How is your daddy takin' all this? How is he doin' anyway?"

"He is doin' okay, but I can't seem to do anything right for him these days. We seem to fight like cats and dogs lately. We really do have a generation gap between us. He is doing well, but he's real busy these days with all that Klan stuff goin' on over there. Every time I turn around we have some FBI agent over at the house asking him questions about something that just happened or something that they are afraid is going to happen. I'm really afraid he is gonna get into some real trouble some day."

"Oh, his heart is in the right place. He wants what is best for you boys; he really is a good man. You know, he is the one man I would trust with my life. I don't know another man in the whole state with the integrity of your daddy." Then he got back to business, "If you open up the back of your car, we can just put that stuff your daddy wanted right back there with the other stuff you need. He told me last week that he wanted some of those table legs that we just got in."

We walked over toward the other end of the building where there were several large wooden bins set right against the large plate glass windows at the front of the store. "Those over there are the ones you need for your coffee tables; these bins over here have the long legs for tables. They already have the screws in them, so all you have to do is put a mounting block under the table top to screw them in."

I walked over to where the bins held the longer table legs and picked one up; inspecting the taper on the leg for consistency and the three-inch square top with a large wood screw installed into the end of it. Mister Payne said, "Those are all machine lathed from a template, so they are all identical."

I picked up another one of the legs and stood facing the building as I held them at eye level to compare the lathing. Just as I was about to reach for another, something hit me at the back of my knees hard enough to knock me off my feet.

Mister Payne blurted out excitedly, "Hey, what was that for, Jackson? You coulda hurt that boy."

I immediately recognized the big white Cadillac that had just struck me. My blood ran cold when I heard the big man's voice. "That's just what I intended to do anyway. This mouthy, loud-mouthed little bastard has back-talked me one too many times this year. He got me kicked out of the rally over at Ruston."

"I don't think you ought to be messin' with him. That's Ed Blanch's boy. He's here mindin' his own business. He ain't done nothing' to you."

"Not here he ain't, but he done crossed me twice now, and I ain't lettin' no little bastard disrespect me like that, I don't care whose kid he is."

While they were talking I picked myself up and turned toward Jackson, "I didn't get you kicked out of anywhere. You got yourself kicked out by acting like you're acting right now. Besides, if you can remember anything past your morning coffee today, you might recall that you started both incidents before, just like you're starting this one. I don't want no trouble with you."

"Leave him alone, Jackson. That boy ain't even half your size."

Mister Payne was right. Jackson Smith was nearly six foot four and weighed about two hundred seventy pounds; I was five foot eight and weighed about one hundred thirty pounds—soaking wet. I turned and started to walk away from him, but he reached to grab my shoulder and spun me back around to face him. He took his right forefinger and poked me in the chest, "You been talkin' to the wrong people, boy. You been tellin' the Feds what we been doin' and who has been doin' it. The only boys in Natchez that trust you work for the law—only the law. You been shootin' off your mouth all over the place."

"What are you talkin' about? I haven't talked to any of the FBI agents or haven't seen any of the police in Natchez since they held that rally over in Ruston. I don't know where you're getting your information, but you need to find another source."

Smith continued to poke his finger into my chest as he continued, "You gonna call me a liar, boy. I seen you talkin' to those feds over in Ruston that night, then I heard some more talk that they been comin' by your house when your daddy ain't there. They been gittin' too much stuff pointin' to some of those boys over in Franklin and Adams; some of that stuff is stuff only we should know. I know how you listen in on all the talk at them Klan meetings over there."

I could feel my face flush and the tears coming to my eyes because I could see no way out of my situation, so I felt I had nothing to lose. I took my forefinger and poked him in his chest as I shot back, "Before you go around accusing people of talkin' to the FBI or spying on the Klans, you need to get your facts straight. I haven't been to any of the meetings since Ruston; I don't know and don't care about any of those assholes over in Franklin County Klans or anything they've been doing. And if you knew what you're talkin' about, you'd know that the FBI has been snoopin' around my house ever since my daddy became the Grand Titan. I never told them anything at my house, I never told them anything where I work, I never told them anything at college, and I didn't tell them anything at the rally in Ruston."

Towering over me like a tree, Jackson snarled, "You nigger-lovin' little bastard." When he hit me, I reeled back into the large wooden bin and crumpled into a heap on a bed of table legs. The square, unlathed ends of the legs cut into me everywhere; I could feel a trickle of blood running down the back of my neck. When I looked up, the bright July sun temporarily blinded me as I slipped to the edge of unconsciousness. Panic overwhelmed me.

After I lay there for a moment trying to regain my wits, I tried to lift my way out of the bin. Every move I made hurt because of the square ends of the legs and the screws protruding from the tops cut into my shoulder, arms and hands.

Mister Payne was yelling at Jackson, "What the hell did you do that for? We're gonna have the whole Monroe Police Department over here in about two minutes. That boy didn't do anything to you that you didn't do to him first."

"I ain't lettin' no boy poke at me like that. He needs to learn some respect."

I finally worked my way out of the bin and found my feet. As I stood at the corner of the bin, I steadied myself on one of the long, tapered legs and realized how badly I had bitten my tongue when I had fallen back into the bin. Smith was so busy trying to justify his attack on me that he had not noticed me climb out of the bin. I stood there for a moment before my anger boiled over and the tears welled into my eyes so badly I could hardly see. Now I knew what the chickens felt like when I used to corner them just before I caught them as a kid; they always fought back. With my mouth full of blood, I called out, "Hey, Jackson."

Even before he turned around, he started, "That's Mister Smith to you boy."

When he turned to face me, I spit the whole mouthful of blood right at his face. He recoiled while I reached back and took a baseball grip on the table leg. He regained his footing and made a lunge at me. I stepped toward the clear spot next to the bin and took a wild swing which Jackson tried to dodge by jumping backward with both feet. The square end of the leg missed him, but the screw tore into his shirt and his side, then got hung in his shirt. I tried to pull the leg away so I could take another swing but he grabbed it with his left hand before I got it away. He pulled on the leg hard enough to pull me off the ground and he put himself off balance badly enough to have to step back to keep from falling. I lunged forward with all my weight on the leg, stabbing him in the side of his rib cage and knocking him completely over. I twisted the table leg and pulled it away with all my might—it came free. I knew that if he got up, I would be beaten to death. I made one swing that swept his legs to the side, then I stepped in toward him as he rolled over to get himself up. I chopped down into his back with the square end of the leg as if I were splitting firewood.

Jackson swore and threatened me with what he was going to do to me after he got up. Each time he said something, I hit him again. When he tried to get up again, I took a baseball swing at his butt, catching him squarely on the back of his thigh; he went down on his face. I walked around to his head and stomped on his right hand with all my weight then spit another mouthful of blood at him. I stabbed the screw at the end of the leg into his right shoulder and leaned on it enough to let him know I was serious. "Stay down, because if you move again, I'm gonna ram this thing into you right up to the wood and then I'm gonna beat you to a bloody pulp."

Jackson lay quietly on the hot pavement as long as I leaned on the leg. After a minute or two, Mister Payne walked over to me and said, "Give me the leg, Buddy. He's whipped; let him git up now."

"If I let him up, he's just gonna come after me again."

"No he won't. We won't let him. What do you plan to do? Stand here for the rest of the day?"

"I will if I have to. This asshole ain't never hittin' me again. I'll beat him to death first."

Mister Payne reached over for the leg, so I lifted it off of Jackson's shoulder and walked over toward the building where I noticed the reflection of the crowd that had gathered around us during the scuffle. In the distance, I could hear the sound of an approaching siren as it wailed sadly. *God, help me. I am in so much trouble. They will never let me get away with this. Oh, God. What have I done?*

By the time the first police car pulled into the parking lot, I was a nervous wreck. I leaned on the leg and awaited my fate, sobbing and shaking uncontrollably. I still couldn't make myself turn and face the crowd in the parking lot. I watched the reflection as the policeman walked up and started talking to Mister Payne about what had happened. I could only hear a part of the conversation though I could see him gesturing toward me several times then back to Jackson who was now propped against the front fender of his car.

The policeman turned to Jackson and looked him over. "You're beat up pretty bad. That little boy did a job on you. We're gonna have to get you over to the emergency room to get you stitched and get that hand x-rayed. It looks like you got at least one broke finger."

The comments enraged Smith, "I'm gonna kill that little son-of-a-bitch."

"I think you better leave that boy alone or else I'm gonna take you to the jail instead of to the hospital."

One of the men in the crowd blurted out, "Those boys over in Adams are gonna love this when they hear that Jackson Smith was done in by a boy that can't even drink yet. Hey, Jack. You want me to hold him so you can beat him up?"

Someone chortled in the crowd.

Why can't people just keep their mouths shut, I thought. *Ain't this enough already?*

Too late—the comment put Smith back into a rage. He stood up and charged at me before anyone could react. I think I screamed when I saw his reflection coming at me in the large plate glass window—it was like a mirror in the bright sunlight. I tried to step aside, but was trapped by the large bin so I spun around with the leg and took the best swing I could as I fell over into the bin. The leg hit Smith on his side, then ricocheted into the plate glass window just as Smith hit it. The glass shattered as he fell through it and onto the floor inside the building. Before all the glass had even fallen out of the frame, I was up and ready to fight. I wasn't crying anymore, I was just livid. "What a chicken-shit! I let you up and you try to ambush me from behind. I'm gonna break your damned legs, you big asshole."

Just as I started through the hole in the glass, Mister Payne and the policeman grabbed me and pulled me back into the parking lot. I was the one in the rage now. I yelled insults through the window at Smith and told him that I would finish the job. If I couldn't finish it today, I'd finish it when I got the chance if I ever saw him again.

Mister Payne yelled in to the store, "Call an ambulance out here and tell them to get here quick. I don't want that man's blood all over my store."

Jackson tried to get up several times, but was restrained each time. "You need to lay here and wait 'til the ambulance gets here." He had large cuts on his left shoulder and left thigh from his fall through the glass.

By then two more police cars had driven up into the parking lot and I was sure to go to jail. I just knew that they were going to tack some kind of charges on me once they found out who I was and also found out that Jackson was a man of notable influence in Mississippi and parts of Louisiana. After I settled down, Mister Payne walked me over and sat me down on the bin next to the broken window so I could see that Smith was being restrained. I looked up at the damage to the store front and then to Mister Payne, "I'm sorry about the glass, Mister Payne. I'll pay for the damage."

"No you won't. Jackson Smith is going to pay for this one. He started this whole mess here today, and we have a dozen witnesses that will say the same thing. You just don't worry about it. Besides, it was worth the price of this window here just to see someone kick his ass like that. If more of these boys standin' around here watching had acted more like men, they'd have done it a long time ago."

Jackson heard the comment through the window and chimed in loud enough for everyone to hear, "If these boys knew the truth about this boy, they'd be kickin' the shit out of him right now. He's been talking to the FBI. That is why they know so much about what we're doin' before we even git finished."

Before he got the full statement out of his mouth, the door opened and a familiar figure walked over to where he was still lying on the floor. "Hey, Mister Smith. Remember me? Maybe you should make sure your own house is clean before you go trying to clean out everyone else's."

"Yeah, you look familiar, but I don't know you."

"Well, you should. I am Agent Reese with the Jackson, Mississippi office of the FBI. I've done everything but eat supper with you for the past six months," then he spoke up so that everyone could hear. "We got most of that information about what was going in your area right straight out of your mouth."

"You lyin' son-of-a-bitch. I ain't never talked to you before."

"Oh, don't be shy, Mister Smith. Remember? You talked to me at that cross burning over at Ruston just a month ago. In fact, I thought we were going to fight on that day just to see which of us was going to have the privilege of kickin' the shit out of this boy. Remember that? I sure am glad I didn't win that privilege after seein' what he did to you here today."

"That is the only time I ever seen you."

"Well, we've been set up on you for a long time. You know how many times you've yelled at Missus Thomas for picking up on the partly line while you were on the phone. Well, that wasn't Missus Thomas. See, we got in on your party line so we can listen in anytime we want to. You know what, Mister Smith? You talk a lot. You like to let everyone know how much you know, so when you called up Wes Johnson, Ron Priestly, and Art Seymore, you told us everything you told them. That is how we found out about the explosives hidden in the old car over by Meadville, that is how we found the source of all the hand grenades you got, and that is how we got our leads on who did two of the bombings in Franklin County and over in McComb."

Glassy-eyed, Jackson froze like a deer caught in headlights. I could see him trying to process what the agent was telling him, but his mind refused to believe it. As Agent Reese continued, "After we found out your buddy Wes was involved, we watched him close enough to catch him in a little matter of a beating and depriving a man of his civil rights. We took him off to Jackson one day and, after we let him know what we had learned from you, we couldn't shut him up. Shoot. By the time he got through talking, we knew who you were makin' out with, who you were sleepin' with, and who all your pals are. It worked so well, we even started watchin' some of them, too."

Agent Reese looked like he enjoyed badgering Jackson with the little tidbits that disproved all of his theories. He made it a point of punching a hole into each accusation that Jackson had made and then turning each around so it implicated him. "Do you know what I learned from months of studying you, Mister Smith? I learned that you are a very stupid man with a lot of stupid friends and very few smart ones."

Agent Reese paused for a few moments, and the crowd that had gathered seemed electrified by what he was saying. "If you didn't have people like Mister Blanche to cover your butt, you'd be in deeper still. So my advice to you is this, find out who your real friends are and stay closer to town. I didn't find this place by talking to the boy; I found it by following you."

Mister Payne walked up and sat next to me on the edge of the bin. "I found that list you were carrying, so I put everything in the back of your car. I put everything in boxes so it wouldn't be rolling around for your drive home."

The ambulance finally arrived and picked up Smith. He sat slack-jawed on the edge of the gurney as they tended to his wounds and prepared him for transport. As they cuffed his wrist to the rails of the gurney, he looked incapable of comprehending what had just happened. Mister Payne told him that he would look after his car until he returned. Two of the police officers left with the ambulance; the other stayed behind to get statements from the witnesses. After I gave my statement to the police, Agent Reese came out and announced that he would be taking me for questioning for hindering his investigation. He took me to his car and asked for my keys. "Agent Morris will drive your car until we get out of town. I don't trust some of the people still loitering around here. Every time we think we have everyone accounted for, we find one or two new members that we hadn't known about."

When we got onto Highway 80, I remembered my appointment with the dean and said something to Agent Reese about it. He said I shouldn't worry about the appeal today and suggested that I stay out of the area for a while. I told him how badly I had messed up my academics and explained that if I didn't make the appeal, I would lose my eligibility. If I lost my eligibility, I would lose my deferment. If I lost my deferment, I would be drafted and sent to Vietnam.

"Son, you'd probably be safer in Vietnam right now than you are here or anywhere around Natchez. This is not going to go away. Do you really trust that man or any of the men from Mississippi that he hangs around with? Even if he believes the truth now, he's got a reason to come looking for you as soon as he gets healed up."

"Daddy ain't gonna take this very well either. He'll find some way to blame it on me, but it wasn't my fault, Mister Reese. That man was gonna give me a beating no matter what I did. I couldn't take it any more. I walk around scared to death all of the time. I gotta find some way to get away from here."

"Well I think we can light a fire under the Selective Service and get your number called a little earlier. With your training in radio and television electronics, and your experience in truck driving, I am sure they can get you a good school and a lot of training in any of the military services."

We pulled into the truck stop in Rayville for a cup of coffee where we met Agent Morris with my car. He handed my keys to me then sat with Agent Reese as we talked about what would happen next. He explained to me that they would not be going to Ferriday with me because they had to drive to Jackson, Mississippi, and formulate another plan to get back on track with the program in Franklin County. Agent Morris was sure that their operation in McComb had been damaged and it would need to be shored up—he called it damage control. After we finished our coffee, they continued to go east on Highway 80; I turned south on Highway 15 toward Ferriday. It was a very lonely drive home.

When I got home, Daddy was there and had heard the whole story already. He said that someone called him at work right after it had happened and gave him a blow-by-blow account of the entire fight. After he got home, the phone started ringing off the wall; half of the callers wanted to tell him about it, the other half wanted to know the details. I could hear the concern and the pride in his voice when he was explaining the details of the fight. He never bothered to ask me to verify any of the details that he had heard. It was probably just as well because the fight was such a blur to me. By the sound of one conversation, it sounded as if the caller thought I had beat Smith with my bare hands and that I showed no fear whatsoever. Oh, if they only knew the truth. I had been scared to tears and I fought only because my only other option was to have taken a beating at the hands of a sadist.

I unloaded the table legs from the large box in the car, stacking them in the shop with the other wood and material. I found another box in the back of the car that had been closed, so I took it in to Daddy. He popped the flaps open on the box and handed two one-gallon jugs of pelletized smokeless gunpowder to me. "Here. Do something with these. Put it somewhere safe."

I was stunned that I had been driving around in a hot, black car with enough gunpowder to blow me to kingdom come. Worse yet, the car had been driven on a major highway with an FBI agent at the wheel. "I can't believe you had me haulin' that stuff for you. I coulda been blown to hell with just one of these things."

"I knew you were a safe driver. You've been delivering naphtha and diesel for more than a year now, and nothing has happened. That stuff would blow you up worse than that gunpowder."

I didn't feel like debating so I got the short stepladder and brought it into the hall, setting it right under the attic fan. I reached up and pushed the access panel open so I could put the upper half of my body up into the attic. I carried the jugs of powder up the ladder one at a time and carefully placed each one against the right side of the fan frame in a small channel formed between the frame and the rafters. At least they would be out of the reach of my youngest brothers.

I was very careful about the deliveries I took at PedCo, being careful to transfer my pistol from vehicle to vehicle as I worked through the week. I made sure that it was ready to fire at all times because I knew that Smith or one of his confederates would be looking for an opportunity to even the score for what I had done.

Before the end of the first week in August, I received a notice from the Selective Service System stating that I'd lost my 4-S school deferment and had been reclassified to 1-A. I could be called up at any time. It didn't take long. On the ninth day of August, my birthday, I received another letter from the Selective Service System. I opened it up and read, "Selective Service System, Order to Report for Induction. The President of the United States to Edward Blanch, Greeting: You are hereby ordered for induction into the Armed Forces of the United States, and to report at ..."

As I read it, I felt as if a large weight had been lifted from my shoulders. I didn't have to make a decision about how I would escape this mess; it had been choreographed for me by my friendly Selective Service System. I walked into the living room carrying the envelope and letter, "It looks like I need to find my social security card. I have to be in New Orleans on August 29 for my induction into the military. I guess I have to go down on the 28th because it says here I have to report at seven in the morning."

Daddy seemed accepting – almost relieved - by the news. Mama just seemed resigned that all of her boys would wind up in the military. "Well, you will be in boot camp at the same time that Billy is. Maybe you two can get together on the weekends or something."

I pointed out, "By the time I get there, he'll be going to the fleet. I probably won't get to see him until after boot camp."

I gave my notice at PedCo and stopped making deliveries immediately. I went about saying goodbye to all of my friends in the neighborhood, selling my old truck outright and my treasured '59 Chevy to my neighbor for two hundred fifty on the spot and another two hundred fifty later. Since I was letting him split the payment on the car, I was going to keep it until the day before I was to leave. From the proceeds of the sales, I took fifty for myself and gave two hundred to Daddy. "Just pay my bill down at Guice Chevrolet, then you can keep the rest for yourself and Mama." I told him.

One week before my departure, my brothers and I were sitting in the living room watching *The Tonight Show* with Johnny Carson. We had to listen at a very hushed level since Mama and Daddy had already gone to bed. We were laughing as hard as we dared as he finished up his monologue when the quiet was shattered by the blast of a shotgun and the sound of shotgun pellets tearing into the roof of the house. We all dropped to the floor and crawled out of the front room, the younger boys going into the hallway that led to the back of the house while Jimmy and I went through the kitchen toward the workshop. Daddy walked into the hall in his underwear and demanded, "What's goin' on out here. You boys know better ..."

"Get down Daddy. I think someone just shot at the house. Mama, stay back in your room until we find out what is going on."

Daddy ducked back into the hallway and rushed the two younger boys into their room. We all converged at the other end of the hall as we made our way out to the workshop. I ran out the back door and started around the house. I got as far as the corner behind my parents' bedroom when I felt like I was sinking into the ground. I recognized the feeling immediately. "Shit. The septic tank is backed up again."

I hugged the wall and sneaked around the corner to see a cross burning at the front of the yard. In the light from the cross, I could see the familiar Chevrolet pickup; it was the same one that had bumped me on the road almost a year earlier. I was going to try to get my pistol out of my car but couldn't because the front yard was lit by the fire. I knew I wouldn't be able to get back around the house before they drove away, so I ran toward the road through my neighbor's yard. When the light in our front room came on, one of the men in the truck yelled, "We know where you live, you nigger-lovin' snitch. There ain't no way for you to hide."

As they started to drive away, they pitched their beer and liquor bottles out onto the street in front of the house, making a symphony of breaking glass. I reached the side of the road just as they passed in front of me. I yelled, "You're gonna pay for this you bunch of fucking pigs!"

Jimmy ran out of the house with a long board and knocked the cross over on the lawn. We took the hose and shot water across the yard to put the fire out. When we walked back into the house, Daddy snapped at me, "What are you thinking, yelling that word all over the neighborhood? If the neighbors weren't awake before, I'm sure they are awake now. Is that the kind of language they are teaching at college these days?"

"Sorry, Daddy. They really pissed me off this time. They are gonna pay for this in a big way. I'll see to it myself. Enough is enough."

"Did you see who it was? Did you recognize them?"

"No. I didn't recognize them but that was the same pickup truck that tried to get me last year. I thought the police would take care of them well enough to keep them on their own side of the river."

"Are you sure it is the same truck? Do you still have the tag numbers? I have the sheriff on the phone and they are putting a call out to try to get them before they get back across the river."

I ran to the car to get the piece of paper on which I had written the tag number earlier in the year. I ran back into the house and gave it to Daddy, who then read it to the sheriff. After he hung up the phone Daddy shoved the piece of paper back toward me but I just told him to keep it; I wouldn't need it in the navy.

A few minutes later, the phone rang and Daddy picked it up. "Hello. Oh, hi Sheriff. Yeah." Then he covered the mouthpiece and turned to us, "They pulled those boys in the truck over just outside Vidalia. They're gonna hold them until we get over there."

Daddy turned back to the phone and listened for a moment before speaking, "No, just get all their names, take their guns and hold them for a little while then let 'em go. I know how to take care of this. I'll fix it so those boys won't ever want to come to this side of the river again."

Before we went back to bed, I brought the ladder in from the workshop and set it up under the fan as I had so many times before. I took a light up the ladder with me, pushed the access panel open, and looked at the roofing boards at the front of the house. I saw a patch of the plywood that was badly splintered; it was just above and about three feet to the right of the two jugs of pelletized smokeless gunpowder sitting in the attic. As I looked at the splintered plywood I told everyone how lucky we were with such a near miss. I also tried to impose upon Daddy the idea of what could have happened had the shot been a little lower and three feet to the left; the house would have been flattened.

The next day, I asked Daddy if he found out who the men were. He said he knew exactly who they were; three of them were from Franklin

County and one from Adams County. "We've had a lot of trouble over in Adams County with all four of them, so the Natchez Klavern wants us to stay out of it. One of them is Jackson Smith's nephew, so it was a personal vendetta. They want us to lay low and stay on this side of the river until you are gone. We don't want none of this to fall back on you now. The worst of those boys is the son of Fred Miller, that old pig farmer from over in Meadville; that's who the pickup belongs to. So just stay around home here until you have to go."

On the day before I was to go to New Orleans, Sheriff Cross drove up into the driveway and parked. I walked out to meet him, pointing out the new decoration burned into the front lawn. He laughed about it then asked, "Well, are you ready to go tomorrow? You be careful wherever you go and whatever you do. We would like to have you come back here one day and help straighten this mess out."

I shook my head. "No sir. When I get away from here, I'm gonna stay as far away as possible. I don't think I want to live like this the rest of my life."

"Well, you could help change it, you know. You made quite an impact around here in the past couple of months. I know more than a few boys over here that like your brand of justice. Speaking of justice, where were you the other night?"

"I've been stayin' real close to home, Sheriff. Daddy didn't want us involved with any kind of retribution against that Miller boy."

"Well somebody sent him a message that he won't forget for quite a while. Someone killed four of old man Miller's pigs, put them in—ahem—compromising positions in that boy's truck, then lit the whole thing on fire. It burned the truck right to the ground right in his own driveway. When they first found the pig carcasses in the truck, they thought they wuz human; scared the shit out of 'em."

"Do they know who did it?"

"No, but they talkin' over there like you did it. They just don't know how you did it. They had three dogs sleeping on the front porch when it happened. I know a couple of the FBI boys got a good laugh out of it."

I got a pretty good laugh out of this myself, knowing that they were worried. "Well Sheriff, you just let those guys over there think whatever they will. I'm leavin' tomorrow and I want to be a thorn in their sides for as long as I can. After I leave here, I don't think I'll be comin' back for a long time. They really are lucky that only a few pigs and one truck is all they lost, because it would have to be worse than that if I had to stay around here for some reason." My voice seemed to hold a certainty and conviction as I spoke. I realized that it was true—would probably never return. I didn't know what I wanted yet, but I knew what I did not want.

Sheriff Cross looked at me knowingly. "Well, I don't care too much for your politics son, but I do like your attitude and action. You go out there and become a man now. The navy will make a real man out of you."

"Thanks, Sheriff." I shook his hand and went back into the house as he backed out of the driveway and drove down the street.

I got up on Monday and was greeted by a beautiful blue sky. I packed only enough clothes for two days into a small suitcase that I knew I would lose in boot camp. I didn't want to take anything more of this life than I had to. I was going to make a change in my life—a complete change.

The whole family came to see me off at the bus station, which was only a curbside stop at Pasternack's Store. I hugged each of my younger brothers and my mom, and then turned to face my dad. I wanted to hug him, but I hadn't had a hug from him since I was about eight years old. I shook his hand and said my goodbyes and got onto the bus with my small suitcase. I sat on the left side of the bus so I could see my family as we drove away. I waved goodbye as the Greyhound growled away from the station. I watched the sadness of loss in their faces and wondered what each of them was feeling.

I settled into the comfortable seat as we drove through Ferriday. I watched the familiar scenery fall away behind us as we drove through Vidalia. After we left Louisiana and made a scheduled stop in Natchez, I fell into a light restful sleep as the bus bounced rhythmically over the concrete pavement sections of Highway 61. I was going to wake up refreshed to a new life. I would go places I had never gone, do things I had never done, and see things I had never seen, even under the shadow of the nightmare called Vietnam.

My thoughts settled onto the 23rd Psalm; *Yay, though I walk through the valley of the shadow of death, I will fear no evil.*

God help me.

EPILOGUE

After serving nine years in the US Navy, I settled on the West Coast with my young wife and two daughters, eventually settling in Oregon. Though I missed my family and the charm of Louisiana, I wanted my daughters to live without the racial strife through which I had suffered.

In 1968, the schools in Ferriday, Louisiana were integrated, so Wilbur Jones' children went to school in the same school from which I graduated.

In 1970, Mama and Daddy did something unprecedented in the state of Louisiana when, for a short time, they housed a black foster child. For their efforts, they were recognized when the local Klans decorated their front yard with another burning cross. When I think about it, I smile.

I never saw my Aunt Sandy again, nor did I meet any of my black cousins.

Daddy died of lung cancer in February, 1988. Mama lived with Roxie until her death in February, 2012

In 1972, Chief Deputy Sheriff Frank Delaughter was convicted of racketeering for taking protection money from the management of the Morville Lounge in Deer Park, Louisiana. He was also convicted of violating the civil rights of Cliff Davis, a white man, for beating him to death in the Ferriday City Jail. He was sentenced to one year in prison, and could never own a gun or work in law enforcement again.

In 1972, Sheriff Noah Cross was convicted of perjury for having lied to the grand jury regarding his role with the Morville Lounge. In 1973, he also pled guilty, and was sentenced to prison for jury tampering in a previous trial.

Tee Wee Kelly disappeared from Ferriday. He was never seen or heard from after December, 1964.

Wilbur Jones and James Gorham lived out their lives in Ferriday, Louisiana. They suffered terribly from the racial prejudice and poor economy of the area. I still think about Wilbur and wish I had kept in contact with him.

Jackson Smith is actually a composition of two of the Klansmen from Mississippi. Both were later subpoenaed to appear before the House Un-American Activities Committee. The beating at the lumber company was very real.

The murders of Frank Morris and Joe "Ed" Edwards received little attention from local law enforcement and the FBI after the incidents in 1964. The cases went cold almost immediately and were closed and forgotten for more than 40 years. In 2007, Stanley Nelson, editor of the Concordia Sentinel started his investigations into the murders and wrote his first installment on the arson and murder of Frank Morris. Since 2007, Stanley has written almost 200 stories about the Morris arson and other local Civil Rights-era cold cases in Louisiana and Mississippi. For his work, in 2011 he was a finalist for the Pulitzer Prize in the Local Reporting category. Also in 2011, he was the recipient of the Payne Award for Ethics in Journalism from the University of Oregon School of Journalism and Communication for demonstrating "an extraordinary commitment to ethical conduct, even when faced with economic, personal, and political pressure." He was also the first recipient of the LSU Manship School of Mass Communication's Courage and Justice Award for his commitment and courage in his pursuit of justice for Frank Morris.

In June 2009, I called the Monroe, Louisiana office of the FBI and tried to give the local agents information about what I knew of the cases of Frank Morris and Joe Edwards. Without hearing the information, the agent asked, "Do you have any proof?" I tried again, and he asked again,

"Can you prove anyone was involved?" After I told him that I had no proof, he said, "We only want facts that you can prove," then he hung up without hearing a single statement about either of the cases. I still have the agent's name and number in my smartphone.

The murders of Frank Morris and Joe Edwards are still unsolved and the cases have been closed again.